VOICES FROM EXILE

VOICES

VIOLENCE AND SURVIVAL

FROM

IN MODERN MAYA HISTORY

EXILE

VICTOR MONTEJO

UNIVERSITY OF OKLAHOMA PRESS : NORMAN

ALSO BY VICTOR MONTEJO

El Q'anil: The Man of Lightning (Carrboro, N.C., 1982, 1984; Palos Verdes, Calif., rev. ed., 1999)

Testimony: The Death of a Guatemalan Village (Willimantic, Conn., 1987; San Carlos, Guatemala, 1993)

The Bird Who Cleans the World and Other Mayan Fables (Willimantic, Conn., 1991, 1995)

Brevísima Relación Testimonial de la Contínua Destrucción del Mayab' *(Guatemala)* (Providence, R.I., 1992)

Sculpted Stones, Poems (Willimantic, Conn., 1995)

Published with the assistance of the National Endowment for the Humanities, a federal agency which supports the study of such fields as history, philosophy, literature, and language.

Library of Congress Cataloging-in-Publication Data
Montejo, Victor, 1951–
Voices from exile : violence and survival in modern Maya history / Victor Montejo.
     p.   cm.
Includes bibliographical references and index.
ISBN 0-8061-3171-3 (cloth : alk. paper)
1. Mayas—Wars—Guatemala.   2. Mayas—Crimes against—Guatemala.
3. Mayas—Relocation—Mexico.   4. Political violence—Guatemala.
5. Genocide—Guatemala.   6. Guatemala—Ethnic relations.
7. Guatemala—Politics and government.   I. Title.
F1434.2.W37M65   1999
972.81'004974152—dc21   99-27677
                                                               CIP

Text design by Trina Stahl

Tet heb' ya' x'oq' yanma
Yet xuni elilal,
Tet heb' ya' xtzalayih
Yet x'ok nha.
Oxhimi matxa b'aq'inh
Xhjeb'a' kob'ah
Xol telaj, Xol q'eb'taj.
Hulujab' aq'ank'ulal
Ya'a' tzalaoj janma.

Por los que lloraron su desgracia
cuando salieron al exilio,
Por los que ahora estan contenos
por haber retornado a casa.
Ojalá ya nunca
nos escondamos
entre los montes, bajo los árboles.
Que la paz llegue
y nos alegre el corazón.

For those who felt the pain
of going into exile,
to those who are now happy
for having returned home.
We hope that never again
we have to hide ourselves
in the forests, under the trees.
Let peace arrive
bringing happiness to our hearts.

VICTOR MONTEJO
Davis, California
March 1998

CONTENTS

ILLUSTRATIONS

All photographs were taken by the author.

TABLE

ACKNOWLEDGMENTS

I ACKNOWLEDGE WITH gratitude and joy my family: my parents, who gave me life and raised me; my brother and sisters, companions of my youth and companions in exile in Chiapas until they immigrated to Canada in 1986; my brother Pedro Antonio, killed by the Guatemalan army, who always encouraged me to write; my faithful and loving wife, Mercedes Montejo, and my children, Eusebio Marvin, Edda Marilyn, and Victor Ivan, who suffered the years in exile with me and endured slights and lack of concern while I worked on my graduate studies. All these people bring joy to my days, and I live for them and because of them.

We owe our lives and our present happiness to all those people who aided us in getting from Guatemala to the United States during the time of violence: the late Sister Rose Cordis, former director of the Maryknoll Hospital in Jacaltenango, for her help and protection of my family during my absence; Sister Tina, for aiding my family on the journey from Jacaltenango to Washington, D.C.; my friends Wallace Kaufman, Joe Kenlan, and Elaine Chiosso of Pittsboro, North Carolina, who provided housing for me during my first stay here; and Thomas Fricke of the Friends Meeting in Washington, D.C., Victor Perera, Patrice Perilli, Peter Schweitzer, and Priscilla Wheeler, who helped my family join me.

I am indebted to Dr. LaVonne Poteet, Dr. Gene Chenoweth, Dr. John Peeler, Dr. Charles Sackrey, Father John Coyne, and other friends at Bucknell University; to the Joseph Priestley Fellowship, whose members helped me financially through the Montejo Fund during my graduate studies; to my professors at the State University of New York (SUNY)–Albany, Robert Carmack, Gary H. Gossen, and Lyle Campbell; to my friend, Brenda Rosenbaum, whose advice and good teaching were to my intellectual benefit; to my anthropology professors at the University of Connecticut, especially Scott Cook, my major adviser, who generously gave his time and energy to find the necessary funding for me to continue my studies; and to Professors Jim Faris, Irene Silverblatt, and Leigh Binford.

This work would not have been possible without the collaboration of those refugees and friends who shared their lives and their testimonies, songs, poems, and other narratives. I am grateful to Pilin Xapin, the Q'anjob'al Maya who was my guide to the Q'anjob'al camps; Gaspar Camposeco, a Jakaltek comedian, who introduced me to the camps in the Comalapa region, particularly Villa Cocalito; and Juan Pablo Cardona and María Elena, Mexican friends who allowed me to use their pickup to reach the distant camps.

I am also grateful to several Mexican individuals and organizations that aided me personally and refugees in general: Bishop Samuel Ruíz García and Sister Lucy of the Diocese of San Cristóbal de las Casas, who provided constant support to refugees beginning in 1982; and the officials of the Mexican Commission for Aid to Refugees (COMAR), now headed by Dr. Juan José Puerto Salem, for their humanitarian aid to refugees.

The resolution of the refugee problem would not have been possible without Andres Ramirez Silva of the United Nations High Commission on Refugees (UNHCR) in Comitán, who allowed me access to information about the refugees but, more important, worked tirelessly in maintaining the (sometimes tortuous) process of dialogue between the Permanent Commissions of the Guatemalan Refugees (CCPP) and the Guatemalan government through its Special Commission for Aid to the Repatriated (CEAR); the CCPP and the refugees themselves, for their insistence that the solutions to refugee problems could only come about through the participation of the refugees in that process and for demanding collective and voluntary returns to Guatemala; and the Mexican government, for providing protection, humanitarian aid, and asylum.

Thanks are also due to the Maya cultural groups Ah Mayab' (We the Original People of the Maya Land) and Maya-Honh (We Are Maya) for allowing me to tape their songs and music in the camps; the musicians Alfonso Rojas and his brothers, Antonio Mendoza Silvestre and his musical group, and Manuel Santos Montejo; the poet Antonio L. Cota García and his wife; Ambar Past, a Mexican American poet who provided information about the Tzotzil-Tzeltal communities in southern Mexico; and Christine Eber, for the use of her house in San Cristóbal.

Support for my fieldwork among the refugees was provided during the summers of 1988 and 1989 by the African American Summer Fellowship Institute at SUNY-Albany. Subsequent funding was provided by Plumsock Mesoamerican Studies of Vermont and a grant from the Onaway Trust Fund through the kindness of John Morris. I am profoundly grateful to Christopher and Sally Lutz for their encouragement and economic support along the way toward my doctoral degree; to my publishers, Alexander Taylor and Judy Doyle, directors of Curbstone Press, for their friendship and advice; and to Barbara Rossen, who helped edit the dissertation in Connecticut. The University of California's Presidential Postdoctoral Fellowship was awarded to me in 1994 for rewriting my dissertation for publication, a process furthered by Plumsock Mesoamerican Studies and aided by the skills of Marilyn Moors, national coordinator of the Guatemala Scholars Network, who edited the document. The Centro de Investigaciones Regionales de Mesoamerica, W. George Lovell, and Catherine Nolin Hanlon were most generous in permitting the use of their maps. The staff of the University of Oklahoma Press, particularly Randolph Lewis, provided useful assistance and encouragement. With a full heart, I acknowledge their help and support, and I accept the burden of any errors as my own.

VOICES FROM EXILE

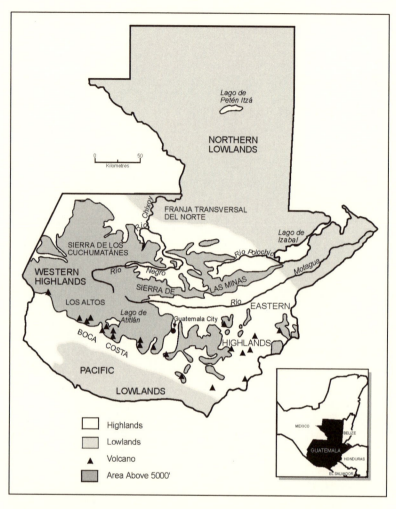

The natural regions of Guatemala. From Nolin Hanlon 1995. Map by Darren R. Stranger, courtesy of Catherine L. Nolin Hanlon.

1

THE ANTHROPOLOGIST
AND THE OTHER

RECENT DEMOGRAPHIC STUDIES of Guatemala estimate that Mayas make up 60 percent or more of the total
population of 9.5 million (Lovell and Lutz 1994: 138).
Despite five hundred years of colonial rule and capitalist
exploitation, these indigenous people have preserved
their cultural identities, as manifest in twenty-two distinct but related languages, religious practices and beliefs
that have maintained their uniqueness while adjusting to
outside pressures, and an astoundingly beautiful tradition
of weaving and native dress. In Guatemala 3 percent of
the population own 70 percent of the arable land, one of
the most inequitable systems of land tenure in Latin
America. Mayas, who for the most part are agricultural
people, suffer from extreme poverty rooted in land shortages and landlessness. This scarcity of land was not the
only inequity in the country, however, and as repression
against all forms of social justice grew, a guerrilla movement developed in the Guatemalan highlands that threatened to extend its activities throughout the country. In

response the Guatemalan army created a strategic plan for control of the highlands that involved the destruction or repression of Maya villages they believed to be supporting the guerrillas. This counterinsurgency war, which began in the late 1970s, eliminated 440 Maya communities (by the army's own count), killed tens of thousands of civilians, and caused hundreds of thousands more to flee for their lives. This book tells the story of one group of those who fled, Mayas from the Kuchumatan highlands who crossed the border into Mexico and sought refuge there.

A Brief Autobiography

I ARRIVED IN the world on Lahunh Tox, October 9, 1951, the firstborn child of Eusebio Montejo and Juana Esteban Méndez, both originally from Jacaltenango in the department of Huehuetenango in Guatemala. When he was young my father could not attend school because there were no schools at that time and because he had to work on the land with his father, José Montejo. When he was twelve years old he began attending a school in Yinhch'ewex that was run voluntarily by a local man, Don Rufino, in a schoolhouse constructed by the village. In return the villagers gave the teacher corn, beans, and firewood to help sustain his family. Occasionally he would ask for a small donation of money from the parents of each of his pupils so that he could obtain medicines or cloth for his family. My father had to walk three kilometers each morning to get to the school, and he also had to carry a log on his shoulder because his father had promised to build a house in that village. This is how my father learned to read, write, and speak Spanish.

My mother had no opportunity to attend school, even though there was a public school in Jacaltenango run by ladino schoolteachers. Education for Maya women was not considered necessary, and her parents did not encourage her. Because her father was often sick, she had to help her mother take care of the other children and travel to nearby towns to sell her weavings. My mother speaks only Popb'al Ti', the Jakaltek Maya language.[1] After my parents married in Jacaltenango, they moved to the Jakaltek village of La Laguna, within the *municipio* (municipality) of Jacaltenango, to cultivate corn, sugarcane, *achiote,* peppers, and beans. It is in this village that I grew up.

There were two more sons and three daughters born into our family. My brothers are José and Pedro Antonio, and my sisters, Maria, Candelaria, and Hermilia Guadalupe. My brothers and I studied to become primary school teachers. My sisters completed their studies up to the sixth-grade level. All of my family were severely affected by the violence in the Kuchumatan highlands in the 1980s. My brother Pedro Antonio, with whom I had the closest emotional ties, was killed by soldiers during the town's patronal festival on February 1, 1981. My brother José and his family are now living in Ottawa, where he moved as a landed immigrant in 1986 after living in a refugee camp in Chiapas. He is studying at a college in Ottawa. My sisters also moved to Canada in 1986 and live there with their families.

As young Maya boys, my brothers and I spent our childhood playing and working in the village of La Laguna. After doing our chores at home, we would gather on the patio of the school and play games like Maxhtik'a No', the Animal Is Not Here. We retold stories we learned at home, and the older children told the younger ones ghost stories. We all knew that we must return home with firewood so that our mothers could cook and make tortillas. My sisters did not play in groups like the boys did. Maya girls had more household chores to do, fetching water, caring for younger brothers and sisters, and making tortillas with their mothers. They played in twos and threes close to their houses. Both boys and girls learned at an early age how to swim, because the Río Azul runs on the outskirts of the village.

I grew up speaking Popb'al Ti', and I went with my mother to various Maya ceremonies and festivities. She would tell me stories about my grandfather, who was an Alkal Txah, a Prayer Maker. When I was a small child and became ill, my mother promised the Virgin Mary, the patron saint of Jacaltenango, that I would dance during her festival if she would spare my life. I remember dancing as a deer in the Xil Wej, the Dance of Rags, on Ash Wednesday, a festival that coincided with the honoring of Witz, the Owner of the Hill and Animals. And I danced as a *chichimit*, a small, red warrior holding an ax and a rattle, in the Dance of the Conquest. I learned the names of the sacred places and the stories of our culture heroes, like Q'anil, the Man of Lightning. We learned all these stories from the elders, who passed on to us through the oral tradition the knowledge of the world around us and the greatness of our people.

My upbringing also included attendance at Catholic church ceremonies, many of which coincided with or were superimposed on traditional Maya ones. For instance, on the day that I danced as a deer for Xil Wej, I also received from the priest the traditional cross of ashes on my forehead. More direct contact with the Catholic church came when a group of Maryknoll nuns arrived in La Laguna to recruit Maya children for a boarding school in Jacaltenango. I was one of the children who decided to attend the Fray Bartolomé de Las Casas school, and at the age of seven, I left my parents and home community for Jacaltenango. I began to attend mass regularly and even became an altar boy, learning Latin so as to make the proper responses during the mass. At this point in my life I became a Catholic because I received my education from Catholic missionaries. I also started to learn Spanish.

I liked school very much and had good teachers, except for one. My second grade teacher would hit me on the back of my hand every time he caught me writing with my left hand. Because of this punishment, I began to use my right hand, and now I can write with either hand. I dreamed of continuing my education after the sixth grade, but there were no middle schools in the town. My good grades in the last years of primary school called me to the attention of the parish priest, Fr. Bill Mullan, who obtained a scholarship so that I could attend the Seminary of San José in Sololá. And so I moved again, this time very far away from my family and home village.

I received my *educación básica* (basic education) at the seminary, which was run by Benedictine priests. I learned a great deal there, but the distance from my family and the culture shock of being in a different town where the spoken Maya was different from my language gave rise to some adjustment problems. I became a sleepwalker, traveling down the dark corridors of the buildings and often waking up far from my dormitory. It was at this school that I discovered world literature and found in ethnohistorical books such as the *Popol Vuh* and the *Annals of the Kaqchikels* that these ancient stories bore great similarity to those in the oral tradition in my small village. We had not considered those stories very important, nor had we paid much attention to them. This was the beginning of my interest in writing and of my strange dreams. In one dream I found myself in the middle of a cornfield showing the people (the corn) books on whose covers my name appeared as author.[2] When we came to study *The Divine Comedy* by Dante Alighieri, I remembered my mother telling me the experiences of my grandfather who had died and revived again. It seemed to me that my grandfather's story was worth writing down, so I began to work on it, asking my mother for more details during my holidays at home. I finished writing the story when I was in *diversificado,* the equivalent of high school.

After three years at the seminary, I received a scholarship to study at the Instituto Indígena para Varones Santiago in Antigua, Guatemala. This school was run by the Brothers of LaSalle, who were very strict but who also inculcated in us great respect for ourselves, our people, and our culture. I had, by now, decided to become a schoolteacher and work among my own people. I did my training as a teacher in a private school for girls in Antigua, and after graduating in 1972, I moved back to Jacaltenango to look for a position. I became a primary school teacher in the village of Yinhch'ewex in January 1973.

In Yinhch'ewex I met Mercedes, the lovely woman who was to become my wife. She had just finished attending school, and I was introduced to her by one of her sisters. I would pay musicians to serenade her house in the evening, or I would bring my record player to provide music, but her parents did not like that. Once I joined the monkey dancers during the festival of the patron saint of the village to get into her house and buy a soft drink without being recognized. Her parents were opposed to their daughter seeing me because they did not believe that I was serious about marrying her. Then I obtained a teaching position in another village, and Mercedes followed me there, against her parents' wishes. We were married in Jacaltenango. Since then we have raised three children: Eusebio Marvin, born in Yinhch'ewex in 1975; Edda Mari, born in Jacaltenango in 1976; and Victor Ivan, also born in Jacaltenango, in 1980.

I taught in several rural communities in Huehuetenango, mostly in the Jakaltek region. In Yinhch'ewex I taught with another teacher who disappeared in the violence of 1982. From Yinch'ewex I moved to the ladino community of Peña Roja in the municipio of La Libertad, where I worked for three years. Then I went to the community of Tzalalá (a pseudonym) in Jakaltek territory where I witnessed the events described in my book *Testimony*. In all, I worked for a decade in Maya communities in Jacaltenango, until the violence became unbearable and the massacres forced me into exile.

In early November 1982 I left Jacaltenango and went to Guatemala City to apply for a visa to come to the United States. Wallace Kaufman, a friend of my recently deceased brother, Pedro Antonio, invited me to come to the United States to lecture on Maya culture and to work with him on a translation of *El Q'anil: The Man of Lightning*.[3] I could only get a tourist visa that permitted me to stay for six weeks. After working with Mr. Kaufman and giving my lectures, my visa was soon to expire. As

I was preparing to leave the United States, my wife sent someone to call me with the news that I should not come back to Guatemala because my name was on a death list. The army and the civil patrols were looking for me. They did not believe that I was in the United States but thought that I had gone to the mountains to join the guerrillas. So I did not return to my wife and children and resume my work as a teacher. With great sadness, in mid-December I decided to go to Mexico to search for my parents, brother, and sisters who were living in a refugee camp in Chiapas and to join them in exile.

In the refugee camp in Guadalupe Victoria, I found a typewriter and started to write about the events that had forced me and thousands of others into exile and had caused the massacre of thousands more innocent people in Guatemala. In the tenuous safety of the refugee camp, I decided to speak for those whom the army wished to silence through death, disappearance, or exile. My pain was enormous, because my work as a teacher was finished and my wife and children lived in peril in Jacaltenango. During the first three months of 1983 I tried to find work in Chiapas, but there were so many refugees that there were no jobs. In San Cristóbal de las Casas, I met Victor Perera, a Guatemalan writer living in the United States who was visiting the area. He read my manuscript and thought it should be edited and published in English and Spanish. He was very supportive of my writing and gave me the courage to keep writing and living.

With the help of Wallace Kaufman and Dr. LaVonne Poteet of Bucknell University, I applied for an H-1 visa, for writers and people with special skills, and came to the United States for a second time in April 1983. I stayed for a few months, then went back to the refugee camps again to be with my parents. In February 1984 I returned to the United States with my H-1 visa. I found some part-time work, but my main concern was to get my family to safety. Whenever I sent them money it was stolen, so my wife had to rely on her parents for help. But they lived in another town, making their assistance difficult. Because I did not return to Jacaltenango, the civil patrols began to retaliate against my family. My wife and children were under virtual house arrest and were warned that they would be killed if I did not return. Again my resourceful wife sent someone to call to let me know that she could not leave town because of the civil patrols. With the help of friends in the United States and members of the Friends Meeting House in Washington, D.C., we devised a plan to rescue my family. Congressmen and senators wrote letters to the U.S. Embassy for the appropriate visas, and Sister Tina, a nun from Philadelphia long past the age when such service should be required of her, courageously went to Jacaltenango and helped Mercedes and the children leave the town and the country. It had been two years since I had seen them, and I was overjoyed to greet them at Washington's National Airport on March 4, 1984.

At that time of joyous reunion, we met Gloria Halbritter, an Oneida Indian clan mother from Oneida, New York. She was drawn to us because our children looked like her grandchildren. She welcomed us into her life, her home, and her family, giving us deep and abiding ties to a Native American community here.

The challenge now was to find ways to survive with my family in the United States. Dr. Poteet arranged for me to be a consultant in Latin American Studies at Bucknell University, and I began to study English, reading from *El método cortina*. Soon I was giving talks in English to practice my language skills, and I began to dream of studying at a university in the United States. I spent a great deal of time in the Bucknell library reading books on Maya culture. I knew I could write about my culture, but I needed the tools and the academic training to do it well. I decided that I wanted that training to be in anthropology, and I began to search for universities where there was both a Maya Studies program and the possibility of scholarships. Robert Carmack, Gary Gossen, and Lyle Campbell from SUNY–Albany gave me the opportunity to fulfill my dreams. I received the equivalent of a bachelor's degree and began work on a master's degree in anthropology. By this time *El Q'anil* had been published in a bilingual Spanish/English edition, and other Maya stories I had written appeared in anthologies and journals published in the United States. My limited scholarship stipend was augmented by the Montejo Fund, created by friends at Bucknell through the Joseph Priestley Fellowship. And, of course, the faithful Mercedes took all kinds of jobs to help support us. In 1987 *Testimony* was published.

I graduated from SUNY in the spring of 1989 and moved to the University of Connecticut to work on my doctorate. I was honored to be awarded the prestigious Edward Burrows Fellowship for Anthropology and to have the support and friendship of Scott Cook, my adviser. To supplement my scholarship, I received help from the Lutz family, making my Ph.D. a reality.

Anthropology and the Other

RECENTLY THE FIELD of anthropology has seen much discussion on the relationship between the anthropologist and the people studied, the "other." Usually the anthropologist is from a dominant Western culture or a former colonial power while those studied are less powerful, less literate, and less sophisticated in the ways of the "first" world (Asad 1988). This dichotomy is not as relevant in my case. I am a Maya, I was a refugee, I lived in exile, and as an anthropologist I returned to the refugee camps to investigate the situation of those remaining there. I have the advantage of a Western education *and* a Maya upbringing. I speak two Maya languages, Popb'al Ti' and Q'anjob'al, in addition to Spanish and English. However, I have lived outside my culture for the past ten years and have acquired some Western and academic ethnocentrisms from that experience. Because of my double identity, this work is directed to two audiences: the Maya themselves, so that they have this document as a commemoration of their struggles; and the general Western community, academic and nonacademic, so that our work becomes relevant to and respectful of indigenous cultures.

Stephen Tyler states that "it is the anthropologist who represents native speech within the context of anthropological writing for his/her own reasons" and that "anthropologists write of the native not for the native's sake, but for themselves, out of their own interests or as an act of contrition or atonement" (1992: 5). But oral history and ethnography can also serve the "native." It can begin the process of preserving individual and group experience. It can heighten consciousness of communal suffering and injustice, and it can begin the awakening of political comprehension both for the natives and for the larger international community. Anthropology has been strongly criticized because of its colonialist and elitist practices; indigenous people are seen only as the providers of information to be processed and interpreted, thus deleting the native presence in the writing of ethnographies. "The absence of the native as a speaking subject in anthropology has (rightly or wrongly) been read as a continuation of the colonial situation in which the 'other' was gradually destroyed" (Hastrup 1992: 120).

Native anthropologists and intellectuals, mainly from third world countries, have been writing from, for, and about their cultures to balance or to complement the outsiders' perspectives. Ethnographic representation and the critiques of colonialism and anthropology have been important projects in the past (Asad 1988; Said 1979). This tradition has been continued in the current outpouring of autoethnographies. Native anthropologists who have been the traditional subjects of ethnographic writing are now writing ethnographies of their own cultures and adding to these writings their autobiographical experiences (Reed-Danahay 1997). I am within the tradition of Maya intellectuals and scholars, advocates of pan-Mayanism, Maya cultural revival, and Maya self-representation (Warren 1997). In this work I often take on the roles of informant and ethnographer at the same time. My task is to decolonize this Maya experience of exile and to write critically from my insider perspective about its causes and outcomes. That this development in ethnography comes under fire from the traditional academic hierarchy is clear.

> *The alarm about the "nativist turn," I suspect, does not center on the "ethnic of the researcher" (although the last two decades have seen a rapidly growing number and greater visibility of formerly excluded subjects in academe) but exists because of the associated trend of a more radical, politically engaged scholarship advocated by many of these scholars.* (Motzafi-Haller 1997: 217)

Although many non-Western anthropologists have criticized the discipline and continue to do so, anthropology is likely to continue its hegemonic practice of representing the other (Shahrani 1994).

In this study I provide an anthropological analysis of the data I collected in my fieldwork in the refugee camps in Chiapas. The data collection and analysis are enriched by my personal experience there. This personal experience goes far beyond the usual participant observation that is the sine qua non of anthropological fieldwork. Because I have been personally affected by the political violence against the Maya people and because I have experienced the bitterness of life in exile, perhaps "study" is not the correct word. Instead I find that I have a moral responsibility to make evident to the world the plight of my people in exile.

Indigenous people have always complained that anthropologists do not listen to them, that anthropologists have represented them as "primitive," or "a minority," or "backward," or even just as "informants." As Mayas we find it hard to deal with the academic world, because if we tell the "experts" what is Mayan, they are reluctant to listen. Instead they find it more scientific (or perhaps more comfortable?) to tell us what it is to be a Maya or how to define Maya culture. We know that there are many perceptions of any situation. We know that we do not possess the sole truth. But it is our culture that is at stake. We regret that our views are not taken seriously and that we are continually placed in the position of being listeners. Our stories and knowledge have been treated as data to be processed into ethnographies by and for the academic interpreters. I hope in this book to be both a Maya researcher and a listener to the voices of those in exile and to present to the reader a view of the exile experience that is simultaneously "inside" and "outside."

As a Maya anthropologist, I am also aware of many areas of the exile experience that are subject to various political interpretations and manipulations. The process of cultural representation is seen in the camps, where Mayas are engaged in a constant struggle to make themselves visible in a world that works to dehumanize them and erase them from public view. Their struggles, which sometimes result in division and conflict, are exploited by those, both Mayas and non-Mayas, who wish to gain political advantage from their turmoil. Here my efforts as a Maya scholar are strongly directed toward the revitalization of Maya cultures, and this revitalization transcends much of the divisive fallout of living under difficult conditions.

Maya Refugees

UNTIL RECENTLY MANY studies of refugees have concentrated on the immediate needs of the people and on relief programs to aid in survival in the camps. The alarming incidence of poverty and desolation in restricted refugee camps calls for this type of study, so theoretical discussion of refugees in academic terms has been limited. But if we are to take refugees seriously, we must help them to grasp an understanding of their situation in political and cultural terms and to gain visibility in the world. Often, particularly through media accounts, we know the statistics of a refugee situation but nothing about the conditions that caused the flight into exile. And many researchers prefer to remove themselves from situations of war and political turmoil, thus leaving history bereft of the insight they could have provided.[4]

In part this has been the case in Guatemala, where the lack of information and the misinformation about the violence against Maya communities persist. Was it just coincidence that when Guatemalan government violence against modern Mayas was most intense, the research receiving media attention in the United States was that on the archaeological past, which provided new versions of old theories for the classic Mayan collapse, stressing warfare and human sacrifice? These accounts replaced current news of the Maya in U.S. newspapers.[5]

But, fortunately, the Maya have also been studied by researchers and anthropologists who have worked hard to bring about an understanding of the violence and its roots in Guatemalan social reality. The work of Beatriz Manz (1988a, 1988b, 1988c), Robert M. Carmack (1988), Ricardo Falla (1992), Carol A. Smith (1990), Kay B. Warren (1978, 1993), Duncan Earle (1988), and others not only contributed anthropological insight but also demonstrated a deep concern for the Maya people and their future.

The political and armed conflict in Guatemala has dominated life there for a period of at least thirty years. The players in this conflict have been both civilian and military. On the civilian side, workers, students, peasants, and indigenous and Church people have sought solutions to problems of racism and injustice rooted in a society ruled by a landed oligarchy and magnified by the lack of land for ordinary peasants and indigenous people. On the military side, the Guatemalan army battled in opposition to the insurgent guerrilla forces of the Guatemalan National Revolutionary Unity (URNG) and all those the army believed to be URNG collaborators and sympathizers. As this conflict took place during the cold war, it came to have international connotations and connections, particularly to the United States.[6]

Life in exile involves notions of both space and identity

(Gupta and Ferguson 1992). Migrants and refugees who remove themselves from their home communities carry with them their ways of life, which they then replicate whenever it is possible or whenever they see it appropriate for their survival in a foreign land. At the same time they enter into contact with cultures different from their own and make use of selective aspects of these cultures for their survival. This transnationalization of culture can be seen in the actions and reactions of Maya refugees in Florida,[7] who have tried to replicate their culture in the middle of previously well defined spaces marked out by Mexican, Haitian, and Jamaican migrant workers and by Cuban and other Central American refugees. In Chiapas the refugees struggled to reestablish their culture in the spaces previously defined by Mexican Mayas, Mexican campesinos, and Mexican officialdom. In these actions, "transnational communities have established deep footholds in receiving countries that reduce the risks and uncertainties that generally accompany migration" (Camposeco and Griffith 1990: 6). This process of the replication of a native community on foreign soil so as to continue to express the identity of a specific ethnic group makes Benedict Anderson's (1990) "imagined community" a relevant concept for this study. Or as stated by Akhil Gupta and James Ferguson,

> *Remembered places have often served as symbolic anchors of community for dispersed people. This has long been true for immigrants who use memory of place to construct imaginatively their new lived world. Homeland in this way remains one of the most powerful unifying symbols of mobile and displaced peoples, though the relation to homeland may be very differently constructed in different settings. (1992: 11)*

While people in exile have probably existed since warfare came into being, current numbers indicate a growing use of refuge by more and more people. At present some 40 million people worldwide have crossed international borders seeking security and protection. This is the case for the Mayas of Guatemala who sought refuge in Chiapas, Mexico, in 1982. In Guatemala these indigenous people, with a language and culture different from that of the dominant society, were marginalized and exploited. The conditions of marginalization and exploitation were not altered when they reached refuge: the refugee camp was a restricted space and place, dislocated from the land that gave Maya culture its roots. In this new place the maintenance of their culture was threatened and disrupted. Their marginal status became more evident when formerly hardworking farmers became landless peasants, dependent on international humanitarian aid for survival.

> *With the reorientation of economic and social life away from independent subsistence farming toward dependent ration collection, the ethos of self-determination is being subtly undermined. Instead of looking to oneself, to one's kinsmen, and to the land for subsistence and survival, it is now possible and, for some, necessary to look to an external agency for assistance. (Edwards 1988: 321)*

For the past one hundred years the Maya of Guatemala have been the subject of anthropological studies, many of which focused on the ancient Maya, leaving the inheritors of that great civilization almost unnoticed. When ethnographic accounts of present-day Mayas began to appear about fifty years ago, many ethnographers, but by no means all, attempted reconstructions of traditional Maya culture or looked at issues of Maya-ladino relations, giving secondary importance to the contemporary land problems and economic issues that Mayas faced (e.g., Bunzel 1972; Hawkins 1984; Tumin 1952).

But beginning in the mid-1970s anthropologists studied and wrote more about the actual economic and community parameters of Maya life (e.g., Hinshaw 1975; Smith 1977; Warren 1978). These Western Mayanists have given Maya culture a solid place in the array of complex and challenging world civilizations. Their work and that of linguists, ethnologists, archaeologists, epigraphers, and ethnohistorians have made Maya civilization a focus of world attention and admiration. As these scholars share their knowledge with Maya people, their work will become more relevant to Mayas and Mayanists alike. Mayanists will then have to deal with subjects who question and challenge the traditional anthropological approach. As Anthony Giddens writes, "Here the question plainly isn't only the disappearance of the exotic, the far away places which were so inaccessible. Anthropologists used to deal with individuals and groups who by and large didn't answer back" (1995: 273).

In turn Maya people can offer an understanding of a deeper relationship with nature and the universe, and they can present Western thinkers with new ways to understand our current ecological and economic crisis. A more helpful and engaging anthropology may develop as collaboration between Mayas and Mayanists becomes more common. Toward this end the work of Manz (1988a, 1988b, 1988c), Carmack (1995), Warren (1997), and Robert Carlsen (1997), among others, sets a goal for the anthropological community to emulate.

Certainly the anthropological studies of the Maya by North American academics and published in the United States in English did little to disabuse the Guatemalan ruling class and even Guatemalan intellectuals of their pervasive ideas that Mayas were a drag on national development, that they were backward, incapable of moving forward in a changing world and unable to deal with modern technology. The Maya reality is something different. We consider ourselves to be the major movers of the Guatemalan nation, not only ideologically, as in the use of Mayan symbols to give the country its national character and identity, but also economically, as Mayas have made major contributions to Guatemala through the construction of its modern infrastructure, much of this under the duress of forced labor in the past, and through our continued exploitation today on modern plantations (Castellanos Cambranes 1988).

This book concentrates on Maya life in the refugee camps because there is a great need to document the hardships, the hard work, and the triumph of Maya survival and growth in exile. Our generations yet to come will benefit from knowing of this struggle to maintain and transform our cultural traditions during this time as well as in previous centuries. Thus we reaffirm our place and presence in Guatemalan national life as visible human beings making history even in our exile.

Field Research Methods

THIS STUDY IS based on field research in Guatemalan refugee camps in the state of Chiapas, Mexico. My intention is to analyze the dynamics of cultural resistance and transformation that occurred in the refugee camps largely as a result of the interrelationship between several Maya ethnic and linguistic groups represented in the camps, among them Q'anjob'al, Popb'al Ti', Ixil, Chuj, and Mam speakers and some ladinoized Mayas who spoke only Spanish.[8]

In 1982 there were some two hundred refugee camps scattered along the Guatemala-Mexico border, but between 1982 and 1992 some of the camps were relocated or dismantled. Over the last fifteen years small camps were integrated into bigger ones, then bigger camps were dismantled into smaller ones. Thus there can only be an accounting of the number of refugee camps and their locations at any one time.

My research was conducted in two major camps, La Cieneguita and La Gloria, each containing approximately three thousand people, and in several small camps of one hundred to two hundred families, Guadalupe Victoria, Villa Cocalito, Nicolás Bravo, and Las Maravillas Tenejapa in the same region. These

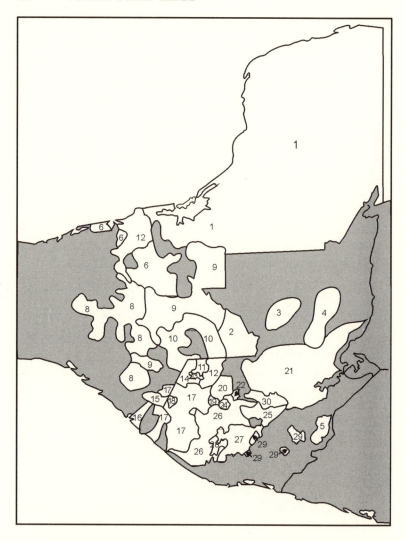

*Maya languages. From England and Elliott 1990. Courtesy of
Centro de Investigaciones Regionales de Mesoamérica.*

refugee camps were chosen because at the time of my research
they were the best organized. I speak Popb'al Ti' and Q'anjob'al
and have long experience working with people in these languages. In addition, I had Maya friends living as refugees in

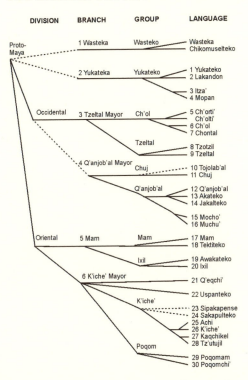

DIVISION	BRANCH	GROUP	LANGUAGE
Proto-Maya	1 Wasteka	Wasteko	Wasteka / Chikomuselteko
	2 Yukateka	Yukateko	1 Yukateko / 2 Lakandon
			3 Itza' / 4 Mopan
Occidental	3 Tzeltal Mayor	Ch'ol	5 Ch'orti' / Ch'olti' / 6 Ch'ol / 7 Chontal
		Tzeltal	8 Tzotzil / 9 Tzeltal
	4 Q'anjob'al Mayor	Chuj	10 Tojolab'al / 11 Chuj
		Q'anjob'al	12 Q'anjob'al / 13 Akateko / 14 Jakalteko
			15 Mocho' / 16 Muchu'
Oriental	5 Mam	Mam	17 Mam / 18 Tektiteko
		Ixil	19 Awakateko / 20 Ixil
	6 K'iche' Mayor		21 Q'eqchi'
		K'iche'	22 Uspanteko / 23 Sipakapense / 24 Sakapulteko / 25 Achi / 26 K'iche' / 27 Kaqchikel / 28 Tz'utujil
		Poqom	29 Poqomam / 30 Poqomchi'

these camps, and I lived for ten months at the Guadalupe Victoria camp where I, along with my brother and others, worked as volunteers in educational programs among Jakaltek, Mam, and Q'anjob'al refugees in 1983 and 1984. I have followed the process of building, dismantling, and relocation of the camps in Chiapas since the arrival of the refugees in that region in 1982.

Among the anthropological methods I used were in-depth interviews, direct observations of refugee life and behavior, identification of linguistic codes and structures arising from the refugee situation, and comparative analysis of refugee life and behavior to determine differences among and between refugee camps. The data collected have been analyzed and interpreted to gain an understanding of the process of change, continuity, and intensification of such cultural forms as weaving, dress, ethnic relations, gender roles, oral traditions, education, religious beliefs, and the culture of resistance operating in the camps. I interviewed the leaders of the refugee camps as well as members of the Comisiones Permanentes de Refugiados Guatemaltecos en México (Permanent Commissions of Guatemalan Refugees; CCPP). I also conducted personal interviews with officials and members of Mexican and international organizations that aid refugees, such as the Comisión Mexicana de Ayuda a Refugiados (Mexican Commission for Aid to Refugees; COMAR) and the UNHCR, whose offices are located in Comitán, Chiapas. In addition, I examined official documents, censuses, and archival materials in Comitán and in the Diocese of San Cristóbal de las Casas.[9]

Another important research strategy was to tape testimonies of adults and children and to collect drawings, poems, songs, and other cultural and literary creations of the refugees in the camps. The early Maya literature and testimonial expression (the *Popol Vuh, Anales de los Kaqchikeles, Título de Totonicapán,* and the *Chilam Balam*) centered on questions of domination, conquest, ethnic conflict, and Maya resistance. For contemporary Mayas, the value of recent testimonies is in the expression of the internal sufferings and the need to elicit solidarity in the struggle to end violence. "Testimonio is, overtly or not, an intertexual dialogue of voices, reproducing but also creatively reordering historical events in a way which impresses as representative and true and which projects a vision of life in a society in need of transformation" (Zimmerman 1995b: 12).

Because of linguistic differences, I was able to interview only in Popb'al Ti', Q'anjob'al, and Spanish, the Maya languages to which I had access. The testimonies that are the collective experience of the different ethnic groups were obtained in the original Maya languages of the informants as well as in Spanish. These testimonies were provided mostly by adult men who had experienced *la violencia* in Guatemala in various political roles or social positions, for example, former soldiers, civil patrollers, peasants, catechists, and schoolteachers.[10]

Several problems arose which had to be resolved to do this research. First, the refugee camps were closely monitored by Mexican immigration authorities, and access to them was often difficult. Most of the time, as a protective measure for the refugees, specific permission from the officials of COMAR was required to enter the camps. This was especially true in 1988 and 1989. Second, the danger and insecurity of exile created the sense of a closed community and a suspicion of intruders among the refugees. On several occasions the Guatemalan army had made incursions into the refugee camps. The real danger combined with the psychological effects of exile and uncertainty prompted cautiousness toward all outsiders.

The big refugee camps such as La Gloria and La Cieneguita were more organized and politicized internally. Representatives of the CCPP maintained control over information provided to outsiders. Insecurity and constant fear were also expressed in the social relations and communal behavior in the camps. During 1982 and 1983, when their persecution even in Mexican territory was constant, refugees concealed their identities and were distrustful of foreigners. A regular exception to this rule was the presence of Church people, particularly Bishop Samuel Ruíz and Sister Lucy of the Diocese of San Cristóbal de las Casas who promoted programs to help the refugees from their arrival in 1982.

In 1992, during my last summer of fieldwork, the situation had changed: refugees were more open to Mexican and international solidarity organizations working among them. One problem in doing this later research was the persistent attempts of some mestizo refugee leaders to control refugee actions and decisions and those of all who worked among them.[11] Another problem related to reassessing the current situation to understand the delicate and shifting sociocultural environment, as the rhythm of life in the refugee camps changed in response to changing situations. The continual insecurity led refugees to

express their feelings in different ways depending on the problems they were currently facing, the types of activities undertaken,
or the situations experienced.[12]

Language barriers were also present, and while my knowledge
of Q'anjob'al and Popb'al Ti' in addition to Spanish was a useful
entrée to the refugee camps, fieldwork remained difficult
because eight other Mayan languages (Tzotzil, Tzeltal, Tojolabal,
Mam, Chuj, K'iche', Lacandón, and Akatek) were also spoken in
the area. Given these problems, especially the tension generated
by COMAR's restrictions on visiting refugee camps, I concentrated my research on small camps where Spanish, Popb'al Ti',
and Q'anjob'al were spoken. The center for my early research on
refugees, in 1983, was the camp at Guadalupe Victoria (one
thousand refugees) located outside the Mexican community of
the same name on land the community allowed them to use. I
was fortunate to live with relatives and friends, especially José
Montejo, a schoolteacher whose insights and experience have
greatly enriched this study.

The second phase of my fieldwork was carried out during the
summers of 1988, 1989, and 1992. At this time the refugee
camp at Guadalupe Victoria had already been dismantled, and
the refugees were dispersed in small camps along the border. I
continued my fieldwork at these new camps, such as Nicolás
Bravo and Villa Cocalito, Spanish- and Popb'al Ti'-speaking
refugee communities of about two hundred each. My assistants
in these camps were mainly Jakaltek refugees. I was accompanied by Gaspar Camposeco, who promoted Maya theater in the
camps. The poet Antonio L. Cota García and his family were also
very helpful in the camps. Cota García was my major link with
Villa Cocalito and Nicolás Bravo. Also, Antonio Mendoza, orga-
nizer of the Ah Mayab' cultural group, gave me support while visiting Villa Cocalito. I occasionally visited other Q'anjob'al
refugee camps, such as Las Maravillas (five hundred refugees)
and La Gloria and La Cieneguita, but research there was more
difficult because they were more politicized. My assistant in

these camps was Pilin Xapin, a Q'anjob'al refugee who recently has moved to Immokalee, Florida, where there is a large Q'anjob'al refugee community. Another important assistant in these camps was Alfonso Rojas, a Jakaltek, who visited most of the refugee camps as a composer and singer of Maya songs. Since my research the camps have again undergone reorganization and dispersed.

During the summer of 1992 I returned to the refugee camps in Chiapas and videotaped cultural representations and artistic performances by the refugees.[13] I recorded songs and dramatic plays, and I helped to organize the activities of the Ah Mayab' group.[14]

Then in January 1993 I went back to the camps and accompanied the twenty-five hundred refugees who took part in the first major journey of organized, collective return to their homeland in northern Guatemala. This part of my work was as a cultural adviser for a film on refugee life in Chiapas and the Kuchumatan highlands of Guatemala.[15] This was the first time I had returned to my country since I went into exile in 1982.

Throughout my research I have been heartened and fortified by the persistence and courage of the refugees. Their determination and endurance are a testimony to the strength of our culture. Their adaptation under conditions of unutterable hardship and their transformation of that culture under duress give me hope for our future.

2

TOWARD A MAYA HISTORY
OF GUATEMALA

Before the Spanish Arrival

OUR MAYA HISTORY is long and powerful. When
Egypt's first pharaohs took office in the Nile valley, our
ancestors were growing corn, building platforms, and
making pottery, developing the basis for Mesoamerican
village life in the New World. The remnants of these cultures can be seen in such sites as Cuello and Kaminaljuyú.

When democracy was flowering in the Attic world,
our ancestors were forming city-states such as Tikal,
Uaxactún, and Quiriguá, with monumental art and archi-
tecture, writing, calendars, and astrological systems. Our
first recorded Maya date, 7.10.0.0.0, was chiseled in
stone before the dawn of the Christian era. Our Maya
ancestors developed regional political organizations in
the lowlands whose trade networks extended into
Mexico. They influenced and were influenced by the civilizations in the Central Valley of Mexico (Henderson
1981: 24). By the time Rome had fallen and Europe had
struggled through dark ages of chaos and disease, our

lowland city-states had also reached their peak and begun the process of decentralization and dispersal.

When Charlemagne ascended to the throne of the Holy Roman Empire, our ancestors had begun to reestablish city-states such as Iximché, K'umarcaaj, and Zaculeu in the Guatemalan highlands, maintaining ancient links to epi-Toltec rulers in the Yucatán peninsula of Mexico and vying with each other for control of land and trade. Trade relations were particularly intense with the Mexica rulers in the Valley of Mexico after A.D. 1400 (Carmack 1981: 142). During the postclassic Maya period, city-states such as the Mayapán empire in the northern lowlands of the Yucatán and the K'iche' Maya in the central highlands of Guatemala developed and flourished. "Both the southern highland and northern lowland Maya states traded extensively with the Oaxaca and Central Mexico core zones, mostly through the mediation of outside, long-distance merchants" (Carmack, Gasco, and Gossens 1996: 95). In the Maya highlands of Guatemala, the K'iche' extended their empire, seeking to incorporate other Maya people in the northern, central, and western highlands. Overall there were more than thirty Maya linguistic communities, or native nations, redefining themselves and their internal relations when the Spanish arrived. In other words, before the coming of the Spanish, we ruled ourselves; we were in charge of our own destinies.

The Conquest and Colonial Rule

THE SPANISH INVADERS landed first in Mexico and brought with them horses, metal spears, and guns. But their greatest weapon of destruction was the diseases carried from Europe to our homelands. These diseases spread faster than the Spanish could, and by the time Pedro de Alvarado reached the highlands of Guatemala in 1524, our ancestors were already struck down by smallpox and pneumonic varieties of the bubonic plague. The *Annals of the Kaqchikels* tell of the great waves of disease that felled our people (Recinos and Goetz 1953: 115–16).

Despite sickness and severely reduced numbers, the Mayas fought off the Spanish as long as they could. But Alvarado made use of divisions between and within Maya nations and claimed victory by turning language groups, such as the Kaqchikel, the K'iche', and the Tzutujil, against each other and pitting elite rulers against common Maya farmers. We remember our Maya heroes of those days, such as Tecún Umán, who fought for our right to remain independent and unconquered. But the Spanish prevailed against our people, sick and dwindling in numbers because of the pandemic diseases brought to our lands.

The Spanish conception of "Indians," as they called us, the indigenous people of the New World, was formed before their arrival. Their purposes, to become wealthy landlords and to return to Spain rich enough to take positions in the Spanish court, meant that they saw our land and labor as a vast resource to be tapped for their gain. Because, even with the rapid decline in our numbers, there were fewer of them than of us, enslavement and forced labor were the rule in colonial society. This was justified by their view of us as savages: "Those people are barbaric, uninstructed in letters and the art of government, and completely ignorant, unreasoning, and totally incapable of learning anything but the mechanical arts; that they are sunk in vice, are cruel, and are of such character that, as nature teaches, they are to be governed by the will of others" (Sepúlveda, quoted in Las Casas [1552] 1974: 11).

These ideas about the nature of the Indians, combined with the desire of the Spaniards to be masters and landlords, encouraged a great emigration of Spaniards to settle in the newly conquered territories. To facilitate the colonial project the foreign masters were accompanied by Roman Catholic clergy, who promised to save Maya souls through conversion and to raise Mayas culturally by destroying what they considered to be devilish traditions. In the light of such beneficent intentions, indigenous resistance was seen as inhospitable, ungrateful, and even satanic. In the face of Maya resistance, Alvarado destroyed entire communities and forced Mayas out of their homelands. He documented the expulsion of the K'iche' from their lands in his own words: "And as I knew them to have such a bad disposition towards the service of His Majesty, and to ensure the good and peace of this land, I burnt them [the K'iche' kings], and sent to burn the town and to destroy it, for it is a very strong and dangerous place, that more resembles a robbers' stronghold than a city. . . . [Then] I made an expedition and chased them and threw them out of the entire country" (Alvarado 1969: 63–64).

The conquerors brought with them to the New World the Spanish feudal system and began by establishing *encomiendas* (feudal land grants), expropriating Maya land and assigning the Mayas living on it to work for the Spanish landlord. But even more precious than the land was the right to the work of the Maya population, as land without workers would produce nothing of value. "In all cases, the rewards to the conquerors were Indians, taken either as slaves or assigned to individual Spaniards to whom they owed tribute and labor" (Sherman 1979: 9).

In the Kuchumatan highlands of northwestern Guatemala, for instance, Huehuetenango was given to Juan de Espinar, a conquistador who accompanied Gonzalo de Alvarado in the conquest of the Kuchumatan region in 1525. As *encomendero*, or landlord, Juan de Espinar enjoyed the labor of between two hundred and three hundred *indios de servicio*, and he accumulated so much wealth "he could afford to lose twenty thousand *pesos de oro* through gambling" (Lovell 1985b: 96). Most of his labor force worked the mines around Chiantla. If Mayas resisted his control and exploitation, Espinar could call on the governor to reduce the Indians to slavery. "When the *principales* [Maya chieftains or elders] of Huehuetenango refused to serve Juan de Espinar, their encomendero, Jorge de Alvarado [the governor] gave the encomendero license to convince them otherwise by putting them in chains. Later these *señores* took revenge by burning some houses in the pueblos of Espinar" (Sherman 1979: 289).

Mayas did not remain passive in the face of colonial domination. Sometimes they openly challenged colonial forces through acts of retaliation or uprisings and rebellions, but more often they fled the Spanish-controlled core or simulated accommodation to the system. "The Mayas were aware that resistance would provoke armed reprisals and they found it more prudent to feign submission, and then relocate their settlements" (Farriss 1984: 16). In some cases they managed to avoid the conquest for a long time. The area of the Petén inhabited by the Itza Maya remained unconquered until 1607 (Cambranes 1997: 228). Continuous pressure on Maya communities led Mayas to seek refuge in less controlled places.

From time to time full-scale uprisings have also been part of the Maya resistance to outside domination. The Tzotzil-Tzeltal rebellion in 1712 (Bricker 1981), the Caste War in the Yucatán in 1846 (Reed 1964), limited uprisings in Totonicapán and Patzicia in the ninteenth century, and even the recent Zapatista rebellion in Chiapas all confirm an active Maya opposition to domination, exploitation, and control.

Caught in a developing colonial system, the "collective enterprise of survival" of the Mayas was severely tested (Farriss 1984). Despite ongoing struggles against everyday forms of oppression, any attempt at rising up against the colonial landlords brought fierce retribution. Punishment for resistance to Spanish dominion was swift and relentless. To ensure obedience of the indigenous population, the Spanish made clear with public punishments that whoever opposed the will of the ruling masters was an enemy of the government.

By the seventeenth century *repartimiento* (a system of enforced labor) had replaced the encomienda as the labor distribution device of choice. Many colonists, not all of them landlords, wanted access to a still-dwindling Maya labor pool (see table). To facilitate the repartimiento labor drafts, Maya communities faced massive reorganization through the processes of *reducción* and *congregación*. Ostensibly to encourage their conversion to Christianity, the reorganized and consolidated Maya communities made possible easier access to a labor force for those assigned their labor by the colonial government.

These pressures and the unending, daily colonial brutalities pushed Mayas to establish villages in more mountainous or remote areas, away from the developing Spanish urban centers. Throughout this time there was constant movement and migration, some of it at the behest of the colonial government, some of it a form of resistance as part of the collective enterprise of survival. The heavy weight of tributes and forced labor that characterized repartimiento provoked movements by persecuted Mayas toward uncontrolled regions of refuge. "In fact, it [the area beyond the frontier] became the home of large numbers of refugees who fled colonial rule to form independent settlements of their own or to join their unconquered cousins" (Farriss 1984: 16).[1]

Throughout the colonial period Maya labor built the colonial cities and churches, transported Spanish goods and supplies, provided the Spaniards with housing, food, and drink, and created their wealth through the mining of gold and silver and the production of cacao and dyes (Moors 1988: 67). Spanish men, who went or sent home to find "suitable" women to marry, often impregnated Maya women; their children were *mestizos* (later *ladinos*) if they were acknowledged by their fathers but Mayas if they were not. The Spanish had a great talent for crafting racial and ethnic pigeonholes for different degrees of racial inheritance in their society, but the greatest gulf was always between the true Spaniards—both those born in Spain, the *gachupines*, and those born in the colony, the *criollos*—and the true Mayas.

As colonial society grew, ladinos, who were often bilingual, were used by the Spanish to control Maya life. Attempts were made to assimilate Mayas into Spanish patterns of life, to convert

ESTIMATES OF THE MAYA POPULATION
OF GUATEMALA, 1520–1992

Year	Maya Population	Total Guatemala Population	Maya Population as Percent of Total
1520	2,000,000	2,000,000	100
1550	427,850	—	—
1575	236,540	—	—
1595	133,280	—	—
1625	128,000	—	—
1684	242,020	—	—
1710	236,208	—	—
1770	220,500	315,000	70
1778	248,500	355,000	70
1804	292,000	417,000	70
1820	350,000	500,000	70
1820	416,500	595,000	70
1830	—	600,000	—
1830	469,000	670,000	70
1840	525,700	751,000	70
1850	592,900	847,000	70
1860	665,700	951,000	70
1870	756,000	1,080,000	70
1880	844,384	1,224,602	69
1893	1,005,767	1,501,145	67
1914	—	2,183,166	—
1921	1,343,283	2,004,900	67
1940	1,560,000	2,400,000	65
1950	1,611,928	2,870,272	56
1964	2,185,679	4,339,204	50
1973	2,680,178	5,589,543	48
1973	2,984,500	—	—
1980	3,230,393	6,873,176	47
1988	4,000,000	7,500,000	52
1991	5,423,000	—	60
1992	—	9,500,000	—

Source: Lovell and Lutz 1994.

them to Christianity, and to stop the use of their Maya language and inculcate the speaking of Spanish, that is, to "ladinoize" them.

Independent Guatemala: The Nineteenth Century

ALTHOUGH THE MAYA uprising in Totonicapán in 1820 may have moved Guatemala closer to independent status, the actual separation from Spain brought few changes to the lives of the Mayas. Liberals fought Conservatives, those in favor of a unified Central American state fought those wishing independent status for various regions. At the final outcome nation-state lines on maps divided us from our brothers and sisters in El Salvador, Honduras, and Chiapas, but little else changed. Liberals, who argued that it was necessary to compel Indians to work for plantation owners if the nation was to progress, dominated the early years of independence. For instance, the Decree Law of November 3, 1829, stated that the laziness of Maya *campesinos* stunted Guatemalan agriculture: "Wage laborers who do not have a known way of making a living and those who work with machines and are not exercising their profession will be forced to work on the *haciendas*. The mayors will make sure that the people comply with this law, and the omissions or excesses in the application of it should be known by the chief officials" (Skinner-Klee 1954: 20; my translation).

When the Liberal Mariano Gálvez came to power in 1831, Maya communities were exposed to even harsher land appropriations and labor drafts. In 1838 Mayas flocked to join the uprising of the Conservative Rafael Carrera, who obtained the support of the Jakaltek, the Q'anjob'al, the Chuj, and the Mam of the Kuchumatan highlands as he organized his rebel forces in Jacaltenango (Recinos 1954).[2] In general, for the Mayas Conservative rule in Guatemala under Carrera was more benign than that of the preceding or following Liberal periods. Maya communities felt more empowered to deal with their cultural and internal affairs without outside intervention (LaFarge and Byers 1940; Stephens 1841). In the Kuchumatan highlands Carrera is still known as the "President of the People," and he appears in the legends and oral histories of the Kuchumatan Maya communities.[3]

Coffee cultivation was introduced in the middle of the century, and its requirements for land and labor placed additional burdens on Maya communities. The coffee planters stood in opposition to both the mercantile elites and the rural population who supported Carrera, and ultimately his dictatorship was overthrown in 1871 by Gen. Justo Rufino Barrios. Barrios was a Liberal who supported the expansion of coffee cultivation, the introduction of foreign capital, and the encouragement of North American and European immigrants to Guatemala. He wanted to build Guatemala as a whiter nation, able to benefit from European trade and culture (Woodward 1993: 469). Liberals were less concerned with the rights of Indians and more concerned with the coffee growers' need for cheap and readily available labor (McCreery 1994: 172). Land for coffee *fincas* (farms) was obtained by the expropriation or nationalization of all Church property. In support of this policy the government wrote, "One of the major obstacles to the prosperity and development of the Republic is the existence of property in dead hands which withhold capital from commerce, agriculture, and industry" (*Recopilación . . . Guatemala*, 1:210, quoted in McCreery 1994: 182).

The religious property nationalized included that belonging to the Maya *cofradías*, or brotherhoods. Of even greater impact on Maya communities was the selling of "state-owned" *terrenos baldíos* (barren lands), land often claimed by Maya communities, and the leasing of *ejidos* (lands under community control). When the Mayas of Cobán refused to lease more land for coffee cultivation, the departmental governor declared their possession illegal. In January 1877 the Barrios government allowed the conversion of rented land to the private property of the coffee grower (McCreery 1994: 183–85).

Seasonal migrant workers were needed to pick the coffee, so Barrios revived the *mandamientos,* or forced labor drafts, on a national scale. Decree 177 created three types of workers for the plantations: resident workers (*colonos*); seasonal workers who were bound to the plantation by wage advances (*mozos habilitados*); and seasonal workers who received no advances (*mozos no habilitados*). Maya workers carried work books, or *libretos,* in which their contracts, debts and credits, and days worked were recorded. But Mayas resisted these laws, and the Barrios government was forced over and over to strengthen the labor laws, extending extraeconomic coercion through the threat of unpaid labor on roads under military command (McCreery 1994:188–90).

The Barrios government also retaliated against those Maya communities that had been strong supporters of Carrera. According to the oral history of the people in the Kuchumatan highlands, ladino emissaries of the Liberal government came to Maya towns and deceived the people by asking them to rebel against the new government. The emissaries convinced the towns to enlist in such an uprising, giving them a date when the leaders of the rebellion would come. On the appointed day government soldiers arrived and put the local Maya leaders to death. In Jacaltenango six Alkal Txah, or Prayer Makers, were shot at the church by a firing squad. The deceit of the ladinos on this and other occasions has not been forgotten. Regional and local leaders, both Spanish and ladino, such as the *jefe político* (political chief) of Huehuetenango, Evaristo Cajas, used their familial and political connections to Barrios to amass property through widespread killings (Casaverde 1976: 241).

More complex forms of resistance developed during these years. Maya communities became more closed to outside interference, developing what Eric Wolf (1957) called "the closed corporate community." Cultural resistance took the form of enacting conflictive ethnic relations in plays and traditional dances. During Holy Week Mayas satirized ladino landlords and local officials as Judas the traitor or as Juan Noj, the image of the devil, expressing their hatred for the oppression to which they were subjected (Wagley 1949; Warren 1978). And Mayas continued to flee, moving to Mexico or higher into the mountains or into the Ixcán jungle.[4]

The project of nation-state building, begun earlier in the independence era, took on urgency in the face of international trade and the promotion of white immigration. By the end of the nineteenth century it was based in a romantic nationalism, which Benedict Anderson terms "the imagined community" (1990: 15). This idealized image of the nation was a creole-mestizo project that marginalized Mayas and excluded them from any political or economic benefits (Martínez Peláez 1971). According to Anderson, many of Guatemala's current problems are rooted in this truncated and poorly developed sense of nationhood.

The creoles, mestizos, and ladinos came to call themselves Guatemalans and believed that a true nation must be "white by blood." The Mayas had not been eliminated, and indeed the plantation elite needed Mayas for their labor. But Mayas could not be considered equal partners in the nation of Guatemala, because that would call into question their treatment since the conquest. As Mayas were seen as inferior, they not only needed to be controlled and directed, but the proportion of Europeans to Mayas needed to be tilted more in favor of the former.[5]

Barrios remained in power until 1885, and his land and labor policies had a dramatic impact on the socioeconomic life of Maya communities. Like Carrera, his name and image as a Guatemalan tyrant have persisted among Mayan people.

The Twentieth Century

THE LIBERAL POLICIES of the late nineteenth century continued under Manuel Estrada Cabrera (1898–1920) and Jorge Ubico (1931–44). Under Ubico vagrancy laws replaced debt peonage as a device for forcing labor to the coffee plantations. Based on the amount of land an individual owned or his "ability" to support his family through nonagricultural labor, Maya men were forced to work one hundred or one hundred fifty days a year and to give two weeks of labor on the national road system or pay a two-dollar tax (Moors 1988: 69–70). By this time land for Maya communities had become quite scarce, and the work drafts took time away from producing corn and beans on what little land Maya families had. Population increases in the country as a whole and in Maya communities exacerbated land problems and depressed the wages paid for plantation work (see table above).

Although Ubico was appreciated in some Maya communities, the Mayas of the Kuchumatan region saw him as the cause of their persecution as laborers and said of him (and still say of him), "Najuwico tu' kaw matzwalil naj" (That man, Ubico, was an evil one). In contrast, Carmack (1995: 193) reports that in Momostenango, where Ubico and local ladino rulers enforced a strong centralized government, his rule was seen as a good one that brought important changes to the community.

When the growing middle class in Guatemala City overthrew Ubico in 1944 and opened the period known as the Ten Years of Spring, first Juan José Arévalo (1945–51) and then Jacobo Arbenz (1951–54) initiated laws that brought about changes for Maya communities. Most important, there was an end to forced labor. Mayas who could support themselves without working on the plantations did so, and the 1940s and 1950s saw an increasing diversification of Maya economic activity (cash cropping, trading, transportation, craft production, etc.), especially in areas close to decent roads. Many Mayas were still forced to the plantations by poverty induced by land shortages and low wages. Labor contractors, both Maya and ladino, provided loans against work that were called in when particular fincas, now including cotton and sugarcane plantations, needed laborers. This reform period also introduced major political parties into highland communities, and in many villages the appointed ladino officials were replaced with elected Mayan mayors and town officials (Moors 1988: 70–71). In the Kuchumatan highlands social relations within and between Maya communities were affected. Political organizing and political parties challenged the older civil-religious *cargo* system of community leadership, so that in Santiago Chimaltenango (Chimbal) by the mid-1950s, elections had superseded the age-graded, ritual obligations of the cargo system (Watanabe 1990: 192). And in an area where arable land was in short supply, conflicts arose between Maya communities and between the landless and the landed as agrarian reform drew near.

Arbenz's attempts to deal with the problems of landlessness led in 1952 to the Agrarian Reform Law, Decree 900, which sought to expropriate unused land from fincas larger than two *caballerías* (1 caballería = 45,125 hectares) in size, or from national or municipal land, and redistribute it in various ways to peasants and workers (Handy 1994: 86–90). Elite private landowners fought against the implementation of this law with all the tools at their command, but it was the largest landowner in the country, the U.S.-based United Fruit Company, that broke the land reform and all reform measures by pushing for the intervention of the U.S. Central Intelligence Agency (CIA) to overthrow the Arbenz government and by bringing charges of communism against all in favor of land reform (Gleijeses 1991: 229 ff.; Schlesinger and Kinzer 1982: 89–95). This prevalent cold war, domino theory, "communist conspiracy" language was accepted and used by the U.S. Department of State and the news media as a justification for intervention. The Catholic church, then solidly behind the ruling classes, voiced concern about Guatemala's drift toward totalitarianism. The CIA trained and armed a counterrevolutionary force under Col. Carlos Castillo Armas and overthrew the Arbenz government.

The succeeding Castillo Armas regime reversed many of the gains of the Ten Years of Spring. Former owners reclaimed their lands, and corruption, graft, and inept rule made life harder for ordinary Guatemalans.[6] Now that Guatemala was safe for international capitalism, U.S. corporations made money and credit available for an expanding agroexport economy. Coffee, cotton, and sugar exports, with their concomitant demands for labor, increased during the 1960s and 1970s (Moors 1988: 72).[7] In addition to the persecution of former Arévalo and Arbenz supporters, the general pattern of elite rule coupled with occasional open military attacks against Maya communities was again established. A small uprising in eastern Guatemala was decisively crushed by the army.

Maya resistance, as always open to migration and flight elsewhere, followed new paths this time. With the help of outside organizations, primarily Catholic Action and the U.S. Agency for International Development, Mayas formed cooperatives to enable the bulk purchase of seeds and fertilizer. The ideology of Catholic Action was to rescue Indians from the evils of communism and to purify the Church of the syncretic Maya-Catholicism in which the traditional Maya beliefs resided. It denied a religious role to the traditional leadership of Maya elders and to the civil-religious cargo system.

> *Catholic Action ideology, as it has been elaborated by Indian converts in San Andrés, asserts that spiritual membership in the universalistic Catholic Church should supersede ethnic identities; singles out local ladinos as the major stumbling block for the actualization of economic equivalence for all individuals; and proposes ladinoization as a means to achieving social and economic equivalence of Indians and ladinos in the broader society. (Warren 1978: 94)*

Some communities preferred to face the uncertainty of starting over, and moved people, animals, and saints to new cooperative communities in the Ixcán. They invested in the education of their children, hoping to spare them a life of hated plantation labor. As Mayas found ways to free themselves from economic dependence on ladino shopkeepers and labor contractors, ethnic tensions in highland communities increased (Frank and Wheaton 1984: 31–34).

Guatemala in the 1970s

GENERAL SUCCEEDED GENERAL as president of the country. The military entrenched itself in all major Guatemalan institutions (political parties, banking, construction, etc.) and did not compete against the landed elite for wealth but sought to acquire other sources of wealth for itself. It opened to military ownership vast tracts of land in the Petén and the Ixcán, land often claimed by Maya communities and cooperatives, and it sponsored mining, oil exploration, and cattle ranching in these areas. In May 1978, 100 of the 600 Q'eqchi' Indians seeking an answer to their letter protesting their impending eviction from their lands by the military were massacred in the village of Panzós (Frank and Wheaton 1984: 55).

For ordinary Mayas, wages for plantation work did not increase, but the price of fertilizer, corn, and beans did. By the mid-1970s 75 percent of Guatemalan children, most of them Mayas, were malnourished, and in 1976, twenty-two thousand people, again mostly Mayas, died in an earthquake that caused extensive damage from Huehuetenango to Chimaltenango. Peasants and workers, Mayas and ladinos, rural and urban dwellers began to protest the conditions that forced them into poverty (Frank and Wheaton 1984: 38–39).

Guerrilla groups, remnants of the 1960s struggle, reappeared during the 1970s and grew into three major insurgency groups working in the cities and the countryside. Their growth paralleled the increasing army repression in the highlands and the growing desperation of people for survival (Moors 1988: 75). This then was the backdrop to the violence of the late 1970s and early 1980s. It was only necessary for the military and the dominant elite to invoke the word *communists* to legitimate the genocidal and ethnocidal war against the Maya people that followed. The threat of communism attracted military aid from the United States for the purpose of keeping the Americas safe from this cursed evil. Over the course of five hundred years, the dominant rhetoric has shifted from Indians as "savages" to Indians as "communists" who threaten the status quo with seizure of private property and the introduction of totalitarianism (Arias 1990; González 1992).[8]

3

THE ADVENT OF
VIOLENCE IN THE
KUCHUMATAN HIGHLANDS

THE GUATEMALAN GOVERNMENT began its program of repression to discourage the growing tide of peasant and labor organizing, protest, and dissent following the earthquake in 1976 in the departments of Chimaltenango and Quiché, south and east of the Kuchumatan area. This first wave of violence was selective, aimed at decapitating the leadership of organizations the government found troublesome and deemed subversive. Between 1976 and the end of 1977, 68 cooperative leaders were killed in the Ixcán, 40 in Chajul, 28 in Cotzal, and 32 in Nebaj. The earthquake and its resulting chaos were the pretext for increasing militarization in these rural areas (Davis and Hodson 1982: 15). Hundreds of religious leaders, priests, Protestant clergy, lay preachers, and catechists were kidnapped or killed, including Father Bill Woods, a Maryknoll priest involved in the Ixcán resettlements. Other foreign priests received death threats or were forced out of the country. Maya-language radio stations were closed by the government. The violence continued in the rural areas against development workers, health workers, teachers, and journalists who reported on these events, and in the city against opposition politicians, trade unionists, and labor organizers (Davis and Hodson 1982: 21–24).

The growing activity of the Guatemalan guerrilla groups, combined with events elsewhere in Central America—the war in El Salvador and the victory of the Nicaraguan Sandinistas over Somoza—forced the Guatemalan military to rethink its strategy to preserve the status quo. Gen. Benedicto Lucas García, the president's brother, was responsible for drawing up plans for a massive campaign of strategic warfare against civilian populations thought to be collaborating with the guerrillas. These plans were first implemented in 1981 and came into full force after Gen. Efraín Ríos Montt came to power in a coup d'etat in March 1982. The army saw civilian populations, particularly Maya communities, as indistinguishable from guerrillas and guerrilla bases. The guerrilla group targeted was the Ejército Guerrillero de los Pobres, the Guerrilla Army of the Poor, or EGP. This group had been working in northern Quiché, the Ixcán, and Huehuetenango and had experienced more success recruiting than training or equipping its growing insurrectionary force and was therefore overextended. Under the new military plan, the worst excesses of military violence during the preceding decade became daily occurrences. Over the next eighteen months, four hundred highland villages would be eradicated, families torn apart, husbands tortured and murdered before their wives' eyes, women raped, babies bayoneted, fields, crops, and homes burned, and life in the highlands irreparably shredded (Manz 1988a: 17).

Violence in the Kuchumatan Highlands

THE PEOPLE IN the Kuchumatan knew through radio and word of mouth about the massacres that had occurred in the late

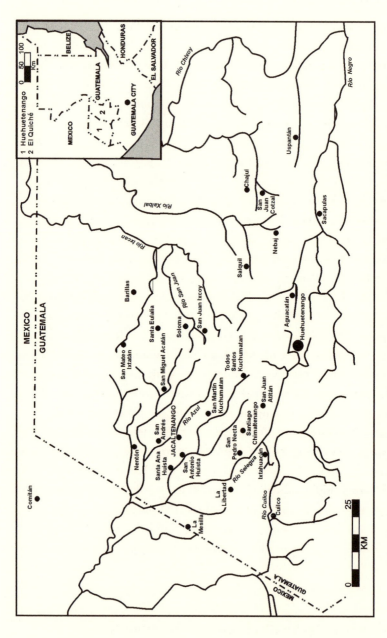

The Kuchumatan highlands. Adapted from Lovell 1985b. Courtesy of W. George Lovell.

1970s, the Panzós massacre in 1978 and the Spanish embassy massacre in 1980, but these events seemed far away and unrelated to their lives or their communities. But each community had its own special circumstances. In Chuj and Q'anjob'al communities where land was poor and scarce, many people had listened to the guerrillas' recruiting messages and had joined or supported their efforts. And in the Chuj community of San Mateo, people organized and fought the big lumber company, Cuchumadera, owned by powerful politicians and army officers, to preserve their community forests. Manz reported, "In December 1980, before any trees were actually cut, the guerrilla forces of the EGP, already strong in the region, entered San Mateo. The Cuchumadera company quickly pulled out" (1988a: 216).

At the end of the 1970s the guerrillas planned to focus their operations in the Jakaltek region, but the people were afraid of them. The Jakaltek people thought of the guerrillas as long-haired, unshaven ladinos who were adept at avoiding danger. When the guerrillas entered the municipios of Jacaltenango, San Antonio Huista, Santa Ana Huista, Nentón, and others to hold meetings, that image changed. Summoned to listen to the guerillas' speeches, the people realized that the guerrilla forces were made up of ladino leaders who spoke in Spanish *and* Mayas who translated their message into the local language. They were cautioned not to denounce the guerrillas and were asked, instead, to collaborate with them to overthrow the repressive government of Romeo Lucas García.

After the guerrillas' visits, many people were confused and fearful, as it was known that the army arrived soon after the guerrillas did. Army spies, *orejas* (informers) and *comisionados militares* (military commissioners), regularly reported on guerrilla activity and, indeed, were the source of information about army violence in other communities. This was the beginning of the killings, robberies, and disappearances of Mayas in Kuchumatan communities as the army started its counterinsurgency campaign. The following Q'anjob'al account, typical of accounts retold later by refugees, tells of the pattern of destruction.

Kaw lananxa yul kamik ko k'atan, lananxa skam amina, lananxa stz'a-toj na' haktuxin xma kon tit yetoj sunil hunin ti smasanil. No' Kaxhlan, no' tx'i', no' txitam, ay ma xkani, ay ma xtita. Ma kankan awal, smasanil xma kankanoj.

Death was approaching us, people were being killed, houses were burning down, that is why we left, all of us, with our children. Chickens, dogs, pigs, some were left behind, some came with us. The cornfields were abandoned, everything was left behind.[1]

This Is How Our Misery Began: Dreams and Portents[2]

BEFORE 1980 THE political situation in most Kuchumatan highland communities was calmer and less dramatic than that in the Ixcán and northern Quiché.[3] But when the army began to set up military barracks in our municipios in October, November, and December 1980, the rhythm of life changed and the conflicts began. It was at this time, well before the violence reached its peak, that Kuchumatan people began having dreams and visions and seeing omens. Dreams are as important to modern Mayas as they were during pre-Hispanic times.[4] Similarly, modern Mayas use dreams to understand and prepare for future events. "[Mayas] dream to live a full life. They dream to save their lives" (Laughlin 1988: 4). This is what occurred among the Mayas of the Kuchumatan highlands and what I also experienced living there at that time.

As 1980 drew to a close, there were many signs and omens of terrible events to come. Close to the Mexican border packs of wolves appeared, howling on the outskirts of villages. This upset many people because wolves had disappeared from the area long ago. But apparently the wolves returned, escaping from the forests that were being burned and bombed by the army in northern Quiché, Huehuetenango, and the Ixcán. Animals whose presence carries a strong omen, such as foxes, mountain lions, and owls, messengers of death and destruction, announced their proximity by howling during the dark nights. Dogs also foretold trouble. Perhaps to console each other, they went out onto the patios and barked sadly, as if they knew their masters would soon die. At other times they ran through the streets in pursuit of invisible things. Mayas know that when these strange things happen it is a signal that death is imminent. Some people, in their attempts to explain, said that dogs can foresee the future with more clarity than humans.

In the villages people reported having seen crosses without their tops and balls of fire rolling in the sky. Others said that the devil chased them along their paths, throwing stones and laughing or whistling to them at the darkest places in the roads. Women and children stopped coming down to the rivers to wash clothes late in the afternoon because undressed men whose bodies bore signs of torture appeared to them in visions. These strange-looking men with long noses appeared to them, making dramatic gestures as they climbed the trees on the edge of the river. For a long time people talked about these apparitions.

Many people had similar dreams that were told and retold in the communities, passing from mouth to mouth.

In my dreams, I saw big, golden letters in the sky.

In my dreams, I saw sharpened machetes falling from the sky to the earth. Many, so many, well-sharpened machetes were falling as rain from the sky.

It is almost like Mrs. Matal's dream. She said that she saw well-sharpened axes falling from the sky when the clouds opened.

Also, Señor Antonio said that a rain of boiling drops reached the village. He said that the drops entered the thatched roofs, making holes in the floor as they hit the ground.[5]

The village elders also dreamed, and their dreams were heard as tales of caution and retold in the highland communities.

Our ancestors came with red handkerchiefs tied to their heads and passed in the air in a procession that headed toward the west.

Mrs. Candelaria was sad when she saw in her dreams that the Virgin of Purification [the patron of the town] had abandoned her niche, and with lighted candles at her feet, she left her children [the people of the town] to go to Mexico.

Many people dreamed that the patron saints of their communities abandoned their chapels and went west toward the Mexican border, forsaking this land. And many people dreamed of fire that destroyed cornfields, animals, entire villages. The women wept over these dreams, and the elders sighed.

Army Bases in the Kuchumatan

IN THE TOWNS where the army established bases at the end of 1981, horrible events began to occur. Helicopters would arrive with gagged men transported in bags, brought in from distant communities to be tortured and executed inside the military barracks. Local townspeople could hear the screaming of men being tortured late at night. These nocturnal screams and the almost constant noise of submachine gun fire instilled panic among the local people. Skulls and dismembered parts of human bodies were found on the outskirts of towns, and dogs and buzzards fought over the carrion. Then the army began to kidnap villagers. At night drunken men were kidnapped from local houses where liquor was sold and taken to be tortured. In these dangerous circumstances fewer and fewer people came from nearby villages to sell their products in the local markets. Everyone knew that the soldiers could kill anyone with impunity. During the year so many Mayas were killed by the army that the soldiers created clandestine cemeteries to bury their victims.

In the town of Jacaltenango, two weeks after the army constructed its barracks, five young men were kidnapped. Three of them later reappeared, but the other two were never found. Then during the feast day for the town's patron saint, the army killed a young schoolteacher in the town plaza.[6] This event changed the life of the town and confirmed the local belief that the army was the most criminal institution that the Mayas had ever seen.

By July 1981 the army began to kill openly, invading small, isolated communities in the department of Huehuetenango, bringing death and destruction. Their bombing of the Q'anjob'al community of K'oya' on July 19 gives evidence of their tactics: "Two hundred soldiers attack the village of K'oya', San Miguel Acatán, Huehuetenango, killing more than 150 people. Helicopters surround and bomb the village, while soldiers throw grenades and fire machine guns on women, children and old people" (Manz 1988a: 246 n. 85).[7]

El Limonar: A Jakaltek Maya Village

ON SEPTEMBER 7, 1981, the people of El Limonar celebrated the feast day of their patron saint, the Virgin of the Nativity.[8] As was the custom, the villagers gathered to play the marimba and dance in the patio of the small chapel that housed the Virgin's statue. At about 8:00 P.M., without warning, a red pickup appeared on the newly built northwest highway (the Transversal del Norte) close to the Mexican border. The vehicle stopped some distance from the village and turned off its lights. A few minutes later several armed and masked men sprang out at the celebrating villagers shouting, "Long life to the EGP! Unite with the guerrilla movement!"

The leader of this group was masked and hooded but wore a long black jacket, the traditional dress of Q'anjob'al men. All of them wore the rubber boots typical of the guerrilla forces, but their weapons were *galils*, the Israeli-made rifles that the Guatemalan army used. The leader ordered the people to shout "¡Viva el EGP!" Then he stood on a chair and addressed the group: "We are from the EGP and we ask all of you to join us to overthrow President Lucas García and his army of assassins. We will give you training in the mountains and ten quetzals for joining us."

No one responded, so the leader continued, prodding the people, "Everyone say, 'Long life to the EGP!'" The armed men who had joined the crowd shouted their response, and again the leader asked the people to do the same. Pressed or motivated by the armed men, a group of five drunken men who had come to the fiesta from neighboring villages shouted, "¡Viva el EGP!" The armed men approached and told them that they would be given the ten quetzals as announced and, in addition, one hundred quetzals for the support of their families while they were away. Four of the men were young; the fifth was a married man with several children. They were led to the pickup while some of the armed men looted village houses and the Catholic chapel, from which they stole the Virgin's gold earrings, the village's gift to their patron saint. One of the villagers, a former soldier, noticed that his brother-in-law (the man with several children) was among the drunks taken to the truck. He approached the armed men and asked for his brother-in-law's release. Instead of freeing the brother-in-law, the armed men forced the protesting man into the truck, and they were all taken in the direction of the Río Selegua.

When the car started, the armed men took off their masks and identified themselves as soldiers from the military barracks at Camojallito, near the city of Huehuetenango. The car went at full speed and stopped at the edge of the bridge over the Río Selegua, a short distance from the international highway. Here, the captives were taken down and told to speak. But since they did not know what to say, they were ordered to lie face down on the ground while their arms were tied behind their backs. One soldier was ordered to dispatch them. The soldier opened fire on the first, killing him instantly. Then the soldier approached the second and opened fire at his head, . . . then the third victim.

As the soldier killed the fourth victim, the sixth man, lying on the ground with his hands tied, lifted himself up and jumped off the cliff above the Río Selegua. The soldier immediately fired his weapon at him and was joined by other soldiers who pursued him with the aid of flashlights. But the night was very dark, and their search was in vain. Although shot twice in the right leg, he escaped death at the hands of the army. Later, one other captive, taken by the same soldiers to the barracks at Camojallito, also bravely escaped that fate.

The deception of El Limonar was well planned by the army. The next day a group of soldiers came to the same village, asking if it was true that the "guerrillas" had passed through the community looting and kidnapping. When the people did not answer, the soldiers distributed flyers on which they had written, "Guerrillas: thieves and killers."

By the end of 1981 the killings and massacres increased in the northern regions of Huehuetenango. The army bombed and massacred entire communities. These attacks against the Maya people in the region were similar to those experienced in Maya communities in the Cobán, Quiché, Chimaltenango, and Sololá regions. Mayas were being killed by the thousands, and no one had the will or the authority to stop it. But if 1981 was bad, 1982 was worse.

The Darkest Year in Modern Maya History

THE VIOLENCE AND massacres that once seemed distant and unrelated to people in the Kuchumatan highlands began to touch their lives in 1982. No one was safe: the army's intent was to kill all suspected guerrillas, and all Mayas were suspect. The following chronology documents the major events of the first week of the year, most of which I witnessed personally.

JANUARY 1: In the community of La Laguna close to the Mexican border, people were at home. Many were preparing recently harvested corn for storage. Without warning, at 7:00 A.M. an earthquake shook the area. "Oh God, the corn, the corn!" cried the women. Those who still followed Maya traditions sprayed water over the ears of corn and said, "Paxanti Miyaya," meaning "Return to us, Mother." As corn is the center of Mayas' lives, they believe that the corn as "mother" contains the spirit of abundance. They also believe that earthquakes are bad omens and their power can swallow the spirit of the corn, bringing a shortage, and consequently hunger the following year. "This year that is entering will be a year of misfortunes," commented the elders.[9]

JANUARY 2: Frightening rumors reached the community involving a ladino military officer located nearby who refused to let his relatives leave their houses and travel to Maya villages. The army had plans to bomb all the Indian communities along the new road, especially the most isolated ones. Their scorched earth policy was to start with the destruction of Santa Catarina, then El Limonar, next La Laguna, and so on. Although the officer's relatives were cautioned against disclosing this information, many people learned of the secret plan to massacre them in their villages and were frightened. "The [army's] idea was, kill ten people, for sure there will be one guerrilla among them, even if the rest are innocent" (Montejo and Akab' 1992: 45).

JANUARY 3: A unit of the army based in Nentón came to the

Jakaltek village of Santa Catarina. There they gathered all the residents, and the commanding officer said, "There is a barricade closing the road and we are sure that you put it there to create an obstacle to prevent the mobilization of the army. Now, all the men will go with me to clear the road. After that you will form a line because I have a list of those of you who are guerrillas." All the men went a few miles outside the village where a barricade of stones was obstructing the road. After the men had cleared the road, the officer told the villagers, "I will let you go now, alive, but if something happens to any of my soldiers, you will be held responsible, and then I will return and kill all of you." He and his unit then left the village. As they were marching back to the barracks at Nentón, the region's only bus passed on the new road, and as it was empty, the tired soldiers boarded it to avoid the long walk. A short distance down the road the bus was attacked by guerrillas, and the two soldiers on top of the bus were killed. The people in Santa Catarina heard the noise and suspected that the army had fallen into a guerrilla ambush. With fear and sadness they remembered the officer's words. They were not an empty threat.

JANUARY 4: At 1:00 A.M. *kaibiles,* an elite army counterinsurgency unit, encircled Santa Catarina and killed men, women, and children. A woman who survived reported the events:

Yinhmi a la una de la mañana, yet x-apni heb' naj soldado Santa Katal. Komo xin kaw sti' carretera aynahay nixtej nha, x-Ichinakoj heb' naj yanikoj q'a' yinh nixtej nha tu'. Wayoj chu anma yet xtz'ahay nixtej nha tu'. Yet xab'en anma yay tzaq'a' yib'anh, xtzab'lokoj yeltij yinh anhe yul yatut. Chinhetik'a eltij yul yatut tu' xin, listo yenakoj heb' naj sulnihayoj anma tu'.

It was one o'clock in the morning, more or less, when the army arrived at Santa Catarina. And because our houses were on the edge of the road, they started by setting them on fire. While the houses were burning, the people who were sleeping felt the heat and fire falling on them. Then when they jumped up and ran outside, the soldiers were right there, ready to kill them as soon as they got outside.[10]

Seventeen people were killed, but the rest managed to escape in the darkness, running toward the forest to avoid being hit by the bullets and grenades directed at the houses. The survivors were left without houses or property as everything was burned. No one had as yet sought refuge in Mexico, and the survivors made their way to the larger towns in the region, Jacaltenango, Huehuetenango, or even Guatemala City.

JANUARY 6: The villagers in El Limonar had just finished constructing a new house with a thatched roof. In El Limonar, as in many Maya towns, there is still a tradition of communal labor, and the house had been built according to this custom.[11] After the work was completed the house builders and their families, members of a charismatic group, gathered in one of the biggest houses in the community to offer thanks and prayers.

At 7:00 P.M. the army arrived and encircled the village. One group of soldiers went to the house where the people were praying and took the men outside. There the men were ordered to kneel on the ground. The soldiers opened fire, aiming for their heads, then opened their chests with knives and took out their hearts. Meanwhile other soldiers set fire to the houses. They put the women inside the houses and raped them in front of their husbands, who were then butchered.

Again the people who could escape ran in the darkness to the ravines, pursued by soldiers firing their weapons in all directions. Eighteen men were killed in El Limonar. Two who were inside their houses escaped death because of the quick action of the women. One young mother saw her husband being kicked by the soldiers and pleaded for him, offering one hundred quetzals for his life. The soldier moved the barrel of his rifle from the man's head and waited for the woman to bring the money. She found barely ninety quetzals, the end result of years of saving, and gave it to the soldier, who pocketed it and left.

The darkness helped entire families to escape the massacre. The only way out was to run to the cliffs of the Río Azul. Nothing could be seen, only the sound of the rushing water, but people jumped off the edge into it and tried to reach the other side. Children, who could not move as fast as their parents, became separated from them. Parents lost track of their children. No one knew which child's hands they were holding. It was everyone's goal to save them. A six-year-old boy, carrying his two-year-old brother on his back, was found two days later by people from a different village.

One sixty-year-old woman jumped into the river at its deepest part. Not knowing how to swim and becoming entangled in her traditional dress, she drowned. It was not until the next day that her family discovered she was missing and went to search for her. Her body was found several kilometers downriver.

The next day some of the villagers returned to see the destruction wrought on their town. Everything had been burned, the houses and all their contents, corn, beans, chickens, clothes, and some of the corpses of people killed in the houses. Outside dead bodies lay everywhere in puddles of blood. It was a horrible spectacle.

Waltu' matxa mak slanh sb'a. Ha'tu' xhjalah, ta'an mach xhko yah anma yet kaw xtitkan lemna xhq'il ti', hantaj xu smalkantoj xhchik'il heb' ya' lah. Walonh kaw ay sam konhchi yaj' k'anch'an anma xin. B'atxb'on yek' xhchik'il heb' ya' juhan, xkonh toh janojaytoq heb' ya' yul holan b'ay x'ahtij tx'otx' texah. Oxtajwanh, kanhtajwanh chuytoj heb' ya' yul holan juhan.

Nobody wanted to eat. We would say that we didn't dislike the dead people when we were really angered by these actions. The victims' blood was spilled everywhere. Usually we say that blood smells bad, but under these circumstances, it was the blood of innocent people. We took their blood in our hands and deposited it with their bodies in the holes where tiles are made. We put three of four of them at a time in the holes to be buried.

People in nearby La Laguna heard the thunderous fury of the attack and saw the fires at El Limonar, and many made plans to leave. According to the reported sequence of military actions, the village of La Laguna was certainly the next to be destroyed. The people packed whatever belongings they could carry, took some food, and attempted to escape that same night, crossing the border into Mexico. The border was only five miles away, and in their flight they were joined by hundreds of other Maya families, Popb'al Ti', Mam, Q'anjob'al, and Chuj speakers, carrying with them whatever they could. The commitment of the army to the destruction of Maya communities was now clear, and it was better to abandon houses, animals, and crops in the hope of saving their lives.

The number of refugees in southern Chiapas increased during the following days. Hundreds of families continued to arrive, especially from the Q'anjob'al and Chuj regions, including people who had to hide in the mountains for several days before crossing the border. South of the Pan-American Highway and close to the Mexican border, hundreds of Mam-speaking Mayas also arrived, escaping death and persecution. The refugees were fearful of the Mexican authorities, and so they did not travel far from the border but built camps about one kilometer from Guatemala. Their intention was first to protect their lives. If they were to be deported from Mexico, it would be preferable to return to Guatemala and try to hide from the military rather than face torture and death.

JANUARY 7: Five thousand refugees gathered at the hammock bridge at Dolores, a small Mexican village at the border. Among them were old men, children, and many orphans and widows. Women were crying and trying to construct makeshift tents of nylon and branches. Some pregnant women had given birth to their babies in the forests, just as jaguars do, and continued on the trek to the border. After two days of hunger, thirst, and cold, having found only bananas to eat in the forests, some of the men decided to undertake the dangerous journey back to their villages to get corn and other foods. Since La Laguna was one of the nearest villages and the army had not burned it down, at least before the people left, some of the La Laguna men decided to try to smuggle some food back to the people in the camps.

One of the men was Gilbertino, who had left several *quintales* (100-pound bags) of corn at his house.[12] Although army helicopters were searching the area, Gil entered the abandoned village, hoping to obtain food for the hungry refugees. He reached his house and began filling a smaller bag from his stock of corn. He had almost finished his task when a unit of four hundred kaibiles entered his house and demanded to see his *cédula*, his ID card, which he did not have with him. Instead he showed them an old card from his military service days. This document was not acceptable, and the kaibiles tied his arms behind his back and took him to the bridge crossing the Río Azul where they tortured him, shot him, and threw his body into the river.

At the same time five campesinos and their burros from a nearby village were coming down to the bridge, men and donkeys loaded with corn. As they approached the bridge the soldiers shot the donkeys and tied the men together by their hands and feet. They were tortured and their bodies thrown into the river.

The soldiers again returned to the village and tore the doors off the most prosperous-looking houses, looting them of everything they could carry. While inspecting the houses in La Laguna, the soldiers came upon a small hut where an old villager named Tumax lived. Tumax, a man of eighty-five years, was a widower who cared for Pilín, his forty-year-old deaf-mute son. The soldiers questioned the old man, but he did not speak any Spanish and was killed on the spot. Meanwhile Pilín paid no attention to these activities, and the soldiers who had killed his father recognized that he was mute and decided to let him go. He was known in the village as the man with an eternal smile. Pilín took his gourd and started to the river to fetch water. On his way another group of soldiers accosted him and saw only a strong, tall man who had fallen into their hands. When he did not answer their questions, but only smiled in response, they suspected that he was a guerrilla and tortured him. When he still did not utter a word, the soldiers became angry and finally killed him. Later they broadcast the news that they had captured and killed a top guerrilla commander on the Transversal del Norte, and the La Laguna refugees realized that it must have been Pilín. The horror and irony of this event prompted my pen to write a poem some years later, in 1995:

> *On the new highway cutting across*
> *northwestern Guatemala*
> *the kaibiles captured*
> *a young*
> *and strapping deaf-mute named Pilín.*
> *The military officers*
> *began torturing him to make him*
> *denounce the others*
> *and show them the way*
> *to the guerrilla camps.*
> *But since Pilín would only smile,*
> *the military officers, furious,*
> *went on beating and torturing him*
> *without his uttering a single word.*
> *Struck with admiration*
> *at the captive's obstinate silence*
> *the kaibiles then decided*
> *to cut out his tongue,*
> *gouge his eyes out*
> *and burn him alive.*
> *Days later we hear*
> *from army communiqués*
> *that on the new northwest highway*
> *they killed several subversives*
> *and among them*
> *"one of the top guerrilla chiefs."*

It appears they meant
the placid villager, Pilín,
deaf-mute, always smiling
and innocent of politics.

JANUARY 8: After pillaging the remaining houses, the soldiers continued on their way, destroying communities along the new highway toward the Río Selegua. They took the villagers' horses, mules, and donkeys to carry their spoils from the abandoned villages. The soldiers did not burn down the houses in La Laguna because they wanted the people to return so that they could come back at night to massacre them. Meanwhile the villagers preferred to suffer hunger and illness in the improvised refugee camps in Mexico rather than return to their villages and be killed by the Guatemalan army.

WHEN THE HIGHLY irregular elections of 1982 were aborted by a military coup and the genocidal General Lucas García was replaced by Gen. Efraín Ríos Montt on March 23, there was rejoicing among the refugees. But the rejoicing was short-lived.

On July 17, 1982, the worst massacre in the region took place at the Finca San Francisco in the municipio of Nentón, when the Guatemalan army wiped out almost the entire population. Survivors, interviewed later in Mexico, reconstructed a list of 302 men, women, and children who had been brutally murdered (Amnesty International 1987: 59–62).[13]

Shortly after the Ríos Montt government took control, a brief period of amnesty was announced during which the guerrillas were to turn in their weapons and surrender to the army. When this did not occur, Ríos Montt announced a state of siege and put in place a far more comprehensive counterinsurgency campaign than had been waged up to that time.

4

MILITARY CONTROL
OF THE HIGHLANDS

Military Organization and Training

THE GUATEMALAN ARMY that implemented the state
of siege announced by General Ríos Montt in July 1982
had taken on a very different shape from the military
force that had overthrown the Arbenz government not
quite thirty years before, in 1954. The intervening years
had seen the creation of a military force that, bolstered
and reinforced by U.S. training and aid under Alliance
for Progress programs, was larger, more technologically
sophisticated, better trained in counterinsurgency warfare techniques, and supremely confident of its ability
and even its destiny to lead the country (McClintock
1985). By the early 1970s this army had imposed a year-
long state of siege and defeated a small guerrilla movement in eastern Guatemala led by army officers who
had defected. "Although the insurgents were defeated
they were not extinguished, probably because the
socioeconomic and political injustices that led to their
emergence not only persisted, but even worsened"
(Aguilera 1988: 155).

The Estado Major, or High Command, of the army was responsible for developing the policies and strategies of the counterinsurgency campaign and the state of siege and for supervising the five major tactical commands under its control: Personnel, Intelligence, Operations, Logistics, and Civil Affairs. The small Guatemalan navy and air force commands were not directly under the control of the army, but divisions of these military branches were under the authority of the army commanders of the zones in which they were located (Barry 1989: 39).

Most army officers received their training at the Escuela Politécnica, Guatemala's equivalent of West Point. Those above the rank of lieutenant also received training at the School of Military Studies, and many officers were sent to the United States for a variety of courses funded by the Alliance for Progress and the International Military Education and Training section of the U.S. foreign aid budget. The officer corps of the army has been exclusively European and ladino in its ethnic makeup, and the military has long been seen by middle-class ladinos as an organization in which they could attain power, privilege, and wealth.

In the 1960s the army began to expand its control over the political structure of the nation, eliminating all left-of-center parties, rendering ineffective most of the center political parties, and moving into positions of power within the remaining right-wing parties. In the late 1960s death squads with names like Mano Blanca (White Hand) and Ojo por Ojo (Eye for an Eye) appeared as extrajudiciary arms of military action, aimed at students, trade unionists, and other loci of political reform. By 1970 it was clear that electoral politics could not solve the problems facing Guatemala, and from 1970 to 1985 Guatemala was ruled by a succession of military officers, some taking office through increasingly fraudulent elections and others through coups (Handy 1984: 158–164).

At the same time the army expanded its economic base so that it was not totally reliant on Guatemalan tax revenues for support. Funds from the United States played a large role in this expansion, as did the development of a military bank (Banco del Ejército), a construction company, and the opening of "vacant" land in Alta Verapaz, the Ixcán, and the Petén to exploitation and ownership by military officers. That these lands were claimed by Maya communities or cooperatives was of no concern to the military. More important was the development of a financial base that would allow remuneration for military service in a way that did not compete with the oligarchs for plantation land. The conflict at Panzós in 1978 and the construction of the Transversal del Norte are evidence of this expansion. The military also took control of, among other state and private agencies, the national airline, the telephone and electric companies, and a major television station (Barry 1989: 41).

In the late 1970s the army began a program to expand its military bases into all departments and major municipios. Control over the countryside was managed by a network of comisionados militares and orejas. These civilian men were usually former noncommissioned officers now living in the community and loyal to the army. Sometimes self-appointed, they were often recruited by the army without much leeway to refuse. They were allowed to carry weapons, most often machine guns or semiautomatic rifles. They worked without official compensation, except for what could be gained through the abuse of power, and they reported to the military commander of the local barracks on the activities and talk of the local people. They were also responsible for army recruitment and for the supervision of the civil patrols (Americas Watch 1986: 42–44).

In theory every Guatemalan man was required to perform military service, but in truth most recruitment was forced. Army trucks would enter a village or town on a market or saint's day and the local military commissioner would point out the young men, Mayas and poor ladinos, to be pressed into service (Barry 1989: 43). Some poor rural youth enlisted for the $35-a-month pay, plus $20 sent to their families, along with bed, board, and other privileges of the army uniform. Once shanghaied into military service, the young men were brutally indoctrinated into the ranks. They were promised that they would become real men with the power to order others, but first they must suffer through three months of savage basic training. Spanish speaking was obligatory, and Spanish lessons were compulsory for most Maya men enrolled in the army. To persist in speaking a Maya language was to invite a beating. Recruits were severely punished. Hit, beaten, tied up, and made to perform fifty or more push-ups, they were made to roll on the ground until they vomited. If they complained, they were punished further. If they deserted, they were imprisoned in a hole in the ground and covered with garbage and water for three months and then made to begin training all over again. Weapons training involved live grenades and ammunition, and more than a few recruits died. They were taught how to capture villagers and how to beat them by practicing on each other. They were taught to love their machine guns and to hate "subversives." They were indoctrinated with the basic racist attitudes of ladinos toward Indians, even when that racism was directed at themselves and their families. And above all they were taught to obey all orders immediately and without question. Although Maya men made up 90 percent or more of the lowest ranks of the army, it was army policy not to let recruits serve in the area from which they came. In that way Maya men, forcibly recruited, brainwashed, desensitized, and brutally trained to follow orders, could be coerced into carrying out a violent war against their own people (Sanford 1994).

The Guerrillas

MEANWHILE THE GUERRILLA movement had expanded among the indigenous communities of western Guatemala. In the Ixcán region of El Quiché and Huehuetenango, the Guerrilla Army of the Poor began recruiting Maya peasants into their ranks. As a result, the army intensified its counterinsurgency campaign in those areas. Catholic missionaries, catechists, and peasant leaders became the targets of the Guatemalan army (Burgos-Debray 1984). The people of the Kuchumatan highlands heard this news from the radio and from passing merchants. In 1979 the first guerrillas appeared in Kuchumatan villages. Among the Jakaltek people there was no great rush to join the guerrillas because they were considered by most to be dangerous, to be troublemakers. Some people saw them in a more magical light, as extraordinary people with special abilities who were well trained to avoid dangers.

But the mythical images of the guerrillas changed when they came into direct contact with the Kuchumatan Mayas. In May 1980 a guerrilla detachment came into Jacaltenango and summoned the community to gather in the central park to listen to a recruiting message. The ladino leader spoke in Spanish, saying that the EGP combatants were poor, landless campesinos who wanted to fight for a better future. He said that when the guerrillas took power everyone would be equal and everyone would have a piece of land to work; that after the revolution there would be no rich and poor but everyone would be equal. And then he asked the people to join them. The EGP followers were mostly Mayas, but they remained mute. The guerrilla leader invited the people to ask questions, but no one did because they were afraid. While he was speaking his microphone ceased working, and he asked if anyone there could repair it, but again no one answered for fear of being considered a guerrilla sympathizer.

As a result of this first visit, people became more silent and more distrustful of each other. They asked, Why had the guerrillas come? Had some people been in contact with them? Would the incident be reported to the army base in Huehuetenango? The situation was problematic as the people knew that army repression followed guerrilla appearances. There was nothing extraordinary about these poorly armed and sick-looking peasants following the ladino guerrilla leader, however intent they were on fighting to overthrow the Lucas García government. They were only simple people and, like themselves, rural Guatemalans.

The repercussions from that visit began almost at once. The EGP flag, a red banner bearing the face of Che Guevara, appeared the next morning in front of the municipal building. No one saw who did it, no one wanted it up there, but no one wanted to be the one to pull it down either. Finally the municipal authorities called the security police to remove it and burn it. Almost every night thereafter a flag or a placard was placed somewhere on the outskirts of the town urging people to join the guerrillas. By engaging in these clandestine activities, the EGP wanted to make the people believe that they represented a strong and defiant front against the army. But the EGP did not know that these very activities were increasing the fear among the people and causing the people to reject them. People began to see that this was a dangerous game, and it would draw them into the conflict.

But it was the guerrilla practice of setting traps for the army at strategic points close to villages that greatly angered the people. This guerrilla provocation of the army had several consequences. The guerrillas saw it as a way to recruit people; they believed the people would join them in reaction to the army's retaliatory attacks on nearby villages. But most became even angrier with the guerrillas for putting their lives in danger. Some abandoned their communities and sought refuge in cities or across the border in Mexico. The army did retaliate against those villages where the attacks occurred. In the long run some Mayas joined the EGP, and guerrilla activity spread throughout the Kuchumatan highlands. By 1981 the guerrillas had become strong enough to take direct military action against the army, attacking convoys, destroying bridges, and damaging electric transmission. And thus armed conflict was generalized in the region by early 1982.

Military Control

AS THE FURY of the massacres of 1981 and 1982 abated, the army replaced terror and brute force with several forms of more direct control over highland populations. In some areas "model villages" were established to house the displaced people who could not flee to Mexico. Derived from the strategic hamlets policy of the Vietnam War and constructed close to army bases, these jerry-built communities replaced the dispersed settlements destroyed by army sweeps and congregated suspect populations under direct military surveillance. Their construction, the reconstruction of other villages, and the construction of military roads was carried out under a variety of "food for work" programs, including *fusiles y frijoles* (bullets and beans) and *techo, trabajo y tortillas* (roof, work, and bread).[1] Ideological indoctrination of those considered supporters of the guerrillas was carried out in reeducation camps under direct military control (Anderson and Simon 1987: 30–31). But the most pervasive system of control and the most destructive to Maya culture was the civil patrols.

In 1981 the army expanded its Patrulla de Autodefensa Civil (PAC), the civil patrol system that was first inaugurated in Alta Verapaz in 1976. When Ríos Montt came to power in 1982 he made the civil patrols a cornerstone of his counterinsurgency program. The army said that the patrol would allow a village to protect itself from the guerrillas, but its primary purpose was to put all highland men under military control and force them to monitor the activities of village people, which would free the army for other military duties (Manz 1988a: 38). The patrols reported to the local military commissioner, who in turn reported to the military commander. Thus the army replaced locally chosen authorities with people whom they appointed and who were under their control. By 1984 "the system incorporated nearly one million men and included virtually all male Indians in the western highlands between the ages of sixteen and sixty" (Smith 1990: 272). Any conflicts within the village—land disputes, robbery, drunkenness, household conflicts, and the like—were taken to the military officer at the barracks for resolution, and the civil authorities in the village were divested of their traditional power and influence.

PAC members were required to patrol several days a week. Although participation was always referred to as voluntary, in fact it was just the opposite. Not to patrol was to identify oneself as a guerrilla and incur denunciations, threats, beatings, and death. Patrollers were scarcely trained and mostly unarmed, carrying only wooden sticks and machetes. In truth the army did not trust an armed civilian force. Their duties included reporting all suspicious movements and conversations and capturing any suspect villagers and bringing them to the military commissioner. They were made to go on patrol in the forests and along the roads around the village, looking for guerrillas. In some areas they cleared forests guerrillas could use for ambushing the army. And they acted as point patrols for the army when they were searching for guerrillas. With army guns at their backs and guerrilla guns ahead, they were often cannon fodder as the highland insurgency continued (Robert F. Kennedy Memorial Center for Human Rights 1993: 20).

It was now the army, with the decisive support of the civil patrol, that controlled every aspect of village life. For example, during the government of Ríos Montt the civil patrols were very active, capturing suspicious villagers and taking them to the army. Army officers soemtimes ordered the PAC to execute fellow villagers by clubbing them to death (Montejo 1987). In 1982–83 the civil patrols helped the army destroy communities and crops as they hounded and persecuted those fleeing across the Mexican border. Thus "the civil patrol system, which the Guatemalan army established as the cornerstone of its rural counterinsurgency program in the early 1980s, stands out as the dominant institutional legacy of the period of violence in rural Guatemala" (Davis 1988a: 27).

The persistence and effectiveness of the civil patrols helped the army rule the Guatemalan countryside through fear and terror. The civil patrol commanders were given the power to decide the life or death of the villagers or to punish those members of the civil patrol who somehow failed in their duties. Having been given such power and authority over their fellow villagers, "some civil patrol commanders and military commissioners [took] advantage of their power to enrich themselves on the land, animals, or goods of those who [had] fled, been murdered, or [were] too frightened to complain. Some [made] use of the power to rape women without fearing reprisal" (Manz 1988a: 40).

The disruption of Maya communal life by the civil patrols has been remarked in a number of areas. For example, among the Q'eqchi' Maya of northern Guatemala, the civil patrol was potent in its destruction of Maya values such as communal solidarity. This rupture became evident when Mayas tried to practice their traditional ceremonies and sacred rituals.

> For rituals to take place, it is stated that people must trust and have confidence in one another, an elusive element given the suspicion generated by the civil patrols. They must be "happy," another difficult criterion to meet in conditions of poverty and military domination. To carry out the rituals in a situation where the necessary criteria are not met is worse than not enacting them at all. Villagers told me a story about a divided community which offered a large candle to the Tzuultaq'a only to watch it split in half, symbolic of the mountain god's rejection of the gift. (Wilson 1991: 53)

To better understand the impact of the civil patrols on Mayan communities, let us now turn to the accounts of the people who have suffered from them, allowing the refugees to speak for themselves.

Formation of the Civil Patrols

THE DREAMS AND visions of the villagers became real when the army settled in the Kuchumatan towns. Death and destruction struck in the Maya communities. During the months of June and July 1982, after Ríos Montt took office, terrorism in the towns and villages increased dramatically. The army constantly patrolled the communities and terrorized the people with machine-gun fire. In July 1982 the army announced the formation of the "civil patrols." Soon thereafter, when the patrols were initiated, villagers were directly ordered to club to death anybody who they thought was suspected of guerrilla involvement. Similarly, they were ordered to capture and send to the army barracks those people who did not carry a cédula at the moment they were stopped and interrogated. People from big towns and small villages protested against this abusive strategy of the army, because they understood that this type of paramilitary organization would serve only to disrupt the life in the villages and lead campesinos to kill fellow villagers. The reaction against the formation of civil patrols in Maya communities was forceful. Mayas did not need a paramilitary organization to control and take care of them. In some regions there was strong opposition and resistance, but the army insisted on this military control, even calling it, ironically, "voluntary." But for Mayas it was obligatory and a heavy burden. Thus in the Kuchumatan highlands

> *the response to questions about "voluntary" duty was most often a laugh. A number of informants recalled that when the patrols were first established, people talked about protesting and complaining. When those first resisters were killed or otherwise severely punished, others realized that there was little alternative but to comply. (Manz 1988a: 79)*

Despite the people's opposition, the army commanders continued to apply pressure. When the military commander arrived in Maya communities close to the Guatemala-Mexico border in 1982, he gathered the people in the plaza and preached, "You must be united in order to reject the guerrillas' offering of a national revolution, and to achieve this unity, all of you must join the civil patrol in order to control your villages, day and night."

The men became fearful of opposing the military orders, so women argued instead of men: "You, soldiers, are the one who are obligated to control and protect the communities. That is why you are paid by the government. Our husbands and sons shouldn't be in armed groups because it is too dangerous." The officer replied, "Listen, we will leave this town some day and then who will protect you? That is why I urge you to train yourselves now. Also, I have to tell you that other towns are already doing their duty as members of the civil patrol." All the people responded, "We have always worked together, and when we do, it is because a communal project is needed. Right now what we need is a road that could link the municipal town with its villages toward the west. Starting tomorrow we will show you that we are united, and we will organize ourselves but for a beneficial purpose."

This general meeting occurred on Sunday, when the people from Jacaltenango and its surrounding hamlets were concentrated in the town square by orders of the army commander. So on the next day, people organized themselves in work groups. People from distant villages came to the municipio to participate. The officer was angry, but he said only, "I hope you won't be sorry for this."

Then work began on the construction of the road that would link the Jakaltek villages. It was impressive to see almost one thousand people working together. Everybody had to do five meters of road space, so with picks and shovels people started to work. The project was proceeding well until the army officer called the people together again and said that everybody was now a member of the civil patrol and that he did not want anybody to protest. Those were military orders, and they would have to be obeyed if people did not want to suffer the consequences of their opposition to the army. And he added, "I don't want the women to speak for the men. Whoever opposes my orders will be put in jail."

The road was not completed. All the villagers of the surrounding hamlets and villages became members of the civil patrol. Their freedom was erased; their cornfields were neglected. Now they were just objects of the army, and easily manipulated. Groups of eighty to one hundred were ordered to patrol the outskirts of the towns and villages each night, from 6:00 in the evening to 6:00 in the morning. The army did not care if the older people had health problems; they did not care about sick children or the demands of the cornfields. There were no excuses.

The formation of the civil patrols, the maltreatment the villagers received, and the army's disrespect for native cultural traditions brought about a loss of confidence in the newly imposed president, Ríos Montt. The army resumed indiscriminate killing of anyone who got in their way, and now with the help of the civil patrol it had a greater capacity to destroy entire communities. The helicopters again began to drop grenades and bombs on the villages. In Santa Teresa and Santa Rosa, Q'anjob'al hamlets located close to the Mexican border in the municipio of Nentón, the army killed randomly. Using civil patrollers to destroy dwellings, the army looted them and took the horses, cows, and chickens that the people left behind in their flight to avoid death (Montejo and Akab' 1992).

The Maya communities on the border again took refuge in Mexico. The campesinos abandoned their cornfields, animals, and everything they owned. This time the army accused everybody in these communities of being guerrillas or collaborators. As the survivors of various communities reached the safety of Mexico and compared their stories, they found them to be almost the same. Different ethnic groups from the provinces of

Huehuetenango and El Quiché were reunited in a foreign country as brothers and sisters dispossessed from their ancestral lands.

Those Mayas who had previous knowledge of the hardships of life in the refugee camps or who had large families decided to stay in their villages and agreed to do whatever the army asked of them. The army instructed them to carry out its orders, even to kill if necessary. Their function was to rid the place of guerrillas. In some villages the army gave a few rifles to the heads of civil patrols, but the majority had to defend themselves with sticks, stones, clubs, slingshots, and machetes. Civil patrol commanders had to win the trust of army officers to carry real weapons. As Americas Watch reported at the time, "The most common arms are M-1s, Winchesters, and pistols. Maryknoll priest Ron Hennessey has observed that in San Mateo Ixtatán, Huehuetenango, the type of armament given to a patroller generally reflects the degree of trust felt by the army: 'When the army really trust the patrol, they give them carbines; when they don't, they give them Mausers'" (1986: 29).[5]

In the village of La Laguna where the army issued an M-1 rifle and two other small-caliber weapons, the head of the civil patrol asked the military commander if they could use the weapons to shoot a deer should the opportunity arise. The officer replied angrily, "Don't be stupid. You should order your followers to kill only people. Every stranger that enters the village without identification should die at that same place where he or she is found" (Montejo and Akab' 1992: 31).

The army told the civil patrols that after each search in the mountains they were to bring in a captured guerrilla. The villagers were pressured to report constantly on their searches. Rivalry between villages grew as personal problems triggered communal conflicts. Sometimes a village would accuse another of hiding guerrillas in the mountains or, even worse, of hiding guerrillas among themselves or letting them pass through the territory without reporting their presence to military authorities (Americas Watch 1986).

To show that they were carrying out their duties as ordered, the civil patrollers had to stop all travelers and ask for their personal identification cards. The testimony of Tumaxh K. and his companions recounts the brutal actions of the civil patrol. He and his companion were captured just as they were crossing into Mexico. He was taken to the military barracks but managed to escape after being tortured. His companion, Jesus, was killed inside the barracks (Montejo and Akab' 1992).

A similar tragedy happened to a Q'anjob'al named Miguel from the nearby hamlet of Poza. The civil patrol captured him as he entered the town early in the morning. He was asked for identification, but he said that he forgot it at his hut and that he just came to town to buy some seed for planting. The civil patrol took this poor campesino to the military barracks, from which he never emerged. His family brought his cédula, but the army responded that they did not have him inside the barracks. In this way the civil patrol helped the army and made possible the disappearance of many poor villagers from other towns or hamlets (Americas Watch 1986). To travel to another place and have any kind of security, a villager had to carry his cédula and his civil patrol ID card.

Most Mayas tried to avoid civil patrol duties, and many of them became refugees rather than blindly obey military orders. In the Q'anjob'al region "many of those who refused to participate in these acts or who tried to escape from civil patrol duty were punished by local authorities or sent to the regional army base for punishment" (Davis 1988a: 28). The army was the sole owner of the people's lives, and the soldiers could kill whomever they wanted. These were the darkest periods of Maya suffering in the Kuchumatan mountains, under the consecutive military rulers of Guatemala.

The Policy of Fear and Intimidation

DURING THE MONTHS of July and August, after the government offer of "amnesty" to the guerrillas, more refugees crossed the Mexican border. The guerrillas believed the amnesty was a deception, a strategy of the army to identify, capture, and kill rebels, and military actions increased in the Kuchumatan region.

After the amnesty period expired the army began its military offensive, an offensive so violent and repressive that even the military officers called it *agosto negro* (black August). There were large-scale massacres during this period, and civil patrol duties became more dangerous. Akuxh Lenam, a campesino from a community close to the Mexican border, was a civil patrol member for many weeks. But when he became exhausted he abandoned his post and fled to Mexico. He provided the following testimony of his experience during this period of extreme violence.

We, the civil patrol or villagers who remained in the village, were fixing the water pipes of the community across the Río Azul when the kaibiles passed by. As we were just a few villagers working in such an isolated region, we were scared, even though we served them as they wished. Obviously, we did not have any confidence in them. Because of the course of action that they had set in motion with massive killings, nobody could say "I will live tomorrow." Our lives were in constant danger. That morning, the army patrol passed the place where we were working without saying anything, but we knew that they were going to a nearby hamlet. Two hours later, they returned bringing three campesinos very well tied, one to the other, with a rope tied to their waists. Among them was a child about twelve years old. We continued to work without looking at the miserable campesinos who were prisoners of the army. Since there were very few people left in the village, we also had to patrol the outskirts at night. This is how the group was sent to guard the bridge on the Río Azul. The army ordered the villagers to protect it against guerrilla sabotage. They threatened to kill us if the bridge was destroyed. The army needed the bridge to mobilize their troops along the Guatemala-Mexico border. I was among the people defending it. We hid close to the bridge that night when we saw the lights of a car coming downhill. We were ordered to stop any passing vehicle, but because we were scared, we let the car cross the bridge without interference. It was dark and we couldn't see the color of the car. The car stopped at the middle of the bridge, and the lights were turned off. We could hear that some men came out of the car and were whispering. We couldn't see them, because the night was so dark, but what we could hear clearly were the moans of a wounded man. The moans were silenced after some hard hits and blows. Then we heard the noise of something splashing into the river. Then another, and another. . . . Three bodies were heard splashing into the water. When this was done, the men who were in the car turned on the lights and returned to Nentón. When the car was gone, we came out of hiding with our flashlights. A puddle of blood was on the bridge where they stopped. Upon seeing this, we congratulated ourselves for not stopping the car. Now we knew for sure that the army used the rivers to dispose of their victims and make them disappear. It became a common practice for the soldiers to kill the people inside their barracks and then take the bodies to throw them into the big rivers. That night we saw blood and several bodies being thrown into the river and we heard no gunshots. At 11:30, we returned to the village, leaving the bridge unguarded.[6]

Having instilled fear in the Maya communities, the army knew that it could give orders that would not be questioned. It became increasingly abusive and caused panic among the local people. The situation in the Kuchumatan highlands became unbearable for many of the civil patrol members. The testimony of Akuxh Lenam is supported by another civil patrol member, Kaxh Pasil, who witnessed the same military action described above.

The next morning, about eighty soldiers arrived at the village. They summoned the people to the center of the village in front of the chapel.

Everybody who lived in the village came to hear the words of the military chief. He said, "All of you should be patrolling as you were ordered. Are you guarding the bridge down there every night?" "Yes, sir," the people responded. "Okay, from now on you should know that bridge is your own life. If you let the guerrillas destroy it, you all will die." The people were silent. It was a heavy and very delicate load on their backs. People knew that the guerrillas had destroyed other bridges along the international highway to the provincial capital of Huehuetenango. Since nobody wanted to talk, one of the old leaders of the community decided to express his disagreement: "Captain, we do not have weapons to guard that bridge. I think it is not good to blame the community if that bridge is destroyed someday . . . " The captain did not let him finish and said, "Listen, all of you, how do the guerrillas oppose our decisions? They are never in agreement with our orders. Look at his face, he is a guerrilla." The old leader was not disturbed and replied, "Señores, I do not know anything about what you are saying. I am a campesino, a hard worker. If you want to convince yourself, you can enter my house and see the quantity of corn, bean, and chile pepper that I have harvested. That is the product of my decent work. Also, I should mention that I do not know how the guerrillas look." The captain continued to point at him, saying, "Listen, all of you. That is the way the guerrillas speak. This is the way they defend themselves. Look straight at his face." The old man decided to look to the ground, avoiding the inquisitorial attitude of the army commander. "Look at the man. You can see how the guerrillas avoid looking at us." The old man changed his tactic and he looked into the officer's eyes, with anger. The captain continued, saying, "Look at his face. The guerrillas look like this man." The people were scared so everybody answered, "Yes!" We thought that the captain would kill that good old villager of ours, but he did not. He walked among the people, looking into the eyes of each villager. Suddenly, he took among the people another person. Maltixh, a villager (68 years old) who had a scar on his nose. "What happened to your nose?" the commander asked. "It is an infected pimple, my Captain." "Mmm . . . let's see it. It seems to me that it is a scar from a bullet," said the officer, while he checked the old man's nose. Then the officer started to shout, "All of you are guerrillas, and I will kill all of you if the bridge is destroyed." (Montejo and Akab' 1992)

The military commander so intimidated the people that the whole community was traumatized. The bridge was more important than the lives of hundreds of villagers, and the people already knew that the army was capable of such killings. The proof could be seen in Finca San Francisco, Nentón, a nearby village. The people were terrified of the power and violence of the army. They knew that the army could also destroy the bridge, simulating a guerrilla action (as they did in El Limonar, Tzisbaj, etc.), and then they could justify the killing of the villagers. That same night, after the army returned to the barracks at Nentón, many families decided to seek refuge by crossing the Mexican border. It was in this way that many civil patrol members also abandoned their duties and fled, but those who had no choice or who wanted to serve the army remained and were complicit in the killing of fellow villagers.

In the refugee camp in Mexico the former civil patrol members who were hidden at the bridge the night the army threw the bodies into the river came to the edge of the Río Dolores to wait for the bodies. They rescued the bodies that were thrown into the river. Some bodies were recognized by people from other villages. Some had bullet holes; one did not have an arm; others had been castrated. From then on the refugees rescued bodies from the river constantly. In some cases the bodies could not be rescued because of turbulent waters. In one instance the body of a woman without an arm, and with her baby tied to her back with ropes, floated by, but there was no hope of rescuing it (Montejo and Akab' 1992).

The Army's Effects on the Highlands

THE FORMATION OF the civil patrols was a major blow to the unity of Maya communities. Those communities that opposed the formation of the civil patrols, arguing that patrolling was the duty of the army, were threatened with death or jail if they opposed the army commander's decisions. The army created an environment of fear and mistrust among the native populations. The army also sent orejas into Maya communities and collected information about the private lives of the villagers. After the establishment of military barracks in a town, girls and women were raped by soldiers. Some young women helped the army locate and even control and monitor the movements of suspected men in town. Open prostitution appeared in the towns. Some girls became friends of army men and were used until they and their babies were abandoned.

Among men the mistrust was almost absolute. It was impossible to sit down with friends and talk or tell stories, because other men, especially those who wanted to remain on good terms with the army, might report the gatherings. Communal ways of life disappeared; people did not talk as friends but saluted each other as if they were strangers. Confidence in friends and neighbors was obliterated. In cooperation with the army, the civil patrol set villager against villager, harassing and often killing any strangers who came into town without papers or identification.

The duties of the civil patrol were delicate, and each patroller was suspicious of the others because anyone could be an army informant. The army often arrived to announce it was in possession of anonymously prepared lists of guerrillas who lived in town. These allegations were perhaps only tactics used to create more fear and mistrust among the villagers, but they had an even more negative effect. They produced mistrust even among members of the same family. Thus a son might be afraid of his parents or vice versa. A *compadre* might be afraid of his friends, or a neighbor suspicious of his neighbors. The negation of the self

was appalling, and this affected traditional Maya beliefs and rituals. The army provided the only voice to be heard, and its decisions always were counter to the will of the villagers.

During the army's tracking of guerrillas in the mountains,
the civil patrollers were sent in first to check the forests, so the
army could move safely behind them. On other occasions the
army tested the civil patrols by approaching them unexpectedly
at checkpoints. This provoked conflicts among the army and the
civil patrols. In some communities soldiers broke into the houses of civil patrol men to abuse their wives while they were away
on duty. The army thus promoted the destruction of moral values, honesty, cultural traditions, and life itself.[7]

After so much devastation in the countryside, life in Maya
villages will not easily return to normal. The presence of army
barracks in the highland Maya communities has continued,
although the intense violence has subsided. But the militarization of the countryside and the formation of civil patrols has
drastically changed life in Maya communities. The soldiers
abuse women and threaten the young people to maintain fear
and control over their daily activities.

As late as December 1992 Manuel, a young Maya, told me
that in a village close to the Mexican border where an army barracks is still operating the soldiers have terrorized the young people in the community. Young men used to sit at the edge of the
road waiting to talk to the marriageable girls who walked through
the village doing their errands. But now the soldiers threaten
young men and hit them to discourage them from talking to girls.
According to one of these young men, the soldiers say that all the
girls are already theirs, and they will beat or kill the boys if they
get close to the young women. It seems that the army has con-
spired to destroy every facet of traditional life.

As of this writing, under the terms of the peace accords
signed by the government, the army, and the guerrillas, the civil
patrols are slowly being dismantled. Some are being reorganized
as "peace and development committees," which will allow the

army to maintain control in local villages. In most cases the leaders of the civil patrols are former soldiers, those who are loyal to the army because they have been brainwashed. But not all the former soldiers are manipulated by the army. Some have also suffered while serving their tours of duty, and now find it more important to understand their experience differently and to criticize the army for its brutality (see chapter 5).

In some areas the civil patrol leaders assumed powers that had hitherto belonged to the army. They were given the right to execute anybody without permission from the army chiefs (Paul and Demarest 1988). Civil patrol leaders, with the army's tacit or direct approval, have carried out massacres in which dozens of campesinos, their fellow villagers, have been murdered (Americas Watch 1986). This systematic destruction of the indigenous culture has also been noted by Manz:

> Today the role of the military and paramilitary organizations in even the most isolated communities has engendered divisiveness, fear, and mistrust. Not since the Spanish Conquest have the highlands seen such a general cultural breakdown. Moreover, although Indians were aware of their powerlessness vis-à-vis economic and political elites and army, fear for their lives did not dominate their activities and consciousness. (1988a: 12)

Unfortunately for the Mayas, the civil patrols were the army's most effective instrument against them. When other villagers abandoned their duties and became refugees, the civil patrols considered them enemies. The civil patrols even joined with the army to oppose the repatriation of refugees. As a paramilitary organization, its leaders received periodic training and information from army officers, thereby learning to reject the refugees as the army does. In some places civil patrol members have usurped the land of their neighbors who are now in refugee camps, and they do not want to give it back (Manz 1988a). It is instructive to compare the actual behavior of the civil patrols with their often-recited code of conduct.[8]

Many Mayas have asked the soldiers to return to their barracks in the distant cities. Guatemalan refugees in Mexico have insisted that the highlands be demilitarized and the civil patrols dismantled, so that the people can live peacefully and once again practice their cultural traditions freely.

5

ONE MAN'S TESTIMONY

NOT ALL THOSE who sought refuge in Mexico remained on the border or in the camps. In southern Mexico the aid programs of the Diocese of San Cristóbal de las Casas provided a starting point for Guatemalan Mayas looking for work outside the area. Educated refugees migrated to larger cities—Cancún, Puebla, Acapulco, and Mexico City. After a few years of living in exile there, some made their way into northern Mexico and then to the United States and Canada. This was the experience of Chilin Hultaxh, whose testimony is presented below.

In 1988, while still a graduate student, I received a small grant from the African American Institute of Albany and used the funds to visit refugees that summer. I was nearing the completion of my master's studies and wanted to research various options for my Ph.D. dissertation. My trip included several weeks of interviews in the camps and a visit with a refugee who had learned of my progress in the university and who had written a letter of congratulations to me. Through a mutual friend I made contact again with Hultaxh, a man I knew well in Jacaltenango. With his wife and four children he had moved out of the camps and into the difficult situation of an undocumented person living outside of Acapulco, in the state of Guerrero. He was under the meager protection of the local Catholic church, which had found him a job as a janitor in one of their facilities. During the day we took the children to the beach to swim and eat mangoes and coconuts. On the last night of my visit, I asked him if I could tape his testimony, and he agreed.

In the evening, when the heat of the day was over, we walked to the top of a small hill overlooking the lights of Acapulco's luxurious hotels. The night was calm, and he narrated his story uninterrupted by me and punctuated only by the chirping of hundreds of nocturnal lizards. Here is the Testimony of Chilin Hultaxh, a Guatemalan refugee and former Guatemalan soldier.

My friends, you who are listening, let me take this short moment to tell you what I witnessed. Sure, compared to the whole tragic situation in Guatemala, my story may sound small, but it is a story of great pain, the pain that I felt when I found out what our military leaders in Guatemala have done to my people.

I joined the army for financial reasons, out of financial necessity. The town where I was born is extremely poor. There is a lack of technical resources, 90 or maybe 95 percent of the inhabitants are peasants. Thank God and thanks to the vision of this very same community, some children (about 5 percent) have been given access to an education that will prepare them for a better life, mostly in teaching. But the daily labors of the pueblo are those of a peasant community.

I was not able to continue my studies because I didn't have the money and I also had personal problems trying to decide which career I wanted to take up. I was interested in government, but I found no opportunity there, and I could not find a place in the private sector either. These professional problems added to the emotional strain of being engaged. I didn't have a specific orientation, or a person who could have helped me direct my interests into something concrete; so I found myself floundering, maybe, if one wants to interpret it that way, but we'll be able to understand later that maybe—and that's what I think—it was the will of God that let me witness what I am about to tell you now.

In one of these years, either 1976 or 1977, I had already completed my secondary-level schooling and managed to finish my preparatory studies [equivalent to high school in the United States], which in my country allows you to go to university. But then there was no work at that time, one could feel the crisis in Guatemala very strongly. There were many teachers but very few jobs and no guarantees. You had to "know people in the right places" in the political parties to stand a good chance.

Unfortunately, I had no way of getting my teaching degree. I only got the *bachillerato* [high school diploma]. Sure, I could have taken equivalency courses to reach my goal. But as I told you a few minutes ago, I was not able to see things clearly in those years; the way I lived left me in a depression. I already realized the sad situation my country was in and knew the need for change in Guatemala, but being totally isolated, I did not know or did not have any clues how to go about it. I even tried to find friends who might help me do something, but it never worked out since my financial situation was so precarious that it paralyzed me. In that time of great despair, a friend came and said, "Look, if you want opportunity, you'll find it in the army." His words gave me a great jolt, just mentioning the army is terrible, no? All the young men in the country, especially the indigenous people, are terrified when they hear about the draft, the raids that the army makes to enlist people into the military service. I was one of these young men who were afraid of enlistment. I still remember the many times when the military commissioners came to my pueblo to assemble all the people. We locked ourselves in our houses or found a way to flee from the "search."

But now my friend said, "There are opportunities in the army. You can work in the office, you don't have to go through the military training. You'll automatically go to work as an office worker. But I'll tell you one thing: it will be quite tough at first because they won't pay you well at the beginning." "Look at me, for example," my friend went on, "it took two, three months of doing simple tasks until they gave me a real post. But since they are leaving the military zone of the Quiché for Huehuetenango, I think there's a good chance they'd give you a job that you wouldn't get otherwise."

I was weighing his words . . . and said, "Listen, give me a chance, get me in touch with someone who will give me work. I need a job. I want to become independent, away from my family. I need to make a life for myself and right now, I'm desperate, man. I don't know where to turn and it doesn't really matter, it's all the same crap."

My friend said, "Okay then, I'll write you." And he left. He had come on a seventy-two-hour leave from the army and had to go back to his post in Quiché. I was very surprised when I received a letter from him a few days later, saying, "Look, they'll give you a job as a worker of the specialized troop in the personnel office 'S-1' in Quiché." So I went there. When I got there, the officer in charge of the personnel office happened to be out of town, but on May 3 they received me. The officer had just come back from a trip delivering pay to the staff in the different army bases of the jurisdiction in the military zone of Quiché, which comprises the departments of Totonicapán, Sololá, Huehuetenango, and Quiché, with the main headquarters located in Quiché in 1978. I remember well. It was May. I was afraid when I saw the soldiers who stood guard at the main entrance of the headquarters in Quiché. I asked to see the officer, and they told me that he was in. I introduced myself. Immediately they gave me instructions on military conduct, how to salute, how to walk, how to turn, how to parade. This was basic, you had to know this just to be able to join the army. In addition, it was very important to know the military ranks by the stripes, stars, and laurels on the officers' uniforms, from second lieutenant to general to major general, and so on. I memorized all this. Thank God I had an excellent memory and took all of this in very quickly. I began to work in the specialized troops, starting out with simple jobs like compiling lists of military personnel on leave, or personnel stationed in a certain place or military base. Accounts were made of how many of the staff were on site, how many were in other places, how many were off-duty. That was my job. As time went by, they showed me how to produce official memos, messages, and military rulings. Little by little I got used to this life. I made friends with other workers in the specialized unit. We were very friendly to each other, being people from the same social class, from the same simple and humble background, who also wanted to make some money. At that time I remember no problem at all with the counterinsurgency war, the guerrilla war, the war that unfolded in all its cruelty in the years 1979, 1980, 1981, 1982 . . . and maybe still goes on today. I had an idea of these things because I'd read something about what happened in Guatemala during 1954 and in the eastern part of the country in 1970, but it was no big deal. Now, at this point in time we didn't know of any such problems and there was no major news about them. I didn't have much information about these troubles and therefore joined the army with confidence, thinking that I would just perform a simple job. But as time passed, I was taught more about military correspondence and little by little got access to the archives. The work became harder and I still only earned what a worker of the specialized troops (of the rank of a second sergeant) made, which at the time was 12 quetzals per month [about US$12]. This was very low pay for all the work I did. Several days passed, and then came May 29. By that time orders had already come in from the highest military command in the military zone in Quiché to launch Operation Puma. This operation, which I'll describe in more detail later on, was started on May 29 at noon, and is perhaps still going on today, maybe just under a different name. But it consisted of distributing and deploying all military personnel in different areas throughout the whole jurisdiction of the military zone because they had discovered so-called subversive groups, guerrilla groups, who were active in the jungle of Quiché as well as in parts of Huehuetenango. In reality the problem was not that serious, and on a national level it didn't get any publicity. The only information the military managed to obtain came from sources they trusted very much, from the military commissioners, the national police, and other paramilitary institutions sympathetic to the military. They started to pass information on to the army about guerrilla groups spreading propaganda, holding meetings, and stirring up people to get them ready for a national revolution. The military operation was started without delay. They deployed the troops. First the military from Quiché was sent to Uspantán, Chikamán, where they had military bases already. Nebaj,

Cotzal, and Chajul, the whole region of the Ixil zone, was surrounded
from this moment on, leaving only one escape route through the Ixcán
and Rubelsanto, an area the army had not yet touched. As I understand
it, they didn't comprehend just how far the revolutionary movement had
spread and therefore didn't come to that area. I think that for strategic situations, for their tactical planning, they had a different military post, the
one at Playa Grande in the Ixcán zone, but this unit belongs to a different zone. During the deployment of personnel we worked very hard, day
and night, all of us in the intelligence unit, the departments of personnel,
training operations, logistics, and supplies. Later, when major revolutionary movements were noticed, the troops from the military zones of
Jutiapa and Zacapa were sent as reinforcements to these trouble spots.
Later this same year, in 1979, the Organización del Pueblo en Armas
(Revolutionary Organization of People in Arms; ORPA) appeared on the
scene, based, I think, more or less in Sololá, Retalhuleu, Quezaltenango,
and San Marcos. It wasn't until then that the military realized the true
scope of the conflict and dispatched troops not only from the eastern
military zone but also from the capital and north of Petén. In Petén they
had their elite fighters, the kaibiles, who had received a type of training
similar to the Green Berets. At this point in time, we are talking about
what was really already the war, unleashed in all its savagery, against the
indigenous population.

In the army, the mestizos, whom we generally refer to as ladinos,
were given preferential treatment. There is strong racism in Guatemala.
There is racial discrimination against the indigenous population. Within
the army the indigenous are considered a very lowly race, ignorant and
incapable of learning the new techniques. So we always have to stay in
the trenches and do the hardest work at very low pay.

At that time the numbers of civilians joining the army grew more and
more each day. The army liked to get poor people, people from the country, the same exploited people whom they had to capture to take them
to the military camps. In the camps they subjected them to very intense
psychological indoctrination. They instilled in these new recruits a high
sense of patriotic duty, that they had to put before all else Guatemala's
freedom, freedom from any influence from communism or socialism;

they told them that these ideologies were devil's work, totally satanical and atheist, and that they had to be extra careful when communicating with any civilians. If they noticed anyone talking about socialism or about changes within Guatemala, that person would be automatically considered a heretic by the Church. That means an enemy of the homeland, an enemy of God, and an enemy of the government. The poor indigenous people who didn't know how to read or write were taught just enough to understand the military language, and they were taught the national anthem. The physical army training was very tough, very rigorous. They treated the recruits, most of whom were indigenous people, very harshly. But maybe I should skip ahead a little now.

Later, when the war had gotten more intense, the army started to draft civilians more indiscriminately and didn't make a great distinction anymore between indigenous and mestizo people. Being poor, all of them fit the army's criteria. They were captured to serve in the military. One of the greatest injustices within the military units is that not one of the civilians joining the army ever gets beyond the rank of a first sergeant to become one of the Brigadas [brigades, sergeant major rank]. These troops wear red caps to show they're a higher rank than the regular soldiers. It's difficult for a Guatemalan of indigenous and poor origin to reach the rank of a second lieutenant; it's not impossible, if a soldier is willing to give himself to the military and defend the cause, but you see it very rarely. For example, there was an indigenous person in Cotzal who made the rank of second lieutenant but only "assimilated." He worked in communications. But in the proper army forces, they select as officers people who go to the military school, the Escuela Politécnica, where the cadets go. There they accept 99 percent people with money and people who they believe are able to lead others. And they must not be indigenous, that's one of the requirements. There are really no opportunities for indigenous people to work their way up through the ranks of military leadership, they just don't exist. As I said a little while ago, it's rare to see an indigenous person climb to a higher rank. The indigenous officer I had the chance to meet (there were maybe two in all) in the whole time I was there still had a certain submissiveness about him. He didn't demonstrate a lot of authority, like saying "This is what we'll do, not that." But the officers we consider ladinos. Whew, what a contrast! They were really bad. One time in Petén, an officer called a soldier "Pigface!" There is an innate, natural spirit of rebellion in the indigenous people. The soldier felt so insulted, he took his gun and killed the officer, then killed himself. There are several cases of indigenous soldiers rebelling. Many of our indigenous brothers are captured for military service; they are terrified and run away, which the army considers an act of high treason. These cases are punishable by death. In times of war martial law demands that deserters be shot on the spot. The soldier who doesn't follow orders from superiors gets punished severely. Sentences range from prison to the dungeon, which is a pit filled with filthy water that has human waste, food leftovers, and other disgusting stuff floating in it. Into the pit they throw soldiers who have transgressed or been disobedient. They leave them there for a day or a night. We know that in Huehuetenango two soldiers died that way. In my own town, during the war when the military got there, two soldiers also died in such a pit. It's a type of torture given to the indigenous soldier to convince him that he should follow orders blindly. It instills fear.

The other major problem I found in the military is the following: for example, let's suppose Juan, Miguel, and Santiago are from the same town, from the same cultural background, it's difficult for them to stay together in the same unit. So that they won't communicate, they are separated. One is put into one squad, the other into a different one or in different units, or different troops. Two friends cannot stay in the same squad. This is an army tactic to ensure that there is not a bit of communication or chance for "rebellion." The punishments are so brutal that they leave a soldier who wants to desert without any courage to do so. They have very strict discipline in the army. They make the indigenous soldiers believe that if their father is a *guerrillero,* then he is their enemy and they have to kill him. This is the truth, there are examples of this in Quiché and Huehuetenango that I know about.

Regarding the things the military did to the civilian population, they chose far-off locations where there are no communication systems, no highways, telephones, telegraphs. It's there that the army carried out their massacre campaigns. There they destroyed entire settlements. Why?

Primarily because these indigenous communities are abandoned. They have no strong links to the outside world and no stronger voice than that of the priests, many of whom were killed in Guatemala. In these remote places there is no one who could protect these small communities.

When the military became aware of how strong the revolutionary forces had become, I had already been discharged from the army. I had problems in the army because, even when I was still a civilian, I knew that this campaign of massacres, which the army carried out largely at the Mexican border, was called Operación Limpieza [Operation Cleanup]. Very simple, that's all they called it. The idea was to kill ten people, because at least one of them would be a guerrilla, even if the other nine were innocent. This was their thinking as aptly described by the governor of Huehuetenango.

Well, I want to give you a rundown of the situation I experienced in Quiché and later in Huehuetenango. It was painful for me who came from a school where I was taught very high moral principles, mostly Christian, where I learned to respect the life of my fellow humans, modesty, serving others, responsibility, which maybe at the time I never fully realized. But the army was aware of my capabilities at work and knew my professional work ethic. Gradually they isolated me from the other specialized workers because I had no experience yet in the specialized troops. When the team of specialized troops was all complete in the personnel department, I was already in Huehuetenango; they told me that they had no vacancy left for me and that there was work for me only in the intelligence section. As soon as my friends heard that I was transferring to the intelligence department, they started calling me "Spy, spy, murderer, assassin!" They knew from experience what type of work I would have to do in intelligence. I didn't pay any attention to them, it was part of army life, but at times we were very hard on each other. When I started in the intelligence section, I found a friend right away, I'll call him a friend because he respected me enough, and showed me respect and appreciation in the army. Maybe it was a psychological scheme to pull me down into the quagmire they were in. This man treated me in a very friendly manner and started to teach me how to do the periodic briefing papers for operations, for intelligence, the statistics, the messages, the official memos, and other documents that had to do with the intelligence section.

Let me at this point explain why I mentioned my simple and humble family background. My parents are peasants. Those are my roots. I grew up with the Catholic religion. This background creates a strong sense in a person to respect others. In the intelligence section I was given access to the general archive. I began to see wounded men in the office. I began to see bloody uniforms, dead bodies, even bodies of special troops who'd been killed in combat or ambushed by guerrilla forces. I saw friends, indigenous persons who'd been killed after being captured by the military. Even though this made me sad, I told myself: I can take this, no problem, it'll pass soon. I was very surprised when one time, after I'd seen all these things for a while, the friend I mentioned before called me and told me a lot about the work of the intelligence troops; until then I had only performed typing jobs.

I was never on the inside of groups like the Escuadrón de la Muerte [Death Squad], Mano Blanca [White Hand], or G-2. They had many names. The OSA or the ESA—it's all the same. It's an invention of the military leaders. They give different names to these groups, as the friend explained; these groups are made up of all the many civilians who help the army. But this is a lie. They're the very same soldiers who pass themselves off as different groups so that they can carry out the heinous crimes they committed in Guatemala.

I want to tell you this friend's name. It was Lito A. Santay. He was from Palmar and has since been killed by the guerrillas. He once invited me to go and look at some "prisoners of war," as he called them. I went with him. "Take a pencil and paper, you'll need to write down information on some of the men," he told me. There were sixteen young men from Parraxtut, from the municipality of Nebaj in Quiché. They had been captured the third week in April, and on April 28 the army started to execute them extrajudicially, without court trials, in their own installations in the military zone. But I'm going too fast. When I went that day to see these boys, they lay stretched out, face down, one hand of one man tied to one hand of the next man. I started to ask them their names. They looked very normal, but you could read the fear in their faces and sense the terror they felt. Behind me were several armed military men of the Policía Militar Ambulante [Mobile Military Police; PMA]. Being from the specialized troop, I went to the captives asking their names, even joked with them. "They'll surely let you go, I just need to take down some information," I told them, really not knowing what the army had planned for them. Then we left and Lito said, "The boys need to get some food." The nice, kind tone of voice in which Lito said this made me believe that the prisoners were going to be set free. We brought them food, and they were fed well.

Four days later I was called and told, "Look, we have a job to do and want you there with us." "With pleasure," I replied. Military orders were never questioned. I had to be there. They called me. . . . They had five young men tied up.

The military execution ground in Huehuetenango has two enclosed cells, three men were in the one on one side, two in the other. They picked them up from the ammunition storerooms where they had been kept prisoner and took them to the execution ground. On the way they told them, "Well, we'll let you go. Get ready because you'll go home. We just want you in here for a little while."

But they lied to them. The torturers prepared some ropes and lassos while the prisoners waited inside. Then they called the first one. These captives had their hands tied behind their backs. They told him, "Get down on your face." The young man obeyed, knelt down, and lowered his head while Lito said, "You're a guerrillero, son of a bitch, you better tell us where your friends are, where the other guerrilleros are, or you'll see what happens."

"I know nothing," said the boy, "I know nothing, Mister. If I did, I'd already have told you."

"Shut up, then," they said, and at that moment Lito put a rope around the peasant's neck and with a stick tightened it and throttled him till he was dead. This was the first shock I got. I was shaking. I wanted to defend this man but couldn't. Very close to me stood a captain by the name of P. Pérez, a native from Tecún Umán, San Marcos. He was armed. So was Lito. And there were two other policemen. I was the only one there without a weapon. They then called the other prisoner and killed him, too. They killed all five young men, one by one.

Lito asked me, "You want to try one?" I couldn't take it any longer and started to vomit. "No!" I said. "I can't stand it. I can't do this." I still saw before my eyes the man's face when they strangled him and heard the poor guy say, "Oh God, oh God," when the soldiers started to kill him. Foam and blood came out of his mouth. I couldn't stop shaking and had to vomit.

"Get a grip on yourself!" the captain told me. "Okay, I will, Captain," I said. While these men were killed, the captives who were inside were not aware of what was going on. The dead were left under a tarp. I even helped drag their poor bodies there under the tarp. I was ordered to help put the bodies into a truck. Without any clothes or IDs, the victims' bodies were put into that truck—which was metallic gray. It was about 11:00 P.M., and they took them away to an unknown destination. Later Lito told me they had to kill the sixteen young men because they were people who for sure would have joined the guerrilla troops. The young men had been caught when the army soldiers had disguised themselves as guerrilleros and had held a "guerrilla" meeting. That's how these friends had been trapped. Their bodies were thrown out of the truck at the highway kilometer marker 313 near Boquerón, where the Pan-American Highway passes by coming from Mesilla. Many of our fellow countrymen were thrown there. Many people who belonged or who did not belong to guerrilla groups were dumped there by the military. This hit me the hardest of all. From this moment on I could not sleep anymore. I knew then what was in store for me. I had to decide whether I wanted to stay in the army. If I got blood on my hands, I'd come out the loser. From then on I tried to get drunk frequently in order to make mistakes so they'd kick me out of the army, for I was afraid to ask for a discharge because if they granted it, they might want to kill me.

I knew the blacklist. Who assassinated Wiwi? One of Wiwi's killers was Lito, who later was killed by the guerrillas. The other was a policeman by the name of Carmelo from Quiché. He belonged to the PMA as well as to the DCI [Destacamento de Contra-Inteligencia], the counterintelligence unit, and was a spy for the army and its G-2, Mano Blanca unit, which is the same as the Death Squad. They are the executioners of the army. They belong to the intelligence sections G-2 and S-2, the same thing. These two men were the main players who shot Wiwi at his law office in Huehuetenango. Juan Yichos, from Cobán, was another one of this group. And I don't know from where he was, but Nul Hernández was another one of these bloodthirsty army killers there.

All the things these men have done were in line with the order that the commander of the military zone had given. But there were cases when the commander did not have to issue instructions anymore whether they should or should not kill a particular person. The soldiers made their own decision. They automatically decided whether to kill someone or not. There were prisoners in Huehuetenango who were lucky and got away. I can still see Wiwi's brother, who was held prisoner in this very same military compound. I still saw him alive, but there was no chance to save him. I admit that I was very scared. For a while there it looked like his mother, Doña Cristabel, would be able to drum up enough support to petition the release of her son from the military zone. Had she continued with her efforts, she might have succeeded, but the son was killed soon after by the army and wasn't heard from again.

What was really driving me insane was this: I was afraid after they told me that I had to kill someone or had to come with them to interrogate or torture someone. I started to plan my escape or leave from the army. Besides, I saw when they caught José Marcos Hernández in Nebaj. This revolutionary was brought to Huehuetenango alive. He had a gunshot wound in his right upper arm and looked totally emaciated, but he was a man of integrity with a great revolutionary conviction. They hit him on the wound, kicked him and all, and he didn't complain. They gave him electroshocks to his genitals, his big toes, and put a hood over his head. I saw who was there with my own eyes, Colonel Mario and Carlos who at the time were commanders together with Colonel Zamora. They watched the torture. And even an officer from the Estado Mayor General, the highest military office in Guatemala, had come. He brought specially trained people to torture José Marcos Hernández but couldn't get any information out of him. Later, José Marcos was taken to Guatemala City.

I wanted to talk to him, but when he saw me in my uniform he just said, "You think I'm going to talk? No." He always was afraid to reveal something. When they led him to the helicopter, I prayed to God that he would die fast since the torture they'd given him in that place was brutal, very, very brutal. . . . Afterward I still heard the screams of this dear man in my ears every night. Many people died, but later I didn't notice what these tortures were like because they let me rest a while. They didn't summon me, they wanted to ease me into this gradually and slowly make me into a member of the Squad of Death. Thank God, they didn't succeed. After what I'd seen and experienced, I knew I had to leave the army.

Back in my pueblo—after leaving the army—I lived as a civilian but already noticed the trauma or psychosis from the war, yet I still felt enough strength to want to confront the situation. I knew for sure that the army would come to my town. They had already received news from the military zone in Huehuetenango. We wanted to help the people (to tell them about the situation) but the people were very closed-minded and there was no chance to do a better job. The people all lived the way they wanted to, and each person did his own thing. When the army arrived, neighbors became more distant. In my pueblo a phase of great coldness began. Even within the same family there was distrust. One can't say that my town was subjected to large-scale repression. People captured elsewhere were brought here to be tortured. This is totally different from what happened in the Ixil Triangle. This triangle is made up of the communities of Nebaj, Cotzal, and Chajul. These people have really suffered the violence of the military counterinsurgency. They have paid dearly for what was the indigenous movement. We know this because the indigenous Ixil Indian has not lost his courage. He has proven that. In the Ixil Triangle the army followed the saying, "El ejemplo de la fuerza es mayor que la fuerza del ejemplo," an example of strength is more effective than the strength of an example. To do this, the army took pains to select the right people for the job. What did they do? They sent personnel from the military zone of Jutiapa who had nothing to do with the great misery and poverty of these indigenous people.

When I was assigned to the advanced command post in Nebaj, a second lieutenant said when he saw the "indiada," a slang term for the indigenous in Guatemala, "These bastards, these animals, they should all be killed. They don't deserve to live. They're not people."

That's how foolishly this second lieutenant talked. "Yes, sir," I answered in a calm manner. But what courage it took. I said to myself: Well, what a smart-ass. He doesn't know shit. As a specialized troop I knew quite a bit more than he; that's why many officers were friendly to me, but at the same time I was also hated by many officers who didn't like that I was capable of work they couldn't do. When I realized this, I got upset and said to myself: What a jerk. What a bastard he is. Just because he has a little stripe on his uniform, just because he has a weapon. They have not gone through what these people had to go through.

He started to explain. "It's because these miserable people are guerrillas, communists, and we have to kill them. If we don't burn their asses now, they will hurt us later. Besides, these people shouldn't live anymore anyway. They are savages, they live in the jungle. Not like in Guatemala City and in Xela where you have good people; these miserable people should be swept from the face of the earth."

He went on like that, brother, as if he was reciting a litany. It left me without any courage. This guy, what about him? I don't remember his name, but the bastard was from Jutiapa. He told me to write a memo and make corrections so it would look good. And I said, "Yes, sir, at your service." "Okay," he said, "tell the second lieutenant who gets this memo that I say they should give me permission to shoot all these people and to send planes to bomb them all. We must kill them." That was it, plain and simple.

This was before the organized army massacres started. This was October of 1981, no massacres had taken place yet. They began at the beginning of 1982. The friends I had in the army frightened me with their views about my people, people so simple and modest. Why didn't they give them what they asked for? Even they [the soldiers] got killed. The people in Nebaj were completely isolated. The army didn't have contact with them other than with the spies. Yes, there were army spies in Nebaj, the military commissioners. But the people in general did not trust the army. One could tell by their behavior in public. And the army saw a guerrilla in every indigenous Ixil. As time passed, this attitude became more pronounced. It became so bad that the army's discrimination against and lack of understanding of the indigenous people led to the extermination of whole communities. We know this from reliable data that have come from other sources. Right now I don't have current information anymore on what the army's treatment is of the indigenous people, but I know the army has won the support of many indigenous people. Even in my pueblo there were people so poor and exploited who gave their hearts and lives to the army and the government. And what was their reward? Nothing, not a damned thing. Just remember the case of the assistant mayor of Chehb'al who was killed by guerrilla forces outside my town on May 26, 1982. Ignorance has been really widespread in my town; it's one of the biggest handicaps and has contributed to the destruction of our communities. There are no schools. The rights of the indigenous people are not respected. There is terrible submissiveness, blind obedience, and tremendous fear. Maybe due to the principle of the right to live, many people have opted to keep quiet and to endure all of this. The instinct to survive is very strong in our people, and it has made us a little more cautious.

Unfortunately, I can't remember some facts anymore that would help me give you a clearer and more consistent account. Back to the topic of how the indigenous soldier was treated in the military zone, that's a tough one. They took away these soldiers' cultural identity. They are no longer indigenous or anything else, just soldiers. And if it's necessary to die for their country, then they'll die for this "homeland" that they don't even know or understand. The soldiers definitely have to pay for any disobedience. There have been many cases of desertion just because of the psychological indoctrination they are given in the army. They teach them many things about military duties that are of highest importance. Without scruples they train them not to be afraid to kill people, and they forget their Christian principles. Probably 99.5 percent of the indigenous people in Guatemala are Christians. Very few belong to other religious sects. But nevertheless, in general, the indigenous people have been discriminated against not only in the military but also in Guatemala's economic, social, and cultural life. There's been a great gap. There are two different Guatemalas, the Guatemala of the rich and powerful and the Guatemala of the poor, indigenous people. The age of colonization and exploitation has turned the indigenous person into a very submissive and fearful person, very obedient but also very friendly. Sure, the indigenous people eventually realized that they had to try to fit in. This war now has the army set against the civilian population and has caused the nuclei of the different cultures within Guatemala to segregate. This is a serious problem, and I am saying that based on both my experience in the army and what I saw in my pueblo before I left.

Allow me to take another moment to talk a little more about what happened before I left the country. After I left the army, I worked very hard with my people and identified almost too much with them. Sometimes when I was drunk I even cursed the soldiers from upstairs in my house saying stuff like "Soldiers, son of bitches, you're murderers." They didn't react. Thank God I got away with this. Many times I could have been killed but I got away. I was okay. That is, until a woman denounced me.

It was May 17 at about 4:00 P.M. when soldiers came to my house. There were about thirty of them. They surrounded my house, and some came in to look for me. They knew I was working at the town hall; all they wanted to do was frighten me. When they couldn't find me, they went back to the army base. My father came to me at the town hall, panting and very upset, telling me I had to leave home immediately. He offered me five quetzals to get to Mexico. I knew what the problem was, but to give my father and myself courage, I said, "No, Papa, I don't have to leave. I didn't do anything wrong. Someone who has done nothing fears nothing." And I continued, "I'll go to them and find out what they want." Thank God I had this spirit and was able to talk like that to my family, but there was a moment when I almost lost heart. I wanted to run away immediately leaving my family, but a friend said to me, "Look, they're not planning to kill you yet. If they wanted to, they'd come by night to get you and wouldn't show themselves. Probably they want something from you. You were in the army, maybe they need you for a job."

His words gave me focus and cleared my mind. Since it seemed sure that they were not going to kill me yet, I would go to them. But, friends,

I went there feeling more dead than alive. My whole body shook from my head down my spine and back, all the way down to my toes, trembling all over. I was afraid to die. My neck felt constricted all around, my throat felt dry with a lump in it, my tongue way back in my mouth. My eyes moved crazily in their sockets, and my whole body trembled. I felt like I had diarrhea, that I'd faint, or was having a heart attack. But I prayed to God, and in those moments when I knew that I might die, I was determined. I wanted to show the army people that I was not scared of them. Yes, it's true I was afraid to die, but I found the courage to confront the army men without a weapon, although I took a very great risk. I left my house and kept praying to God, entrusting my body and soul to him. I began to say the Credo. I was close to the entrance of the military base, . . . and when I arrived there God worked a miracle. All of a sudden, I felt light, was able to stand up straight without dread or fear, and I asked to see the people in charge. They let me enter and go to the officers, a lieutenant and a second lieutenant. Immediately I sat down in front of them and shook their hands, showing that I was not afraid. They said, "Listen you, we sent for you to talk to you about something. There is a charge against you."

"Yes, Lieutenant?" I asked.

"What do you say to that?"

"Well, sir," I said, "thank God you found out. I'm very frightened. For days now I have received anonymous notes saying the guerrillas want to kill me and are accusing me of taking part in the army operations in the outlying villages with you. I wasn't able to come to tell you for fear. I don't want anyone to see me near the base, that's why I haven't come earlier to let you know."

"Shit. That's not what we're talking about," the officer said. "It's a different charge we're talking about. Here are two sheets of paper with three lists. Your name is on them. You are the guerrilla commander in your town. That's what you're accused of. You are a guerrilla bastard."

They frightened me very much. And I knew what would happen next. Finally I said, "Sir, do I have to take that? Please, give me the list and I will put my name on it another ten times, but where is the proof, Lieutenant, where?"

"Never mind proof. If you want to deny, it doesn't matter to us if you deny a thousand times. You're a guerrilla," they said.

"My Lieutenant," I responded, "you are about to do a great injustice. You've seen me go to work every day. If I don't walk by here, I'm taking the other road up there. When the guerrillas come to shoot at you, I even have to run back to my house because I can't go near the base. I'm in the line of fire, but still I'm here at home. So how do you explain that I'm a guerrilla? I don't know who they are or how many. If any are from my town or not, I have no idea. How could I, since I don't know anything about them?"

"No, you're a guerrilla for sure. Your name is on the lists three times."

"Sir, my name could be on there a thousand times, but it's not true, you have no proof."

"Shit, we have photos of you, front, profile, side. We have your fingerprints and footprints. We have all the information on you in our intelligence office. You've worked for us and you know how we torture people and how we kill. You want to die like that?" he asked.

"No, I don't," I said, "and that's precisely it. After working with you and knowing how it all works in the army, do you think I would be stupid enough to join the guerrillas?" I almost smiled at them and talked to them with great courage and serenity. They wanted me to be scared.

"Listen," they said, "you are one of them, and you know what's going to happen to you."

"Sir," I said, "I know you will kill me if you can prove that I'm a guerrillero. But if you want to kill me on your own account, sir, then this crime will weigh heavily on your conscience, for it's a crime. If I were a guerrilla and you killed me, I'd not object, you'd be doing a great deed for justice because we have to protect freedom here in Guatemala and have to kill the damned guerrillas."

"No, you are a guerrilla and you won't trick me."

"No, sir, how would I trick you?"

We went on like this at length until I said to him, taking a high risk: "Lieutenant, let's not be pig-headed, let's cut the crap and play it straight. Confront me with the persons who accuse me so they can prove their charges and then you can shoot me, Lieutenant. I'll give the order myself, but first bring the persons who are accusing me. There are for sure many people in my town who hate me because I've tried to do justice in accordance with the rules of my job, the same when I was in the military. I've tried to work with you and tried to do the best I could. Maybe there is a person who dislikes me or to whom I did something who now accuses me of being a guerrilla. For example, so and so doesn't get along with me and I don't know how many others. The mayor here in town will tell you that I've always worked for the people. Sometimes I go into town to chase away the dirty pigs who are fouling the streets of the town."

"Stop talking about animals," they said to me. "Listen, we'll give you a chance. We were trained in psychology at the university and you can't outsmart us," said the second lieutenant to me.

"But, sir, I'm not trying to argue with you, all I want is to clarify what is being said against me. I have nothing against you."

"Okay, we'll give you a chance to vindicate yourself for your country. You want to work with us?"

"Lieutenant, you should have started like that, I'm a military man 100 percent. You say so and I will work with you with pleasure. I'm afraid the guerrillas will kill me, and I'm afraid to come here to you because they'll go after me more. I'm scared now. You're accusing me, the guerrilla fighters are accusing me, I can't win, I have nowhere to turn to. If you give me a chance to be part of your group, I'd like to, sir."

"All right, I like how you talk now. Here is a list [it had about thirty names on it] you need to work on. You need to spy on all of these people. You know them all?"

"I'd like to look at it, Lieutenant." He handed me the list. There were various names.

"These are guerrillas, right?"

"You are saying that, sir, but I don't know. I won't incriminate myself. If I work with you, I'll find out soon whether these bastards are guerrillas."

"That's your job," they told me. "Once a week you come here to report. If you have any information, you come and we'll give you orders. You can come day or night to bring us information. You must come at any time. To make you feel safer, when the guerrilleros want to kill you, you come immediately to the base and stay with us. We'll get a helicopter to take you to the capital or out of the country."

"Thank you, Lieutenant, I like that. Too bad I disappointed you in Huehuetenango."

"Liar!" the bastards said. "We never believed that you had to quit the army because you drank. You got drunk on purpose so you could leave."

"No, my Lieutenant, how could that be?" I said. "I was scared because the guerrilla fighters came here on September 7 and you did not believe me; instead of helping me you arrested me. I lost hope, and you still don't believe me. Truth be told, I was a target for the guerrillas. I thank God they haven't gotten me yet, but I've gotten anonymous threats." I had gotten out of that.

"All right, we'll expect you here at the latest in a week, but if you have any information earlier, you must let us know."

"Yes, sir, my pleasure." We even shook hands when we parted.

Earlier, when I had arrived at the base, I had seen a rifle, its butt near my hands. It seemed loaded and ready to be used, money and cigarettes next to it. When I entered I was ready for anything. I had this thought in the back of my mind the whole time. As soon as I felt the pressure becoming too much, I'd kill them all. I didn't want to die tortured, my friends. I was prepared to cause my own death, had to provoke it. I was capable of killing so they would kill me. But I couldn't bear that they would put shackles on me. I had seen the horror of their tortures in Huehuetenango. So I told myself: I can take the rifle, I'm not too dumb to handle it or to shoot it; I'd grab it, throw myself down onto the ground and shoot and turn around because there might be someone at the door aiming at me.

This was one possibility, but I rejected it. Why? Because it was likely that the gun was not really loaded and there was no ammunition and that it only looked set to shoot. That's when sadness overcame me and when my spirits sank. I had to listen to all the accusations they hurled at me. They talked to me rough and mean, but I fought them tooth and nail with my answers, never sure whether I'd be able to defend myself in the end or not. I am convinced without a doubt that God spoke through my mouth, not me. I don't remember too well. My answers came out simple and clear, and I stayed calm. The calmness was very important. You have to watch out for the enemy. What helped me was my experience in the army. I knew these guys already, that was my strength. If I hadn't been in the military and had stayed in my pueblo organizing the people, they would have easily killed me. But that's what helped me.

The days passed, but I could not live in peace. Soldiers came by all the time to check on me, watching my every move. That's why I wasn't able to warn the people whose names were on the blacklist, there was no chance. I walked by their houses, but there were soldiers there. What was I to do? I lost hope. To send my wife to warn them was very risky, too. I thought I could go and leave the information at some village outside of town. On May 26 I went to the town hall early to get an advance on my pay. Luckily, I saw one of the people whose name was on the list and told him what I knew. When I fled my country, I had to pass through several villages and left the information I had, but I didn't have all of the details anymore. Some comrades got away. I think they were more careful and didn't sleep at their houses anymore. They moved away and were safe, but others were caught. I found out about this here in Mexico.

This is what it was like. This was the reality and the experience I had with the army in Guatemala. They wanted to manipulate me, and the escape to "another country" they offered me would have been nothing but the graveyard. I knew their scheme, and I thank God that I had a chance to get away. Several times they were going to catch me at night in the streets, but I still had time to run and they didn't shoot me. Every morning soldiers showed up watching my house and I didn't notice. Finally, my wife said, "You'd better go to Mexico." But I didn't want to leave and said to her, "What would I do in Mexico if you and the children don't come with me? What would I do there in Mexico?"

So she decided to come with me. That's why we are here. But there are many things I forget now, maybe due to the time passing, details are forgotten. Maybe we could talk more about this tragedy later on, but for now this is all.

During my visit with Hultaxh I told him about my parents, brother, and sisters who applied and were granted landed immigrant status in Canada. After hearing this, Hultaxh went to Mexico City to explore similar possibilities with the Canadian embassy. I asked a friend to send him the forms and urged him to apply. The application and screening process took more than a year, but finally in 1989 he and his family moved to Canada.

6

THE JOURNEY TO MEXICO

The Guatemala-Mexico Border:
First Experiences

EXILE AND MASS migration are not new responses to
the violent intervention of the Guatemalan government
in Maya communities. Crossing the border from Guatemala into Mexico took place in the past, for example, in
the 1870s when the Barrios government persecuted
Carrera's Maya supporters. In the 1980s indigenous populations fled across the border to save themselves from
the army or the civil patrol. At the time of the first crossings refugees had no legal status, and Guatemalan Mayas
mixed easily among the Mayas in southern Mexico
because their language and cultural traditions were similar. Refugee camps were not created right away, and
massive migration helped to build new villages such as
Guadalupe Victoria in Chiapas.

The refugees from the Kuchumatan highlands whose
stories are highlighted here were not the only refugees
crossing into Mexico at this time. The Guatemalan army
also carried out extensive bombings and attacks on the
Maya and ladino cooperative communities that had been

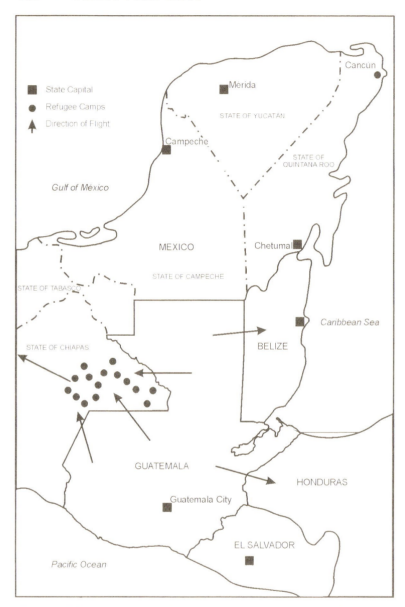

*Refugee flight from Guatemala, 1978–1983. From Nolin Hanlon 1995.
Map by Darren R. Stranger, courtesy of Catherine L. Nolin Hanlon.*

established in the Ixcán and the Petén. These refugees fled into
Chiapas along the east-west border, to the east of the Pan-

American Highway and the major population centers along its length, setting up camps in the Lacandón rain forest. The Guatemalan department of San Marcos was also a target of the military, and many refugees from this area fled into the Soconusco coffee-growing region of Chiapas. For the most part these people did not seek official refugee status and blended into the campesino population that eked out a living laboring on coffee plantations. In addition, as many as five-hundred thousand people were displaced within Guatemala (Nolin Hanlon 1995: 33–37).

The people of the Maya communities of the Kuchumatan highlands were familiar with the Mexican border, because in the past the men had crossed it to work in the seasonal harvest of coffee and cotton in the coastal plantations of the Soconusco. Also, historically, there has been a close economic relationship between Kuchumatan towns (e.g., Jacaltenango, San Antonio, Santa Ana Huista, Nentón, and San Miguel Acatán) and the Mexican frontier towns and cities of Comitán, Comalapa, Motozintla, and Tapachula. Trade and smuggling was a routine activity, carried out on a small scale since colonial times. In their journeys "the ordinary Indians [went] as far as Comitán and Tapachula in Mexico, and Quetzaltenango in Guatemala. They [got] material for making hats from the Mexican Low Country, which they exchange[d] for chocolate and other products of the Guatemalan coast" (LaFarge and Byers 1931: 66).

Socioeconomic and cultural links between the Kuchumatan highland towns and Chiapas have existed since pre-Hispanic times, although the relationship between the larger cities of both regions changed as they became industrialized and fell under the domination of their respective ladino or mestizo cultures. But the Mayas of Guatemala have continued to improve their relationship with the Mayas of southern Mexico, especially with the Lacandón, Tzotzil-Tzeltals, and Tojolabales (Earle 1988). Because of the geographic similarities of the region and its shared cultural expressions, the Maya communities in Chiapas were the

first to become sanctuaries for the Mayas from Guatemala who
escaped the army's reign of death and destruction. This area has
provided Maya refugees with security and protection for the past
fifteen years.

There was great pain among the people who were the first
refugees. Some did not bring anything, not even blankets to
sleep on. But what was more painful were the cries and lamen-
tations of the many who were widows. With their now fatherless
children, they cried and cried inconsolably. All the pain was
shared, for everybody had suffered intensely. Almost everybody
there, reunited in exile, had lost one or more of their relatives
and loved ones, and an immense sadness settled over all the people. On seeing such suffering, some good Mexican families
passed the information to other Mexican communities that there
were thousands of poor Guatemalan families starving near the
Mexican border. Some Mexicans of the region started to bring
some corn, beans, and clothes for the Guatemalan refugees.

Although the refugees knew they were in Mexican territory,
fear prevented them from sleeping. Widows continued to cry.
They were concerned about how they would survive with so
many fatherless children in a strange territory. During the night
the children woke up terrified, calling out the names of their
dead fathers. The violence and death had penetrated deep into
the consciousness of even these little children. Everybody was
frightened because the noise of the Guatemalan helicopters
searching the Mexico-Guatemala border could be heard all
night.

Word of the presence of thousands of refugees along the
southwestern Mexican border attracted many people from
nearby and distant Mexican villages who wanted to see for themselves. Others had different objectives; they sought to gain from
the suffering of the people. Many from Paso Hondo, Comalapa,
Comitán, Tuxtla, and other places came with the intention of
taking the fatherless children from their mothers. Families with
a number of children were asked to give up some of them to the

Mexican people who were eager to adopt them. The people who came to ask for children to be adopted said,

> *Ladies and gentlemen, we know very well what is happening to all of you, and to make your suffering less painful, we come with the desire to take your children with us. We will dress and feed them until the situation in your country changes, and we will return them to you. Don't be sad because we will give you our addresses so you may visit us some day. (Kaxh Pasil, quoted in Montejo and Akab' 1992: 25)*

Others who had come to ask for children showed new clothes to the parents, and said, "Listen, we will dress them well. Here are the clothes, and don't worry." Others offered to buy the children. Because they had nothing to give to their children and because they did not want them to die, some parents gave up their children to these people, who were very aggressive, even pulling the babies from the arms of their mothers. Some children went to caring Mexican families, perhaps without children of their own. Other children, particularly older girls, were pressed into household or workshop labor. It was discovered later that some of these girls were forced into prostitution, even though their parents were told they would be household help. This did not seem to be an organized activity but rather an attempt, by nearby urban Mexicans, particularly those from Comitán, to take advantage of a desperate situation.

Since Jakaltek families do not give children away even under conditions of extreme poverty, the refugees reacted almost immediately to what they had done and began to mobilize at once to recover the children who were given up for adoption. The refugees found out that some people had not acted in good faith and had given false addresses. Others who had acted in good faith and were moved by compassion returned the children immediately when they heard the pleas of their mothers or their relatives. For others, the situation was more difficult. It was only later, with the help of the Mexican authorities, that many parents found the addresses of those who took the children and were able to retrieve them.[1]

After five days in the small Mexican village of Dolores, the immigration agents came to pressure the refugees to go back to Guatemala. The *sub-jefe* (subchief) of immigration and other agents, whose offices are located in Ciudad Cuauhtémoc, a border checkpoint on the Pan-American Highway, arrived at the refugee settlement, where thousands of people were waiting for them. But the refugees became frightened on witnessing the first acts of the immigration officers. The officers grabbed machetes from some refugees who had gone to find firewood to cook their food. The refugees were terrorized. Then the immigration officer shouted to the thousands of refugees gathered at the end of the hammock bridge over the Río Dolores,

"Why did all of you come here? With whose permission have you crossed the border?"

The people answered, "The situation in our country is too bad, and the kaibiles are killing so many people and burning down houses. The many widows and orphans that are among us right now are proof of this. Because of fear of dying at the hands of the Guatemalan army, that is why we left our country, and it is why we are here."

The immigration officer responded, "We don't care about that. If you don't have permission to stay on this side, you have to go back to your country. Also, if the army is killing you, it must be for something."

Again the people responded with pleas: "Sirs, we know that we are in another country, and we also believe that this country can protect us, that is why we took refuge here in this territory. We know that Mexico has a good government, and that is why we have come to seek protection for our children and the elders on this side of the border. But if you have orders from your government to deport us, we prefer that you kill all of us right here, rather than going back to be killed with great torture at the hands of the Guatemalan army. You may not know of the satanic attitude of the kaibiles, that is why you don't believe us, but we, who have all the pain inside because of the killings of our loved ones, can tell you who the kaibiles are. They do not give any value to our lives. They are cannibals. When they capture someone, they hit, torture, and cut him up into pieces. First one arm, then the other. They cut up their victims. They cut the victim's legs, they gouge out his eyes, cut out his tongue, cut off his testicles, and finally, they put their knives into their victim's heart. This is how they kill our innocent people, and that is why we prefer that you kill all of us here, instead of going back to be killed in the places where we have come from. In addition to this, we don't have any houses to return to because the army has burned down our houses and destroyed entire communities."

"I don't care about that," said the immigration officer. "You had better return to your villages because the Mexican army is about to come here, and if you resist going back to your country, the Mexican soldiers will obligate you to go back by force. They won't respect you. They will crack your bones with kicks and will put you in trucks to be deported into the hands of the Guatemalan army."

Terrorized, not only because of what was going on in their country, but also because of the threats of the immigration officer, the refugees did not know what to do. Now they feared not only the Guatemalan army but also the Mexican army, which, according to the immigration officer, could also kill them. For the refugees, armies now seemed to be the same everywhere.

Some refugees opted to return to Guatemala, to seek refuge in the larger towns because the small, isolated villages were being destroyed in the counterinsurgency war. However, other families chose to remain in Chiapas, where they thought it would be safer or where they could be near the children they had given up to Mexican families.

Many Maya women rid themselves of their traditional dress and borrowed clothing from the ladinos so they could hide among the Mexican women in the small Mexican border villages. It was not easy for traditional Maya women to suddenly change their way of dressing. The old women resisted and argued that it showed a lack of respect for their own culture to cast aside the traditional dresses that they had been wearing since they were little girls. The modern clothing felt so simple and thin that they felt as if they were wearing almost nothing. In addition, the borrowed dresses were not the right size. Doña Gertrudis reluctantly wore one of the dresses. It was so long that the moment she tried to walk in it she stepped on the edge of the skirt and fell to the ground. She got up and went into her tent to change it immediately. Thereafter she wore only her traditional Maya *corte* (skirt) and *huipil* (blouse). But the majority, out of fear, began to change their traditional dress, a practice that became generalized in the refugee camps in 1982–83. Nonetheless, the older women continued to oppose the decision of younger refugee women to discard their traditional dresses (Montejo and Akab' 1992: 27).

Afraid of the immigration officers and of the Mexican army, which had supposedly come to force the refugees to go back to Guatemala, thousands of refugees gathered at the edge of the hammock bridge on the Río Dolores and split into small groups. Each group continued to penetrate farther inside Mexican territory, trying to avoid the Guatemalan army, the immigration officers, and the Mexican army. And constantly they heard the Guatemalan helicopters, searching and firing their machine guns in the mountains near the Mexican border.

The refugees lived this way from January until March 23, 1982, when the same Guatemalan army overthrew the president, General Lucas García, and put into place General Ríos Montt, the leader of the military coup. The refugees who had gone back to their villages in Guatemala returned to the refugee settlements in Mexico to tell their relatives the great news, that the genocidal government of Lucas García had been overthrown and now, according to radio broadcasts, there was peace.

Thousands of families received the news with great happiness. They were suffering from hunger and wanted to go back home and start their lives again. Also, as it was March, they could at least clean a piece of land and plant their cornfield to secure food for the next year. This was the time when the fields should be burned for planting corn, to be ready for the first rains of May. Their love for their homeland made their return fast and happy. There was fear among them, but they decided to start their way of life again in these isolated villages, where hundreds of their fellow villagers had been killed. Most refugees returned to Guatemala during April and May, although almost all had little confidence in the Guatemalan army. At the same time the army again started to visit the newly reoccupied communities. They stayed one or two nights in each village, raising suspicion among the frightened villagers. The news from more distant places, which came by radio and by word of mouth from travelers, was that the new military government was even more terrible than the one that had been deposed.

The Flight

IN JUNE 1982 the counterinsurgency war returned to the Kuchumatan highlands, especially to northwestern Huehuetenango. The helicopters began to bomb the communities again, and people fled toward the border, pouring into Mexican territory to escape persecution and death. This time some Maya groups, such as the Q'anjob'al, took their musical instruments and the statues of their patron saints. They wanted their patron saints to accompany them as they would need their help to survive the misery of exile. Meanwhile in Guatemala the army commanders gave notice in Nentón, Jacaltenango, San Antonio Huista, Santa Ana Huista, and other large towns that each house must have a white flag on the roof, signaling friendship with the army. Those houses and villages without white flags would be the direct targets of the helicopter bombing. Overnight the white flags appeared on the roofs of all houses in the Kuchumatan highlands, and those people who remained in Guatemala were subject to the direct control of the army.

In July 1982, when refugees crossed the Mexican border in great numbers, thousands of families were deeply affected. "Guatemalan government sources estimate that 100,000 children lost one or both parents to political violence in the early 1980's" (Manz 1988a: 30). Thus traditional family life was again disrupted, as it had been during the Spanish invasion of 1524. Children were killed and dismembered when they could not run as fast as their parents from their burning villages. Children were separated from their parents when entire communities escaped in the darkness of night, fleeing for their lives. Sometimes the army took the children away in helicopters, and nobody knew where they were sent.

Entire families had to hide in the mountains, so the children had to learn to be quiet to avoid the soldiers who were searching for them. These incredible escapes from death traumatized the children at a very early age. During this time of terror mothers succored their children in the time-honored way, giving them both nourishment and protection.

Hundreds of families have to flee from one place to another, or hide silently from the soldiers, days and nights. Among them, there were many children who were terrified and they cried because of hunger. But since their cries could alert the soldiers, their mothers just lifted their huipiles and fed their children with their maternal milk. . . . In this way, small children were able to overcome their fear, so the soldiers couldn't find them.

Maya women defended their children and their people with the strategy of breast-feeding. The situation was terrifying to even the youngest children. Children as young as four already knew that the army was capable of the most criminal acts. They witnessed helicopters bombing their villages and soldiers firing their machine guns on their parents or village elders.

Sometimes an entire community managed to escape. When the neighboring community of El Limonar went up in flames on January 6, 1982, the residents of La Laguna, near the Mexican border, decided to abandon their village before the army came to massacre them. Sleeping children were lifted up and began to cry loudly as they did not understand what was happening. Kaxh Pasil, a villager who was hiding that night in the bushes, described what happened when another family with several children arrived at the same hiding place.

When the massacre of the neighboring village of El Limonar occurred, we abandoned our village [La Laguna] at night, and some families slept in the woods, before crossing the Mexican border the next day. I was hiding with my father-in-law in a spot we selected on the outskirts of the village that night. We were tired, and when we laid on the ground to rest, my father-in-law immediately fell to sleep and started to snore noisily. I tried to wake him up, but he continued to snore. Suddenly, I heard someone approaching the spot where we were hiding. I wanted to shut his mouth, but I knew he would get scared or he would speak up aloud, so I moved aside and looked at the intruder who was coming slowly where we were hiding. It was a full moon, and with the pale light in the forest I could see just the shadows of a man carrying something as a rifle. I could see the shadows of a man or a soldier with his galil rifle coming toward us. At that distance, I knew he had heard the noisy snoring of my father-in-law, so he walked slowly toward where we were. I was petrified behind a bush, while my father-in-law continued to snore in deep sleep. When the man came a little closer he stopped and shouted, "Oy, Makex" [Eh, who are you?]. When he spoke in Popb'al Ti', then I knew that he was one of our villagers. "Do you think that the soldiers won't come here?" he asked, and I said, "I believe not, they don't know the region and I am sure they won't find us here." "Okay, I will go bring my family which I left alone somewhere else." He went to bring his family. As the night was silent, we could hear him coming from far away, because his children were very loud. We could hear that some of the children were crying, others were fighting and shouting noisily. My father-in-law woke up and said, "You cannot stay here with your children because they make so much noise and they will alert the army so easily." The man said, "It is hard to punish them for speaking. They do not know right now why we pull them up from their sleeping mats and they are angry, furious, and even fearful of following us in the darkness." The man and his wife moved with the children farther from where we were, but we could still hear their cries for a long time until they fell asleep. Poor children, some did ask where their parents were taking them and some only followed their parents without knowing where they were going.

Mexicans, Mexico, and the Refugees

DURING THE FIRST months of the arrival of the refugees in southern Mexico, Mexican families living close to the Guatemala-Mexico border were very helpful. They were hospitable to the Guatemalan refugees because, being poor campesinos themselves, they understood the urgency of the refugees' situation.

> *The arriving refugees were received warmly by most Mexicans of Mayan descent in Chiapas who regarded them as kin. "Today is their turn, tomorrow ours," they would say, as they shared their provisions and offered grazing lands where the Guatemalans could pitch their champas, plastic lean-tos, and erect mud huts. The refugees had reason to look forward to a new start in Mexico, which is universally respected for its tradition of extending asylum to political fugitives from throughout the Americas. (Perera 1983: 455)*

A Mexican peasant recalls the day the refugees arrived in his area: "We remember how they arrived one night and completely wet from the rain, some were injured, while all of them were tired, hungry, to the point that they fell right there exhausted, although they sent people to ask us if they could stay in our lands. . . . Then we understood, for the first time, our capacity and our obligation to help. We understood that nobody is so poor that he cannot do something for others" (Ruíz 1992: 402).

Although Mexico was not a signatory to the 1951 Convention on Refugees, it has had a long record of providing asylum to individuals. Many people fleeing the aftermath of the Spanish Civil War sought and were given refuge in Mexico, and by the early 1980s there was a growing population of Salvadorans who had requested asylum and were living in Mexico City.[2] But Mexico had never dealt with or had to make provisions for such a massive influx of refugees as appeared on its doorstep in 1982. Therefore much of Mexican policy toward the Guatemalan refugees was developed *ad hoc* and reflected a variety of changing pressures and internal political realities (Nolin Hanlon 1995: 54).

The Mexican political system is characterized by constant turnover of elected officials and the view that most problems need only temporary solutions.[3] This, combined with the assessment that the refugee situation would be of short duration, led to a series of stopgap, short-term policies. In early 1982 Mexican authorities granted some refugees asylum and provided documents for them to work and live in Mexico legally, but many other refugees were harassed and deported. By November 1982 the policy of deportation had stopped, but refugees were given only FM-8 visas, which substantially restricted their ability to work and permitted them to live only in official camps within fifty kilometers of the border. These visas, by specifying that refugees would be illegal aliens and subject to deportation if they were found outside the camps, forced them into dependency on the Mexican government for all the necessities of life (Hagan 1987: 84; Nolin Hanlon 1995: 54).

By 1984 the policy had again changed, probably because of complaints from the local Mexican population. Refugees now needed written authorization to leave the camps for specific purposes, for example, to work or to seek medical care at a hospital (UNHCR 1984a, 1984b). The growing antagonism of the local population was a reflection of the injustice and poverty endemic in Chiapas and of the resentment that refugees were encroaching on land and receiving aid that local people needed as well.[4] Another problem for the refugees was that the policies developed in Mexico City by federal officials were slow in taking shape in Chiapas, sometimes because individuals failed to act but more often because of idiosyncratic local interpretations of federal directives.

The Guatemalan Army Reaches into Mexico

IN ITS CONVICTION that the refugees were guerrillas or guerrilla sympathizers, the Guatemalan army was not content to establish its control only on the Guatemalan side of the border. On several occasions it crossed the border in pursuit of refugees, seeking certain individuals or groups and creating havoc along the border. What follows is Kaxh Pasil's detailed account of one such moment of conflict and danger for the refugees on the Guatemala-Mexico border in 1982.[5]

On September 21, 1982, the refugees who were congregated on the Mexican border without a fixed camp were called by Mexican immigration agents (by now, aware of the war going on inside Guatemala) to be registered and given a card for the purposes of working in nearby Mexican communities. Suddenly, while the immigration officers were registering the refugees in the Dolores camp a half mile from the Guatemalan border, the people heard bursts of machine-gun fire. It turned out that the kaibiles and civil patrollers from Guatemala were crossing the border, intending to capture or kill the refugees who had crossed into Mexican territory. When people heard the gunfire, they ran in all directions. There were thousands of refugees congregated in that place when the army and the civil patrol crossed the border. While the people ran for their lives, the immigration agents protected themselves by lying on the ground. They also started to fire their pistols at the invaders. Meanwhile, refugees were frantically trying to cross the Río

Dolores. Everyone was helping each other, especially the elders, women, and children, to cross the turbulent waters of the river beacuse it was the rainy season and the river was high. Doña Catarina, a pregnant lady, was among the people fighting to cross to the other side. She was at the middle of the river when her traditional skirt fell off into the water. Upon reaching the other side of the river, Catarina started to feel the pains of an imminent birth. Fortunately, there were several midwives among the people, and they helped to calm her pains and to bring to life a baby boy. The Mexican immigration authorities reported the invasion to their central government. The refugees heard on the radio that the Mexican government protested the invasion of their territory. But the Guatemalan government defended itself, arguing that the army was prohibited from crossing the border.

A few days later, the immigration officers called the refugees to Dolores and continued giving out the documents that authorized the Guatemalan refugees to stay in Mexican territory. After receiving the papers, the refugees started to move in groups to different Mexican communities in order to be secure from the Guatemalan army's intrusions into Mexico. There were refugees who moved to Aquespala, Colón, Rancho Tejas, Guadalupe Victoria, Comalapa, Paso Hondo, Motozintla, Comitán, Margaritas, San Cristóbal de las Casas, and many other places along the southern Mexico-Guatemala border.

The Guatemalan army's raids were not limited to the one described above. As a result of multiple incursions, the international border region was considered a "national security zone" by the Mexican government (Hernandez Castillo 1992). Again, on April 30, 1984, "some 200 Guatemalan soldiers made another incursion into Mexican territory, raiding the Chupadero camp about six kilometers from the border. Seven refugees were killed" (Manz 1988a: 151).

Getting Settled

THE REFUGEES ENCOUNTERED many obstacles getting settled in Mexico: land, food and fuel resources, and obtaining work and work permits. One of the communities where the refugees encamped for a few months was Colón, close to the Guatemalan border. According to Kaxh Pasil, at the beginning the Mexican residents of this small village were very happy to receive so many people, mainly because it was time for weeding the cornfields. The people of Colón asked the refugees to help weed the milpa in return for being given places to build their hamlets. Because there were so many refugees, the cleaning of the cornfield was done very quickly, but the Mexicans immediately found other ways to take advantage of the free labor of the refugees. For example, they were asked to make channels to drain flooded roads so trucks could pass. Soon supplies of local firewood began to run out, and people had to travel farther and farther to collect wood. The refugees were finally asked to leave the village. Kaxh Pasil told about the dismantling of the camp and the ongoing suffering of the refugees, even in Mexican territory.

A prominent resident of Colón who didn't like the refugees went to ask the immigration authorities to order their evacuation from the village. The immigration agent who came to pressure the refugees was Señor César Marcos Morales. This was a very bad man. He came to tell people to return to Guatemala or he would turn them over to the Guatemalan army. The refugees were then living in constant fear because the Guatemalan army was also crossing the Mexican border to persecute the refugees.

Then another man from Colón named Don Ricardo, who did not believe the stories of terror told by the survivors, began to cause trouble for the refugees. When he heard that the army had crossed the border again, taking the food given to the refugees at the Recuerdo camp, this man went to see for himself if it was true that the Guatemalan army could commit such crimes. Indeed, Don Ricardo was captured by the Guatemalan army. When his family grew tired of waiting for him to return to the village, they went to search for him. The refugees were blamed for his disappearance; the residents of Colón said it was because of the refugees that the man disappeared, so they had to abandon the community and go somewhere else.

They did not know where to go. Meanwhile, the family of the disappeared man went to a spiritist [a ladino lady who was renowned for her divination abilities] to ask the whereabouts of the man. The lady said that the army took him and that the soldiers were angry because of the presence of the refugees in that Mexican community. She also said that the man was already dead: the soldiers tied him to a stone and threw him into the Río Lagartero, "in the deepest part is where they threw him so his body will never surface." Upon hearing this oracle, the people of Colón accused the refugees of being responsible for the man's death. The refugees had to move to other places, and that is how they went to the Rancho Tejas camp where they were given a space to erect their tents. There were already several thousand people at Rancho Tejas, and the people who represented the camp came to show the new incoming refugees where to put their tents. It seemed a more pleasant place to be, as most people had been in this camp since August 1982, when the helicopters landed at Santa Teresa, close to Nentón. The Q'anjob'al people of Santa Rosa and Santa Teresa went back to their villages after the soldiers had left one night and got their marimbas and their patron saints. Because of the presence of the images of their patron saints in the camp of Rancho Tejas, the refugees had built a large tent to be used as a chapel. It was big because there were so many people, mainly Q'anjob'al Maya people. They even brought their church bells and tried to celebrate the rosary as they used to do in their villages of origin. Each Saturday the marimbas played and the Mexican people liked to come to the camps to dance and have a happy time with the refugees.

The Refugees and the
Mexican Immigration Authorities

WHILE THE REFUGEES were trying to protect themselves from the incursions of the Guatemalan army, some immigration officers at the border began to create other problems for the refugees. During September and October 1982 the immigration officers began their effort to split the refugee population into smaller groups. The refugees resisted and did not want to go farther from where they were, so the immigration agents got angry and tried in all sorts of ways to dismantle the camps. In the accounts of persecution recorded by the refugees along the southern Mexican border, the name of one bad immigration officer is infamous. This man, César Marcos Morales, mentioned in the above testimony, was also denounced in the Mexican media. On October 10, 1982, the Mexican newspaper *Uno Mas Uno* reported his crimes against the refugees.

As the agent of Immigration Services in that region, Morales returned an undetermined number of Guatemalans to the army of that country, despite the international agreements established in Mexico's immigration laws and the Mexican government's administrative orders concerning the refugee situation (GARG 1983: 56). These atrocities were also documented by the refugees. According to Kaxh Pasil,

The other major problem occurred when the men selected as *representantes* [leaders] of the camp went to the immigration offices at Ciudad Cuahutémoc, close to the border, to renew the legal status cards of a large group of refugees. These cards, which allowed them to remain in Mexico, had to be renewed every three months. On their way to renew the full boxes of cards, the small Volkswagen in which they were riding was turned over by the turbulent currents of a stream swelled by the rain that afternoon. All the papers were lost in the water, but the representantes continued on their way to the immigration offices. When they arrived at the immigration offices, the chief told them to enter, but they were put in jail. At night they were taken by the immigration officers across the border and turned over to the Guatemalan soldiers. Later the refugees heard that the Guatemalan army had killed them. After that the refugees selected new representantes, replacing the ones who were disappeared. When the immigration authorities heard that the representantes had been replaced, the same immigration officers came again to arrest the newly elected representantes. They knew that without the representantes, the refugees would be easier to control. Among the leaders were Jakaltek and Q'anjob'al men. When they were forced to enter the cars of the immigration authorities, they were very sad. The refugees pleaded for the agents to leave them, but the officers continued to threaten them. Señor César M. Morales said that he could kill the refugees if they opposed him. He said, "I will report that all of you are guerrillas and tried to attack me."

The refugees were frightened, and they left their representantes in the hands of the agents. A few of us wanted to save these refugee leaders who were now captives, and we were joined by some women who began to plead in the Maya language and in Spanish.

"Tzetyuxin che yitoj heb' naj. B'aytu' xka he yinitoj heb' naj he yalni. Tato machuloj heb' naj b'eti', he yetb'i heb'a b'oj heb' naj ay Xeg'a tu', tato che yahatoj heb' naj yu spotx'laxoj. Xhjoche-an tato xhmeltzo heb' naj jet konhob' ti'an, komo k'anch'an heb' naj. Mat noq'oj heb' naj kat he yinitoj heb' naj kamoj."

"Why are you taking them? Where are you trying to take them. If you don't bring them back here, you are accomplices of the Guatemalan army. We want you to bring these villagers of ours back because they are poor people. They are not animals to be taken out and killed."

When they heard this, the immigration officers ordered the people who defended the captives to replace the ones who had been taken as prisoners. These agents started rounding up the protesters. But suddenly a Mexican helicopter started to encircle the refugee camp, looking for a place to land. Upon hearing the helicopter, the immigration authorities quickly abandoned what they were doing. They thought that higher authorities from the Mexican government were coming, so they decided to return their captives. Then they said to the refugees, "If some other authorities come here asking if we have taken anybody from this camp, don't say anything, because if you denounce us, we will come back here and kill you." Then they entered their cars again and went back to the immigration office at Ciudad Cuauhtémoc. This is how the second set of representantes escaped from death at the hands of the Mexican immigration agents who were cooperating with the Guatemalan army without the knowledge of higher Mexican authorities.

Later when the agents heard that the helicopter did not land, they returned. This time they were accompanied by the Judicial Police. They told the people to clean up the place during the night. Their message was publicized among the refugees by their leaders and in their own Maya languages.

"Xj'ochean tato a las 4:00 de la mañana matxa mak ayk'oj yul campamento ti'. Xi heb' naj, mientras xin stzumb'eloj heb' naj anma, kat yanikoj heb' naj q'a yinh yatut refugiado tu'."

"We want you to abandon this place by 4:00 A.M. At that time we don't want to see anybody here."

While the agents ordered people to get out, they also were burning down the tents of the refugees.

At that same moment all the people began to prepare their loads again. People who had small animals like chickens killed and ate them that same night, because it would be difficult to travel with such animals. Nobody could sleep that night, only the babies, because the adults were preparing themselves to move without knowing where they were moving. The materials for building a permanent camp (such as corrugated tin for roofs that had been donated by a priest of the Diocese of San Cristóbal) were abandoned. The immigration officers and the Judicial Police also went to the Mexican colonies of Rodolfo Figueroa, Colón, and Dolores to make sure the refugees would not come to these Mexican communities. When the camp was abandoned, some Mexican people took their mules and wagons to pick up everything that the refugees abandoned, including their animals. The big refugee community was dispersed into smaller groups, and everybody started to wonder where to go. At this time again, some people did return to Guatemala, because they were suffering almost as much as in their place of origin. Others cried without knowing where to go.[6]

Protests from the Catholic church, honest reporting by some Mexican newspapers, particularly *Uno Mas Uno,* and the intervention of international aid workers awakened the human rights community worldwide to the problems of the refugees in Chiapas. The violation of their human rights in southern Mexico became an international embarrassment for the Mexican government, so it had to change immigration policy and personnel in that region. Morales, the immigration officer, denied that he had dismantled the camps of Rancho Tejas and Colón and said that people had voluntarily decided to move or to abandon the camps. But the Mexican government believed the refugees and since that time has given them protection.

The Catholic churches of the Diocese of San Cristóbal and international humanitarian organizations also helped to stop these injustices when they came to the camps to bring humanitarian aid to the refugees. It was at this time (1982–83) that the authorities from Mexico City, under the newly formed *Comisión Mexicana de Ayuda a Refugiados,* began to provide basic support, including food and shelter, for the refugees' survival.

By 1983–84 the possibility of returning to their homeland seemed distant for the refugees, and they began to look for a more secure place to reconstruct their lives in exile. Life in the Mexican refugee camps was difficult and continued to be difficult throughout the years. The refugees were not there out of choice; the brutality of the Guatemalan army forced them to abandon their ancient homelands. This drastic shift in their location, their lifestyles, and their traditional ways was very difficult to accept. Most indigenous people, especially the women, had never traveled farther than their neighboring villages (Anderson and Garlock 1988). Thus their sudden arrival in a foreign land demoralized the people, especially children, elders, and women.

At the beginning of their ordeal, refugee problems were very intense until Mexican solidarity groups, the Catholic church of San Cristóbal, and international aid groups began the work of finding solutions to some of the refugees' problems. At its insistence, all aid was channeled through COMAR, whether from UNHCR or from international nongovernmental organizations (NGOs)(González 1992).

Some refugee families moved to Mexican towns and cities close to coffee plantations, as they preferred to struggle for their subsistence on the plantations, as they had done in Guatemala, rather than live at the mercy of Mexican authorities and camp organizations. Other refugees divided themselves into families and groups of relatives and tried to enter Mexican communities as laborers. These groups tried to assimilate immediately so as to hide themselves from Mexican immigration authorities.

It has always been difficult to determine the exact number of refugee camps. In the early days the camps were often moved. Big camps such as Rancho Tejas, La Sombra, and Puerto Rico, where various Maya ethnic groups lived together with poor ladinos, split into separate camps organized along ethnic lines after their camps were dismantled. But the groups that were controlled by COMAR continued to live in camps composed of various ethnic groups. There were a number of proposals to establish permanent camps and to redistribute the refugee population and condense one-hundred-twenty small camps into fifteen big ones, but for the most part these proposals came to nought (Hernández Castillo 1992; U.S. Committee for Refugees 1993).

After 1984 social relations between refugees who sought work as laborers in small Mexican villages and Mexican peasants were ruptured. The Mexicans knew that the war continued in Guatemala and that the refugees might well remain in their lands for a long period, or might even become Mexicans. To make things worse, the Guatemalan army and the civil patrols continued to cross into Mexican villages and camps to capture refugees. In April 1984 they attacked La Sombra, El Pacayal, and El Chupadero. Some Mexican citizens also disappeared in these raids by the Guatemalan army.[8] Of these illegal actions, the bishops of the southern region of Mexico said in 1984, "We have to denounce to our nation and to the world the violation of our national territory and airspace by the army, warplanes, and civil patrols. In these incursions many lives of defenseless Mexican campesinos and Guatemalans have been lost" (Obispos de la Región Pastoral Pacífico-Sur1984).

As the presence of refugees in these Mexican villages made life unsafe for the Mexicans themselves, they accused the Guatemalan refugees of almost every crime, from robbery to spreading diseases, to get rid of them. And Mexican authorities feared that the refugees could "contaminate the peasants of Chiapas with their ideology of revolution" (Hernández Castillo 1992: 100).

Relocation of the Guatemalan Refugee Camps

COMAR DEVISED A plan for the relocation of the refugees from Chiapas and the Guatemalan border to the states of Campeche and Quintana Roo in the Yucatán peninsula. Relocation was to begin in June 1984 under the direction of COMAR.

The prospect of being moved caused dread among the refugees. Added to their usual burden of insecurity about shelter, work, and daily food, they now worried about how they would manage their lives in a distant place where no Guatemalan Mayans had ever gone before. The refugees resisted the move also because in the previous few years, they had been moved forcibly from place to place like nomads. Many people, including those with large families, women, and elders, wanted to remain close to the Guatemalan border, hoping to return to their home-

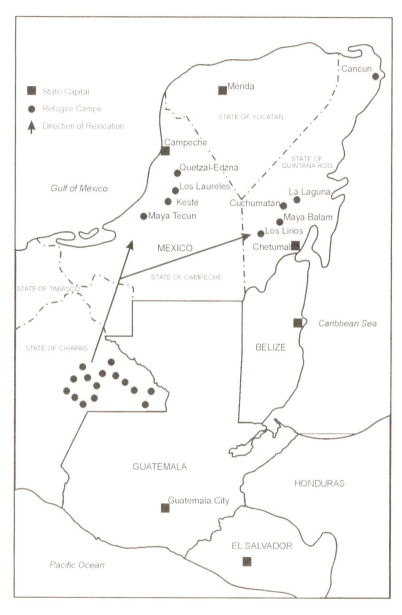

Refugee relocation to Campeche and Quintana Roo, 1984.
From Nolin Hanlon 1995. Map by Darren R. Stranger, courtesy of
Catherine L. Nolin Hanlon.

land. The reasons refugees gave for opposing relocation centered on geographic and cultural concerns. For them, proximity to the border meant being close to home communities, which kept alive the dream of returning and helped to maintain kinship and communal ties (Manz 1988a: 152).

The camps in southern Mexico were built where the refugees could see the mountains of Guatemala. Their exile was softened by their hopes and their constant view of the Kuchumatan highlands, the homeland to which they wished to return. But by the end of 1984 COMAR had already relocated several camps to Campeche and Quintana Roo against the will of the refugees. The refugees protested and sent petitions to the director of COMAR asking to remain where they were.

In response the director of the COMAR Relocation Program sent them letters insisting that they obey the relocation orders and not offer resistance. They were asked to work with COMAR to make the relocation easier and faster. Also a document was sent to the refugees in which COMAR stated eleven major reasons for the relocation of the refugees. The plan was based on the following principles and criteria:

A) To give the highest priority to the interests of the [Mexican] nation;

B) To reiterate the Mexican principles concerning International Political Relations;

C) To respect the ethnic, communal and familial integrity [of the refugees];

D) To serve the interest of their original vocational labor;

E) To search for a habitat similar to that of the refugees' homeland;

F) To provide health services during the process of relocation and in the new camps;

G) To relocate the refugees in a geographical area that could promote their self-sufficiency and eventually their integration [into Mexican society];

H) To provide employment opportunities to the refugees which
would not displace or compete with local labor forces or
affect Mexican Agrarian Rights. (COMAR 1985)

Despite all COMAR's words, the refugees were still distrustful of the relocation. People were already separated from family
members in Guatemala and from relatives who were living in
other refugee camps. Thus the new decision to send refugees
even farther was seen as another threat to their family unity.

In an attempt to starve the refugees into accepting reloca-
tion, COMAR closed off all other sources of humanitarian aid.
The relocation was implemented against the will of the refugees.
Residents of the Chajul camp in Chiapas complained, "Our
future is out of our hands," when they were forcibly relocated on
December 1985. By the end of that year 17,940 of the approxi-
mately 42,000 refugees in Chiapas had been relocated to
Campeche and Quintana Roo (Manz 1988a: 153–55).

The relocation to Campeche and Quintana Roo did not solve
the refugees' problems. Even though the land in the Yucatán
peninsula, the climate, and the availability of water presented
seemingly insurmountable problems, the COMAR plan was to
provide resources in these settlements so that the relocated
refugees could return to basic farming and thus become self-
sufficient. "In Campeche and Quintana Roo, land was allocated
to the refugees by the federal authorities. For those who wish[ed]
to remain in the settlements, at least for the immediate future,
the priority [was] to achieve self-sufficiency as soon as possible"
(Van Praag 1986: 24).

To prod the refugees toward this goal, COMAR decided to
suspend temporarily the delivery of food to the Yucatán camps,
thus forcing the refugees to plant crops and begin farming. This
decision was criticized by the Catholic church and the refugees
themselves. They complained that the reduction of food aid created serious hardships for children, elders, widows, and those too
ill to work the fields. Nevertheless, the project of self-sufficiency

proposed by COMAR continued. Nicholas Van Praag reported that "experimental cultivation of pineapples, bananas, yucca, and sugarcane was begun in an attempt to diversify the refugees' diet and produce a surplus to sell outside the settlements. [But] a limitation on the refugees' ability to achieve self-sufficiency in agricultural production is the lack of available land" (1986: 29).

The refugees felt more physical security in the Yucatán settlements, but they did not achieve self-sufficiency. And because the refugee camps were located far from major population centers, job opportunities outside the camps were limited and it was difficult for the refugees to become integrated into the workforce of nearby Mexican communities.

Conclusion

THE EXODUS OF Maya refugees to Mexico was massive. Over the period 1981–83, probably more than one-hundred thousand crossed the border. The economy of Chiapas could not absorb all these people, and it was difficult for many to compete successfully with Mexican peasants for jobs as agricultural laborers. Some refugees continued to move northward through Mexico. One group of Spanish-speaking Mayas settled in Mexico City. Others continued the journey north, crossing the border into the United States and beyond. Refugee communities formed in Indiantown, Florida; Los Angeles, California; Houston, Texas; Vancouver, British Columbia; and other cities and locations where U.S. and Canadian church people and the Sanctuary Movement gave them aid.[9] Others remained in Chiapas, blending into the local Maya communities and Chiapas towns without benefit of formal recognition as refugees.

The Mayas who have crossed the Mexican border can be seen by the standards of modern nation-states to be engaging in acts of defiance of international borders. They had no choice.

They fled in fear and to save their lives. Their overwhelming desire to remain close to the border to facilitate a return to their homelands in Guatemala is a clear example of "what it means to be rooted in a place" (Malkki 1992: 26).

In general terms, the Guatemalan refugees in Mexico have been categorized by some Mexican authorities, as well as by the Guatemalan army, as rootless and dangerous people who have lost their moral values. The same arguments are used to degrade both the refugees and indigenous people. But the refugees are not "the problem." They are people who have problems. And during their time in exile they used all their physical, mental, and spiritual resources to find solutions to these problems. The following chapters examine how the refugees, some of whom are still waiting to return to Guatemala, developed their lives in the camps in Chiapas, using the strengths of their culture to cope with the limitations of camp life.

7

LIFE IN THE REFUGEE CAMPS

THE FIRST MONTHS in Mexico were precarious in many ways. The earliest arrivals settled close to the border and erected temporary shelters of plastic, nylon, banana leaves, and branches. Many arrived sick or exhausted, especially those whose journeys began far from the border. Poverty was endemic, and malnutrition was evident among the children. Many adults were grief-stricken; children were dazed by the loss of relatives and the wrenching transformation of their lives. The refugees not only left behind their land and houses and came to Mexico with nothing. The reconstruction of anything resembling a normal life in Mexico would require considerable time. In Guatemala their lives had revolved around farming the land, but in Chiapas land was a precious commodity and not readily available for them to farm.

Immediate survival was accomplished in a variety of ways. Some refugees were aided by individual Mexican families, whose support had to be repaid with labor.

Some moved to cities. Others were dependent on the charity of the Catholic church or generous local people. Gradually the Mexican government took over the task of aiding refugee families with food and shelter, and little by little the refugees were concentrated into larger camps.

By 1983 the Mexican government, through COMAR and the UNHCR, had initiated a category of "recognized" refugees, those entitled to live in established refugee camps and receive aid in the form of roofing tin, food supplies, and basic medical care. These camps became "home" to approximately forty-six thousand of the refugees in Chiapas.

The Mexican government's policy with regard to the camps was not consistent. Camps were moved, divided, eliminated, or ignored, and no camp could be considered a permanent base. As camps varied geographically and through time, it is difficult to generalize. This account is based on one camp, Villa Cocalito, in 1989.

Villa Cocalito

THE REFUGEE COMMUNITY of Villa Cocalito was composed of approximately two hundred families or about six hundred people, mostly Jakalteks and ladinoized Mayas from the town of Buena Vista in the municipio of Santa Ana Huista in the Kuchumatan highlands. This refugee community had settled on communal land of La Colonia, on the condition that the refugees provide labor for the Mexican community when it was needed. The center of La Colonia was about one mile distant from the camp. The camp was situated in a small wooded area on the edge of a cattle-grazing pasture. This site provided firewood, a resource that was also greatly needed by the residents of La Colonia. A few natural wells nearby provided water, and clothes could be washed and baths taken in a small canal that emptied into a cement pond constructed by the refugees. Water was abundant during the rainy season, from May to October, and in short supply the rest of the year.

Housing in Villa Cocalito was organized in a circle around an open space at whose center stood a large tree. The tree and its surrounding area provided a common plaza and meeting place for the community. Houses were constructed of wooden pilings and sticks and roofed with thatch. The floors were dirt. All family activities—cooking, eating, sleeping—were carried out in this basic shelter. Each dwelling housed an extended family consisting of grandparents, sons and their wives, their children, and two or three related families. The short streets and paths between the houses and around the community were dirt, muddy during the rainy season and dusty when it was dry. There was no electricity in the camp. People arose when the roosters crowed at the earliest light of dawn, and the sounds of machetes chopping firewood and the slap, slap, slap of hands forming tortillas greeted the sunrise. Soon after sunset activities for the day ceased. Kerosene lanterns and flashlights provided the only illumination after dark.

Housing at the refugee camp at Villa Cocalito

The residents of Villa Cocalito had built a small, one-room schoolhouse and a building that served as the community clinic and as a guest house for overnight visitors. These were constructed of the same wooden walls as the houses but were roofed with tin donated by the Catholic diocese. There was no building constructed for use as a church, and the refugees walked to services at the Catholic church in La Colonia.

Almost every family owned a dog, a pig, and some chickens. The dogs roamed freely around the camp, as did the chickens. Pigs were tied to trees or kept in small huts constructed for them. Eggs improved the basic diet of the refugees, but for the most part chickens ready to be killed for consumption were sold to the Mexicans for cash income. A few families had donkeys, and their owners had to cut a supply of grass for them when the workday was over. They were then tied to trees on the outskirts of the camp.

The refugees traveled mainly on foot, carrying whatever needed to be transported. Those who had donkeys could ride, but most walked wherever they needed to go. Donkeys were also useful in hauling firewood and other carrying chores. When the refugees worked for Mexican campesinos, they were sometimes transported to the fields in trucks. Unlike their home communities in Guatemala, the flatter terrain of Mexico and the presence of dirt roads made bicycles a more common form of transportation in Villa Cocalito. After the first bicycles arrived in the camp, most of the young people became proficient riders and traveled around the area and between the refugee camps. A few refugees even rode their bicycles from the camps to cross the border on dirt roads away from the main border crossings and visit their home communities in Guatemala, a trip of twelve hours each way.

The major local market was held in Comalapa on Saturdays and Sundays, and refugee households tried to send one person to buy whatever items—soap, matches, medicines, or extra foods—they needed. For the most part, the Mexicans of La

Colonia were willing to include the Villa Cocalito refugees in their pickup-truck trips to the Comalapa market. Comalapa was a border town where people came from all over to do business, trade, and meet others. Among those who came to the Comalapa market were refugees from other camps and Mayas from Guatemala with woven goods for sale. From these people the refugees could get news from friends or relatives in other camps, from their home communities, and from relatives who remained in Guatemala.

There was no telephone in the camp, the nearest one being a pay phone in La Colonia a mile away. It was used only when absolutely needed by the camp spokesperson, schoolteachers, or the representative of the CCPP to communicate with headquarters in Comitán. Each refugee camp had a CCPP representative who kept the camp informed about refugee issues or impending visits from Mexican authorities, church people, or international humanitarian organizations. In emergencies the telephone could be used to alert the hospital at Comitán that a sick person was being brought in. The Comitán hospital was under contract with COMAR to provide the refugees with regular and emergency health care. It also served as a special center for treating children suffering from malnutrition.

COMAR provided most of the refugees' food; it brought supplies of dry fish, rice, vegetable oil, bananas, canned pork, onions, corn, and beans every fifteen days, distributed according to the official list of members of registered families. Not everyone liked all the foods that COMAR distributed, and families occasionally traded with other families, exchanging those things they disliked for items that suited them better. Some foods were universally disliked. Canned pork, which was donated by the governments of Canada and Holland, was very unfamiliar, and at first it was often sold or exchanged for something else. And the constant occurrence of infections and sore throats among the children was blamed on chemicals in the dry foods supplied by COMAR. In general, the later years in exile saw better diets and healthier children. Children usually had three meals a day, with tortillas, beans, and canned pork for breakfast and dinner and rice, tortillas, or *pozol* for lunch.

When the refugees had money it was often used to buy supplemental foodstuffs. Some refugees rented larger plots of land from Mexicans and grew an acre or more of corn and beans, the sale of which would pay their rent and make a small profit. But for the most part only small plots of land were available to only some of the refugee farmers, who grew small quantities of corn and beans for their families. The work of the Villa Cocalito refugee men was constrained by the lack of available land and by the need to provide labor for the Mexican community that sheltered them. Some of this labor was unpaid and assessed against the communal labor system under which both refugees and La Colonia residents operated. These projects included fixing the dirt roads and keeping the canal system in repair, and they were usually accomplished quickly because there were so many people to help. Some of the work, however, was done for individual Mexicans, for which the refugees were compensated. This was the only source of cash income for the Villa Cocalito men. Mostly, however, the men were unemployed and without land, and for many the day was long and boring, spent sitting around the camp.

Women came to the rescue of their devastated family economies with their traditional art of weaving. They wove hair ribbons, belts, napkins, tablecloths, and wall hangings in all their free time, receiving help from their daughters (and sometimes husbands and sons) with the household tasks that took away from their weaving time. The woven items were sold by the church groups of southern Mexico, especially by the nuns of the seminary in the Diocese of San Cristóbal who formed the backbone of the movement to aid refugee women by reselling their craft work in a store in San Cristóbal and through international outlets. In good months the women's work could contribute the equivalent of $50 to $60 a month to the family income. Because of their early fears of being identified as Guatemalan refugees by Mexican authorities, none of the Jakaltek people wore their traditional *traje* (clothing). And because they needed to produce weavings for cash income, women preferred to sell *cintas*, belts, and ribbons rather than wear them. Men, women, and children wore ladino clothing that was relatively cheap and could be purchased in a local market. Almost all of the adult women had their traje safely stored away in their houses, but among the Jakaltek women it was never worn in Mexico, even for special occasions. Outside the camps but within the larger mestizo Mexican community, traje marked people as refugees, as Mayas, and as people to be looked down on, abused, and disrespected. It was better to avoid this humiliation by leaving the traje unworn.

The primary school at Villa Cocalito was established in 1985. Approximately forty children from eight to fourteen years of age attended regularly from 8:00 A.M. to 2:00 P.M. on weekdays. There were two schoolteachers who were paid by the UNHCR through COMAR. These teachers had no specific training but were selected by the community because they spoke Spanish well. As Villa Cocalito was home to a mixed group of Jakalteks and ladinos, the children were taught in Spanish. The curriculum changed several times, but by 1989 it had settled into reading and writing, math, social studies, including Guatemalan and Mexican geography and history, health, nature, and agriculture for six grades. There were only two textbooks, one for each teacher.

The small school building was subdivided by partitions, and several grades met in common classes. The children who attended school were only a small percentage of the children in the community, and those who could not attend worked along with their parents to provide for their families. Schooling was free, although parents had to supply pencils and paper unless the school had received some from COMAR or the diocese. Most children attended for a few years, enough to learn to speak Spanish, to read and write a little, and to sign their names.

Despite the crowded conditions, the children liked attending school because their harder studies were interspersed with periods of drawing, singing, and play. Older children, thirteen or fourteen years of age, dropped out of school to help their parents. There was no opportunity to study beyond the sixth grade. After school boys fulfilled their obligation to collect firewood for their families and then ran off to play football on the outskirts of the refugee camp. Girls joined their mothers and carried water, washed clothes, made tortillas, and cared for younger siblings to give their mothers more weaving time. Girls began to learn the art of weaving at about the age of seven, and by twelve they were selling their own woven pieces.

The clinic staff were volunteers, trained to be *promotores de salud* (health promoters) by the hospital at Comitán. Medicine was supplied by COMAR and included cough syrup, antidiarrheals and a variety of first-aid supplies. The *promotores* held clinics in the afternoon when they had returned home from their other work. They handled minor health problems. More complicated cases were taken care of at the hospital.

There were no adult education programs per se, but COMAR officials offered short courses for men and women in primary health care and leadership. These programs introduced women to becoming more active in the community and made them more familiar with political issues. The women also organized a local branch of the organization Mama Maquín in 1989 which advocated programs and policies that aided women and their families. The local Mama Maquín representatives traveled to Comitán or another central location once a month to attend a general meeting of the organization and then returned home to hold local meetings with the women of Villa Cocalito to pass along what they had learned. The community was also served by several catechists, lay teachers of the Catholic faith, who had received their training in Guatemala before the violence. They now worked under the general direction of the priest at Paso Hondo.

The routines of subsistence and daily life were broken by occasional meetings, church and cultural events, and the celebration of rituals of passage. Musicians among the Villa Cocalito refugees would sometimes organize cultural nights when all would gather for singing and dancing. Occasionally musicians from other camps would visit to play and sing. Cultural events were organized, and plays were performed whenever there were visitors—authorities from COMAR, doctors from the hospital, representatives from the Guatemalan government organization Comisión Especial para la Atención a Repatriados, Refugiados y Desplazados (CEAR), and international visitors whom the refugees called *solidarios.*

As in the Kuchumatan highlands, birthdays were not celebrated, but births and deaths were. Babies were brought by their parents and godparents to the Catholic church in Paso Hondo or Comalapa to be baptized. On their return to Villa Cocalito, the event was marked be the sharing of food by the entire family and their friends.

Deaths were of more concern to the refugee community. The body of the deceased was placed in his or her house, and the crying and wailing of women relatives would alert the community to the death. A two-day wake followed, during which the entire community gathered and retold the stories of this person's life, including the violence that forced them into exile and the sadness that now compelled burial in a strange land. After the wake the person was buried in the cemetery at La Colonia.

In addition to participating in the celebration of the patron saint's day of the local Mexican community, the refugees of Villa Cocalito also celebrated the saint's day of their village in Guatemala, the Virgin of the Nativity. Following a religious celebration in the morning, the catechists would remind the refugees of the causes and the history of their exile. In the afternoon there were soccer tournaments against local Mexican teams, the marimba was played, and there was dancing until eight o'clock in the evening. The Mayan artistic group in the camp would sing its songs in Popb'al Ti' and people would remember their origins and the reasons for their exile. On the festival of their patron saint they remembered with sadness the time when the army first arrived in El Limonar. And refugees from other camps came to visit relatives and friends in Villa Cocalito on this day.

These activities attracted Mexican youths from the surrounding villages and often brought them into contact with young refugee women, leading to romance and marriage. A relationship between a Mexican and a refugee woman usually resulted in elopement. The couple would go to live in the Mexican man's community, and there was little the refugee parents could do to oppose the match. More frequently marriages took place within the refugee community, where parents were more knowledgeable about the young man and his family and the young couple were better acquainted. Marriages within one's ethnic community were preferred, but young men would sometimes go to other refugee camps seeking marriageable young women. Weddings were performed in the Catholic church, followed by a celebration in the refugee camp, with a marimba, dancing, and drinking, according to the wedding customs of the Kuchumatan highlands.

When solidarios came to Villa Cocalito, they were housed in the community's guest house. They were warmly welcomed because they were a visible symbol of international knowledge about the refugee situation and a possible source of help in returning to Guatemala. The refugees believed their security was more likely to be assured if representatives of international organizations were involved in their repatriation. After the evening meal the local musical group would begin to play under the tree and people would gather, bringing their kerosene lanterns with them. The visitors would speak of their reasons for coming and their support for the refugee cause. Dancing would sometimes follow, or dramas would be enacted which told the Maya stories of the ancestors or the descent of the Jakaltek people, or of the violence that brought them to Mexico and the problems they encountered as refugees. Occasionally Mexicans from La Colonia would also attend, some of whom in this setting regretted their own ladinoization that had caused the loss of their original culture.

As events brought the return closer, men stopped renting land to work, and mroe people sat around waiting for news about the return. Finally, in 1993, most of the inhabitants of Villa Cocalito returned to Guatemala to found the community of La Esperanza in Chaculá, Nentón, in the department of Huehuetenango. The women's traje has been unpacked, and is again worn, and the Virgin of the Nativity has a new home. The few refugees remaining in Villa Cocalito had hopes of returning in 1998.

THE PATTERN OF life in other refugee camps was similar, but in other camps there were different ethnic groups, different struggles over resource allocations, and different economic opportunities for the refugees. In some, work on the coffee fincas or sugar plantations replaced communal labor for the local Mexican community and supplied alternative sources of income. The geographic location of a camp also meant important differences in people's lives. Those camps far from roads or high in the mountains received fewer services, and, perhaps, less official interference, and those camps close to Mexican towns offered other opportunities for work.

8

STRATEGIES OF CULTURAL SURVIVAL

THE GUATEMALAN REFUGEES engaged in everyday forms of resistance to the loss of their culture and absorption into ladino society (Scott 1985).[1] They participated in the revitalization of Maya culture by retaking aspects of it, reworking and re-creating newer forms and innovations, and merging them into the ongoing continuity of Maya culture (Wallace 1956). Maya ethnic identity is still vital: despite separation, destruction, and reintegration as a result of exile, the culture survives in many forms. The mechanisms of survival they developed and the sociocultural institutions they adapted give evidence that the heart of Maya culture continues and transforms to meet the problems of the present. Through their Maya languages, their weaving and traditional dress, their religious rituals and changes, their gender roles and family relations, their economic strategies and education, the refugees were able not only to withstand the hardships of exile but also to revitalize their Mayanness as a tool of survival. By comparing the survival of these cultural forms to their estimated vitality before exile based on the ethnographic literature, we can assess the strength of cultural continuity and transformation.[2] The dynamics of Maya culture in exile helped the refugees to deny death and search for their own power to flourish in the future. In this way refugee life has become another major expression of our continuing resistance against five hundred years of colonial-imperialist domination.[3]

The major questions are, What has survived culturally given the refugees' separation from their original homelands, the linguistic mix of Mayas from different communities, and the destruction of indigenous social, economic, and religious institutions? And more important, how has this cultural survival and continuity with the ancient and recent past occurred? What are the mechanisms of cultural survival operative among Maya refugees living in the camps of Mexico? Answers to these questions speak to the very heart of cultural and social anthropology, namely, the way cultures survive despite radical social changes. The most visible socioeconomic and cultural strategies developed by the refugees for their survival in the refugee camps are considered below.

The Maya Language

THE MAJOR LINGUISTIC areas from which the refugees came are K'iche', Ixil, Q'anjob'al, Chuj, Akatek, Popb'al Ti', and Mam. I concentrate here primarily on the speakers of Q'anjob'al, Chuj, Mam, and Popb'al Ti', who represented the major Maya ethnic groups in the camps in southern Mexico. These linguistic communities belong to the Greater Q'anjob'alan and Western Maya languages, according to the classification provided by Nora England and Stephen Elliot (1990) (see map on page 000).

The Maya languages have gone through major changes since the Spanish conquest. Although in the past these changes were gradual, the violence unleashed during the 1980s was so dramatic that it had enormous influence on the Maya languages of Guatemala. For example, during the early 1980s the open use of Maya language for social discourse was restricted by native speakers for several reasons. One was the fear of saying something that could be misinterpreted by the orejas, the army's spies. Under these circumstances,

> the language is often veiled or oblique, often condensed into cryptic observations with unspecified agents. The listener is expected to fill in the obvious: that Mayans were involved in the opposition, that it was the government that was trying to eliminate the Mayan leadership. Those unable to deal with strategic ambiguities are by definition strangers with whom it would not be wise to share information. (Warren 1993: 33)

Under these conditions Mayas developed a mechanism of communication that was coded and highly metaphorical (Manz 1988a). People created categories for classifying the different armed groups they came in contact with in their communities. Soldiers and guerrillas were named in Maya languages so the people could refer to them without being understood by non-Maya speakers. Mayas developed these linguistic mechanisms because the soldiers had tried to deceive the people by disguising themselves as guerrillas. By giving new meanings to Maya words, people could distinguish between the Tz'ib'inh (kaibiles) and the Xoltelaj (guerrillas) in Popb'al Ti' and Q'anjob'al.[4] The classificatory names were derived from the attitudes and ways of dressing and subtle or ironic references to places the different armies operated.

> One example that demonstrates resiliency—the ability not to be completely subdued by the militarization imposed on them—is the ability to joke about it. People are constantly deciphering the double meaning in a conversation, acknowl-

*edging the decoding with a responsive laugh or joining back
with another coded statement. Much is communicated by body
language and eye contact. (Manz 1988a: 65)*

It is with their languages that Maya people have kept in
touch with the world around them and by which they have given
names and meanings to things in their native world. It therefore
stands to reason that Maya languages have been a major instrument for cultural survival and for the maintenance and development of security strategies for the individual, the family, and the
community.

For the past centuries the Maya languages have not been
recognized as "real languages" in Guatemala because the dominant society preferred to think of them as "Indian dialects," languages inferior to Spanish in which symbolic and abstract ideas
were nonexistent or difficult to express. This view of Maya languages has been yet another mechanism of colonial domination
and social control. But historically the Maya civilizations were
among the most advanced in the New World. Maya languages
were highly sophisticated, with texts written in hieroglyphics. It
was in Maya languages that the native accounts of the conquest
were narrated to descendants. It was also in Maya languages that
the ancient history and knowledge of the Mayas were written in
ethnohistorical documents such as the *Popol Vuh,* the *Annals of
the Kaqchikels,* and the *Chilam Balam.* As in the past, the present ordeal of the Mayas has been recorded in Maya languages by
the various ethnic groups. The persistence of these languages in
the face of five hundred years of conquest and domination gives
the Mayas hope that these languages will find their rightful place
among the other languages of the Americas and the world.

On their arrival in Mexico early in 1982 the refugees experienced the greatest unease about speaking their native languages,
because it was language that identified them as illegal aliens,
"Indians." If they used their native language, they were more easily recognized by the Mexican immigration officials, whose intent

was to deport them to Guatemala. The refugees began to speak in Spanish and avoided using their native languages in Colón, Aquespala, Paso Hondo, Comalapa, Motozintla, Comitán, Margaritas, and other Mexican communities where the refugees built their first camps. The impact on young people was negligible because most already knew Spanish, but for the elders and especially for the women who did not speak Spanish, the change was radical.

As refugees arrived by the thousands, immigration officers began to acknowledge their reasons for exile and give them more support. With the recognition of their refugee status, the Mayas started to speak their languages openly, without fear of persecu-

Woman with water container at the Aquespala refugee camp

tion. The camps were shared by many different ethnic groups, and several Maya languages were spoken in most camps. One early strategy of the refugees was to live in extended families and keep the linguistic groups together as a means of cooperation and social solidarity. This was especially true within the large, multiethnic refugee camps. But as noted before, the constant relocation of the camps disrupted the solidarity of the refugees.

The use of Maya languages in the camps was preferred, because the refugees wanted to live as they had lived in their home communities. The maintenance of their ethnic identity through language was possible because large numbers of families from the same ethnic group continued to share their values in the exiled communities. Maya languages thus served to unify the people, and it is in their native tongues that they communicated their traditions and history to their children.

For those displaced Maya families that decided to become nonrecognized refugees and sought refuge in Spanish-speaking Mexican towns rather than the camps, the continuity of the Maya language was more difficult. These "urbanized" refugees began speaking in the southern Mexican style of Spanish to hide from immigration authorities. Liisa Malkki found similar practices among the urban Hutu refugees she studied: "Most town refugees did not define themselves primarily as members of the marked collectivity 'Hutu refugees' and, indeed, expended a good deal of creative energy in circumventing this identification. Far from being heroized, refugeeness was instead often negated and supplanted by a series of alternative identities and labels" (1995: 156).

Once the Guatemalan exiles were recognized legally as refugees in Mexico, they became free to use their Maya languages in the camps and in the nearby towns. But even in these settings, Maya languages were not always maintained in their original form. For example, in Guadalupe Victoria, whose Mexican inhabitants were of Jakaltek descent, Popb'al Ti', the

Jakaltek-Maya language was still generally spoken. Here some Jakaltek refugee families had to develop their own particular (pidgin) dialects to avoid being understood by those Mexican Maya speakers of the same language who abused them as wage workers in their small coffee fincas. An example of this is a Jakaltek family that had been relocated many times. Xuwin (Juana) and her husband, Hesus (Jesús), have learned to communicate in a language that only their family members can speak and understand. They speak Maya words or sentences backward. For example, "Tzet cha wu xhi' Manel Xap" (Manuel Sebastian, what are you doing?) is transformed in the pidgin language of the family by inverting the order of the letters and/or words: "U Wach Tetz ixh Lenam Pax." The family members were proficient in their pidgin language and spoke quickly, and each person could understand what was being said. The family was able to voice anger about those who had treated them badly—soldiers, guerrillas, landlords, immigration authorities. They also told stories and communicated daily events to their children. This variant of their Maya language serves the family well as a mechanism for cultural survival.

Another cultural process operating in the refugee camps, especially those in the Margaritas and Marqués de Comillas region, is linguistic sharing and borrowing. The Mexican Maya linguistic groups living in this region are Tojolabal, Tzotzil, and Tzeltal speakers. As most of these adults were monolingual in their own Maya language, as were the Guatemalan Maya refugees, they have been forced to speak Spanish to communicate. But for the children, it has been as easy to learn the language of the Mexican Mayas as it has their own, and vice versa. So both Mexican and Guatemalan children have been learning one another's Maya languages, widening in this way the social and cultural bonds that have existed among Maya ethnic groups of this region.

In the refugee camps the Maya language has continued to be the language of socialization within the community, especially in the region of Margaritas where most of the population is of Mayan descent. Thus learning other Maya languages has enriched the culture of the Guatemalan Maya refugees, as well as the Mexican Maya Tzotzil and Tzeltal communities that have borrowed their techniques of weaving, handicrafts, and agriculture.

Refugee families who chose to live in the big towns and cities of southern Mexico, beyond the control of COMAR, have had their own language problems. They live in constant fear of being noticed by Mexican authorities as illegal immigrants, so they must hide their Maya identity and try to live as Mexican ladinos. In this situation children avoid speaking their Maya languages, and those who attend school with Mexican children must be careful to hide their identity. Neil Boothby refers to a specific case among the Q'anjob'al Maya living in San Cristóbal de las Casas:

> *All along, Hector had kept the family's secret. Then one afternoon he was tripped by another student while playing soccer and, in a moment of anger, the first words that came forth were in Kanjobal. Later, when Hector informed his parents what had happened, he was whipped and told there would be no more school if the same mistake was ever repeated. "That's when I decided I'd never speak Kanjobal again," Hector told me; a pledge he has stubbornly kept to this day. (1986: 50)*

The strategies of cultural survival through language have been essential, and different ethnic groups have reinforced those strategies to maintain their security and subsistence. Of course, the Maya groups living in cooperative communities in the refugee camps have had an advantage in maintaining their languages and their traditional values over those who have chosen to live in the cities.

Maya refugees have relocated throughout the Western Hemisphere, and Maya children living in the United States or Canada have had to learn English or French as well. Many Maya children living in exile are enlarging their view of the world and preparing themselves for the reconstruction of their own marginalized cultural traditions in Guatemala. Meanwhile, these children learn English and French as the most immediate way to adapt and pursue educational opportunities in the industrialized countries. Adults worry about their children being absorbed by the culture of computers, shopping malls, and video games. Therefore, some Maya families living in the United States have made a concerted effort to teach their children about their cultural background and to speak their Maya language with them so they will grow up at ease in both languages. These children have missed much of the flavor of their Mayanness, however, as the cultural context in which they are growing up is very different from the life they had in the Kuchumatan highlands of Guatemala before exile.

The culture shock has also been severe for Q'anjob'al refugees and immigrants who came to the United States, particularly those who settled in Los Angeles and Florida. The language problem is more difficult because they have had to deal with many more people from different backgrounds, countries, and cultures. After twelve years in exile in the United States some adult refugees are now learning English. Their children are more fluent in English and are internalizing U.S. culture and losing fluency in their Maya tongues. American ignorance of the situation in Guatemala and the Maya refugee-immigrants' culture contributes to an ongoing misunderstanding of their situation. This is manifest in the persistent labeling of them as "economic refugees" by the U.S. government and in the discrimination they face in the labor market and when seeking local services; they are seen not as Mayas with a culture to preserve but as just another Hispanic group to be assimilated. Even among people who are sympathetic to the newcomers, American ethnocentrism becomes evident as they discuss these refugees, a prejudice illustrated by a U.S. journalist writing about Maya refugees in Florida:

To a primitive people, America's greatest gift is freedom. . . .
America has provided hope and haven for refugees from many
lands, but few have come with as many disadvantages as the
Kanjobal Indians of Guatemala. These small brown people,
who speak an obscure language, are trying to climb the first
rung of the ladder to success by laboring as fruit and vegetable
pickers near the Florida Everglades. (Santoli 1988: 16)[5]

A Q'anjob'al Maya refugee living in the Margaritas region told me that the language will not be lost. In spite of all the barriers against the cultural survival of Maya refugees, their own languages have played a major role in the transmission and preservation of their cultural traditions. When they return to Guatemala they will be linguistically more powerful than ever. Until recently only the wealthiest Guatemalans had access to the languages of the major Western industrialized countries, and this helped them to maintain domination over the Maya groups. But now the Mayas also have access to these same languages. The Maya languages must be recognized as powerful instruments in the coming development of Guatemala as a pluralist nation. An important achievement in this regard is the Guatemalan government's approval of the Academy of Mayan Languages, for which Maya cultural and linguistic organizations in that country deserve much credit. Mayas understand the importance of their languages in maintaining their cultural traditions.

Maya Weaving and Traditional Dress

THE SKILL OF women weavers has contributed greatly to the survival of the Mayas in exile. Long before their arrival in Mexican territory, women supported the family economy with their weaving. But women's work has been undervalued in Guatemala and exploited by middlemen who have enriched themselves but not the artisan weavers. During the difficult times in Guatemala, economic problems were exacerbated by the men's forced service in the civil patrols, and families became even more impoverished. In many cases it was the women who took the lead in supporting their families through weaving.

When the Maya refugees arrived in the Mexican camps, they had to change their traditional dress because of fear of being recognized as Guatemalan Indians by Mexican authorities. Thus, for reasons of security, "almost without exception the women had abandoned their traje, either selling it to obtain money or forsaking the most visible part of their identity to avoid problems with the Mexican authorities" (Anderson and Garlock 1988: 19–20).

Maya women also changed their traditional dress as a security measure to avoid recognition by the Guatemalan army and civil patrollers who constantly crossed the border in pursuit of the refugees. The same situation prevailed with the internal refugees who moved to the large Guatemalan cities. "Though some . . . abandoned their traditional dress in the city for security reasons they adopt[ed] another area's traditional dress to maintain their self identity as Indians" (Manz 1988a: 62).

As the Maya refugees arrived in Mexico, women started to weave to obtain food for their families. This weaving could provide some income to the family even when there were no other sources of money. In this way, machismo, the usual and almost unconscious male dominance of women, was shaken. Most of the men were without work, and sometimes they would have to look after the children while the women did their weaving. Women's work became an important economic solution to their families' financial crisis.

Maya women inside Guatemala continue to weave the traditional patterns common to their villages and ethnic groups. But in the refugee camps women shared and borrowed the patterns and symbols, developed on the Maya backstrap loom, that once clearly defined the provenance of the weaver. The women worked with weavers from different ethnic groups as well as with Mexican Tzotzil and Tzeltal Maya weavers. Because of this sharing and borrowing, innovations and changes in Maya patterns of weaving among the Kuchumatan women will become evident in the future.

> *One day, generations from now, the son of a Todos Santero will ask his father, "Papa, why does your traje have such different colors?" "Well son, about a hundred years ago my grandfather was a refugee in Chiapas, together with Mames, Jacaltecos, Kanjobales, Huistecos. . . . He lived together with Chujes and Chiantlecos, with people from San Juan Ixcoy. And thus our ways of weaving became mixed." It will be seen that our combining together leads to many questions that future generations will take into account, . . . questions whose answers will illuminate the consciousness of many generations. (Anderson and Garlock 1988: 22)*

In some Maya groups women had lost the tradition of weaving long before becoming refugees. In the camps these women, among them Q'anjob'al women, have relearned and shared with the Jakaltek, Mam, and Chuj this most wonderful art of the Maya backstrap loom. Also, non-Maya or ladino Guatemalan refugees, who had never woven in Guatemala, learned the art from Indian refugee women (Anderson and Garlock 1988).

Although women felt free to resume their traditional dress after they received recognition as legal refugees, children continued to wear ladino clothing because it was cheaper, and because it was preferable to sell the weaving to augment the family's income. In this way Maya weavers received some income for the many hours of work invested in their craft. Even before exile the time and money invested in making a Maya garment was far greater than its sale value. Referring to the traditional dress in the Kuchumatan highlands, Manz wrote,

While the high price of thread has caused some women to begin to dress their children in Western clothing, most women still spend the six months or more necessary to embroider the large and elaborate huipiles that they wear. These are primarily for their own use and most women have more than one. While San Mateo huipiles are for sale in Huehuetenango, Chichicastenango, Guatemala City and other tourist spots, there did not seem to be a working system for widespread export. In San Mateo huipiles that took pounds of expensive thread and months of work would sell for Q45–60. In tourist centers, they were going for more than Q130. (1988a: 250)

In the camps the marketing of the woven products was different. Here the weavers worked on their looms, and their products were then collected by organizations that helped them sell their work in international markets. For example, the Diocese of San Cristóbal has helped refugee women sell their weavings through a store in San Cristóbal to tourists or for export. Thus the marketing was done with the help of the Church and other international humanitarian groups rather than through middlemen who also profited from the women's work.

Traditional dress is a major symbol and visible expression of Maya identity (Otzoy 1992). It was tremendously important in developing friendship and solidarity between the refugees and the host communities of Mexican Mayas. When the Guatemalan refugees arrived in Las Margaritas, Marqués de Comillas, and Ixkán in Chiapas, the Chamula and Zinacantec colonizers of these jungle areas gave a warm welcome to their Maya brothers and sisters. They said,

"We received the refugees because they are like us." They gave them their own clothes to cover the refugees so as not to be noticed by the Mexican authorities. The Indian dress (in this case, Chamulan) is the best passport. The Chamulas do not have to show their identification cards, since their presence

and their Mayan characteristics confirm everything. (Jan Rus, pers. com. 1988)

Among the Q'anjob'al, Jakaltek, and Chuj refugees in this region, women continued to wear their traditional and expensive skirts, or cortes, because small vendors from Guatemala managed to cross the Mexican border to do business among the refugees in the big camps, bringing cortes from Totonicapán and Quetzaltenango.

In the refugee camp of Pujiltik, to the southeast of San Cristóbal de las Casas, Mam women dedicated themselves to the production of weaving when the season of the *zafra,* the sugarcane harvest, was over. In the same region women of another ethnic group, the Huistecos (a more ladinoized group who had spoken Popb'al Ti' in the past), have tried to organize themselves into productive weaving groups, learning from the Mam and Jakalteks the art of the loom. Ladinoized Maya people who abandoned their traditions a long time ago again adopted them. The traditional art of weaving became the major source of income for indigenous people in the camps.

Religious Rituals

FROM THE TIME of the Spanish conquest the communities of the Kuchumatan highlands had to accommodate to the new Christian religion imposed on them by the Spaniards. Each indigenous community was provided with a patron saint, and since then Mayas have prayed to their saints and celebrated their feast days with dances and religious rituals. During the years prior to the general violence of 1982, every Maya community celebrated its saint's day with a festival, part of a cyclical series of celebrations that brought renewed life and solidarity not only to the village but also to neighboring villages. But most of these festivals also incorporated ancient Maya rituals of thanking the

Maker and Shaper of life and nature on earth (Bunzel 1972; LaFarge and Byers 1931; Oakes 1951). Mayas are deeply religious people, and their devotion to the Heart of Heaven (God) has been expressed in a syncretic manner in their religious rituals.

In the Kuchumatan communities of northwestern Guatemala, before the growth of Protestantism in the 1980s, 90 percent of Mayas were Catholics; the remaining 10 percent were non-Christian traditionalists or Protestants. But after the army established its barracks in the highlands in 1982, major changes occurred in these communities. Church meetings were considered suspect, church leaders were harassed, and there was no respect for the religious activities of native people.

The Catholic church had not historically been respectful of Maya religious traditions, especially targeting the ancient rituals as paganism in the 1950s. But by the 1970s the more liberal sectors of the Catholic church in Guatemala tried to speak up for the poor and the oppressed and worked to implement community projects and cooperatives that would ameliorate their poverty (Frank and Wheaton 1984: 29). During the conflict of the 1980s, particularly following the coup that brought Ríos Montt to power, evangelical missionaries were welcomed into Guatemala and Protestant churches proliferated in the highlands (Stoll 1988). Among them were conservative Pentecostal sects that accused the Indians of being pagans and living in darkness. Along with the army, they accused the Catholic church of promoting "liberation theology" as a way to agitate the poor and gain supporters for the guerrillas. The army then stepped up its campaign to eliminate lay Catholic leaders by accusing them of being subversives who had learned the meaning of revolution from the priests.

Despite many obstacles Mayas have been able to retain, transform, and continue their ancestral beliefs, often dressed up in Catholic imagery. The process has been difficult, as even today many priests would still describe Maya beliefs and rituals as the "teachings of the devil." Some leaders of the Catholic church supported the ambitions of the landowners and military officers of Guatemala far more than they cared about the injustices suffered by Mayas.[7] However, many Catholic priests, nuns, and religious workers and some Protestant missionaries have sided with the poor and denounced the injustices in Guatemala. After fourteen priests and hundreds of catechists were killed, most of the priests who served in the highlands of El Quiché and Huehuetenango left the country and formed the Guatemalan Church in Exile, which continued to denounce the violence against the civilian population.

In the Kuchumatan area, in comparison to other localities in Guatemala, the presence of other Christian sects has not been pronounced. But religious conflicts and problems increased when conversions to Protestantism began in the 1960s. These Protestant sects seemed to preach different messages. Some called for peace and social justice; others emphasized salvation, respect, tolerance, submission, and docile acceptance of the "authority" of the ruler, even if it was repressive and genocidal. Through all these confusing circumstances, many Mayas have maintained a strong faith in their ancient beliefs and rituals, although some have converted to the new religions as a mechanism of survival. But outright Maya religious expressions, such as prayers, songs, processions, and burial of the dead, were brutally repressed by the Guatemalan army during its counterinsurgency war against the guerrillas.

Before the massacres in the Kuchumatan highlands took place, people dreamed that their patron saints abandoned their chapels and churches and fled to Mexico. The ancestors also followed them in the people's dreams, explaining that Guatemala was not a safe place anymore and that people should defend their lives against the army's bombs and bullets by following their patron saints into exile. And eventually, in early 1982, this did happen. The army's presence in the communities of the Kuchumatan highlands made it impossible for them to celebrate their festivals. Given the risks, the surrounding villages did not come to participate in the patronal festivities.

As the massacres increased under Ríos Montt's presidency in the second half of 1982, the majority of the villages became desolate and the festivals were almost forgotten. The army took control of the churches and used the bells to call people to obey their commands. Also, the army ordered the civil patrols to use the bells to call the people when there was an urgent need of them or when the guerrillas were passing through the villages. The most sacred places and artifacts—the church, the bells, the saints—were used by the army as tools of repression. Most Protestants remained in their villages and towns in Guatemala and received preferential treatment from the government and Protestant aid agencies.

It was because of the army's lack of respect for religious rituals that some ethnic groups arrived in Mexico carrying their patron saints. One of these was the community of Santa Rosa, which transported their wooden image of the Virgin as Saint Rose to Rancho Tejas, a mainly Q'anjob'al refugee camp in Mexico. They also took the church bell to call people to say the rosary and other prayers every Sunday. Other Q'anjob'al communities close to the Mexican border, such as Santa Teresa, did likewise. In Rancho Tejas, according to the testimony of Kaxh Pasil, after the religious celebrations every Sunday the refugees played the marimba, an essential instrument in Maya festivities. With music and dance, the refugees could recover some of their strength and find relief for their sorrow. The marimba music also attracted young people from the surrounding Mexican villages who came to dance and enjoy this cultural expression of the exiled Guatemalans. Their religious celebrations came to an end when the immigration authorities ordered the dismantling of the camp. Since then Rancho Tejas, which had hosted some six thousand refugees from different ethnic groups, has been called the "Ghost Village." It rose up suddenly and had a life for a short time, and then it was dismantled during the night at the order of immigration authorities. What is left are a few crosses over the graves of the dead abandoned in the pasturelands.

When I visited camps along the southern border during the summer of 1988, the refugees who lived close to or in Mexican villages had decided to join the Mexicans in the celebration of their patron saint festivals. The refugees also participated in communal works in preparation for the festivals and contributed money for the celebrations of their hosts' patronal feast days. Pilin Xapin, a Q'anjob'al refugee living in the Tzeltal community of Las Maravillas, Tenejapa, in the Margaritas region, commented that they indeed remembered their patron saint's festival (San Miguel), but they did not celebrate any festivities on that special date. They only prayed at home and told their children how they used to celebrate the festival in their homelands. Here, as elsewhere, there were major transformations in religious rituals.

Refugee children did not know the folkloric dances, such as the Dances of the Conquest, the Deer Dance, and the Dances of the Moors and especially those performed in honor of the patron saints. They grew up not knowing or participating in these cultural expressions of their communal celebrations that have given life to Maya religious beliefs and rituals. Fortunately, except for the traditional dances, the festivities of the Mexican villages near the camps are similar to those of the Kuchumatan region. Catholic religious devotion persisted in the camps but with less participation by those refugees who found it difficult to travel to Mexican towns to attend services. Priests visited refugee camps only sporadically, not surprising when even small Mexican villages were without pastoral staff. In the larger camps catechists undertook religious instruction.

In the camps traditional Maya religion was not widely practiced. There were no visible activities of Mayan diviners or priests. Most of these religious specialists lived in the larger towns of the Kuchumatan area and were not represented in the refugee population. Much of their ritual activity is location specific and would have been difficult to transfer to the Mexican camps. Because the refugees worked closely with Catholic institutions, they thus have been more closely involved with Catholic ceremonies and rituals such as the Mass and the Rosary. There were no Protestant churches or chapels built in the refugee camps I visited, and those few refugees who were not Catholic did not participate in the religious promotion of Maya culture, as they considered these activities to be pagan. Because Protestants were so few in number, religious differences and conflicts within the camps abated. They cooperated in the economic and political life of the camps without involving themselves in religious activities.

Meanwhile, with the current revitalization of Maya culture throughout the Maya land (Mayab'), religion as expressed by traditional Maya priests has been flourishing. With the help of their recently formed organization, the Consejo Nacional de Aj Q'ijabs (National Council of Maya Priests), these bearers of the ancient Maya calendar and sacred Maya beliefs have come together and performed their rituals in public, giving greater exposure and credence to the ancient faith.

Gender Roles and Family Relations

AMONG INDIGENOUS PEOPLE of Guatemala the daily tasks of a household were always marked by a clear delineation between the worlds of men and women. For centuries Maya men have worked the land as campesinos and their daily life has been linked to the land (Gossen 1974). Traditional gender roles clearly established the authority of men over the work in the fields and the activities of the household outside the boundaries of the house and the authority of women over the household, and most Maya women were important contributors to the family economy.

Each ethnic group had its own economic strategies. Mam, Jakaltek, and Chuj women participated in the family economy by weaving and selling their products in local markets. Q'anjob'al women, who had lost the tradition of weaving, made their contribution to the household economy by making pottery, ropes, and baskets. The same variety of economic strategies can be seen among the men. The Q'anjob'al men, for example, were more dedicated to handicraft production, traveling, and trade, because their eroded lands were very unprofitable or because they had no land. The Mam of Todos Santos specialized in the cultivation of potatoes, which they sold to surrounding towns and villages. Jakaltek men were dedicated to the milpa, and they provided corn to many surrounding communities, especially to ladinoized communities such as San Antonio and Santa Ana Huista, Nentón, and La Democracia. Jakalteks have traditionally enjoyed a wide variety of agricultural crops as their lands encompass hot, temperate, and cold climatic zones.

In 1982, when governmental violence disrupted social life in the countryside, many nuclear families in native communities tried to maintain strong relationships, and men controlled their social activities, especially the drinking of alcohol. Army harassment and punishment of those "drunks" they found out at night was a strong incentive to change. The army disappeared young people who went out in the evening to have a drink or socialize with their friends. When life became too dangerous, the consumption of alcoholic beverages diminished, and, as a consequence, the mutual respect and support at home strengthened the family. Women, in general, became more protective of their husbands and children. The few exceptions were cases in which some wives, beaten or insulted by their drunken husbands, denounced them to the army as guerrillas. For the army, these cases provided opportunities to torture the men to "obtain information." When the women observed the army's actions against the accused men, they commented that it might have been better not to turn them over to the army. It often provoked more problems in the family, sometimes causing husbands to be disappeared or to abandon their wives, which resulted in grave economic hardship.

Civil patrols also contributed to the disruption of families and caused distrust in communities. The army established its intelligence activity in the Maya communities through the G-2 (military intelligence) and paid people to inform on "suspicious" villagers. Social ties and communication were thus restricted. Manz reported, "Villagers are extremely careful in their conversations, both regarding what they say and to whom they say it. In the main squares in the north of Huehuetenango, people would fall quiet if they noticed a few small children listening to the conversation" (1988a: 71).

In addition, the duties of civil patrol service caused the disruption of family life. Patrollers were ordered to spend several days a week searching for guerrillas in the mountains, during which some soldiers remained at the barracks in town and raped Maya women. Such abuse of peaceful villagers was among the most criminal expressions of the Guatemalan army, destroying both Maya values and dignity. Rape had never been a problem in Maya communities, but after the army arrived hundreds of unmarried young women gave birth to children as a result.

Because the violence left behind so many widows and orphans, Guatemalan Indian and non-Indian women have had to care for themselves, for their children, and for other relatives. They have had to be both father and mother, breadwinner and nurturer, the sole physical and emotional support of their children.

For a wife there will be concern for her husband or the grandchildren. . . . Women always have to be thinking of what will happen to their relatives or to themselves; it's something they cannot escape. In the concrete cases, where the repression has affected women, either killing the husband or the children, in those cases the women will have to carry on the economic work by themselves, as is happening in the rural communities in which there have been so many massacres. There are so many

widows and they have to take on themselves all the work of
providing food and maintaining the family. (Anderson and
Garlock 1988: 45)

With the disruption of the family in exile, the social roles of
women and men in the refugee camps had to be adjusted. Men
were restricted from moving beyond the controlled refugee
camps, and they had to learn the skills and undertake handicraft
production at "home" to support their families. The food supplied by the churches and international organizations through
COMAR was inadequate and monotonous. The refugees needed
a greater variety of fresh foods similar to those they had in the
Guatemalan highlands. And the food provided to the refugees
was never enough for larger families.

In the camps men became more tolerant and tempered their
machismo, and problems of alcohol abuse were less visible.
There was also a resurgence of mutual support and confidence
between neighbors because everybody recognized that they were
the fortunate survivors who shared similar hardships and opportunities. But the constant relocation of the camps, the splitting
of large camps into smaller ones, and the relocation of large
numbers of refugees to the Yucatán peninsula presented persistent problems for Maya families in exile as well. The relocation
to the camps in Campeche and Quintana Roo caused divisions
within many families. At that time the options were to relocate
to the Yucatán peninsula, move to another Chiapas camp under
less pressure to relocate to the Yucatán, move to a Mexican town,
or return to Guatemala. The discussion, dissension, and multi-
plicity of poor choices caused family disruption and division.
Some family members avoided being relocated far from the border by escaping to other refugee camps or Mexican towns.
Others preferred to return to Guatemala in spite of the highly
insecure situation there.

The preservation of family traditions has been easier for
those in the camps than for those Mayas who migrated to the

United States, Canada, or Europe. In these distant countries the patterns of family life have been disrupted, and refugee children are growing up learning and accommodating themselves to a very different dominant cultural tradition. It is difficult for Maya families to maintain a strong sense of community and Mayanness when their children have to accommodate to the Western way of life. In this situation refugee parents and children are actually living in two different worlds, and parents must cope with the many other problems of young people that are very visible in those countries: drugs, gangs, crime, high rates of divorce, and car accidents caused by drunk drivers.

The Maya families in the refugee camps in southern Mexico have had the advantage of being in closer contact with the mother culture, the Mesoamerican cultural base of Mayanness. The culture and ecology of the Chiapas region is similar to that of the Kuchumatan highlands. In addition, the refugees in Mexico have kept informed of events in Guatemala through radio and television reports or civil patrollers or community members who have come to Mexico periodically to find work. This relationship with the mother culture has been important for the continuity of the great Maya tradition. This vital connection was reinforced by the refugees themselves, who rejected the idea of relocating to the Guatemalan army's model villages, where people were indoctrinated into a Guatemalan nationalism that was contrary to their social, cultural, and religious beliefs.[5]

Overall it can be argued that family relations in the refugee camps have grown stronger. Egalitarian relationships between men and women have become more possible as the concept of male superiority has diminished. Family responsibility and cooperation in all household chores have been dictated by new economic realities and reinforced by organizations that developed for men and women in the camps. For example, the reaffirmation of women's rights and responsibilities was strongly promoted by their organization, Mama Maquín, which was formed to raise women's concerns in camp policy making and to give women a forum for issues of particular interest to them.⁹ The church also helped men to understand better their responsibilities as parents. There developed a greater tolerance on the part of both men and women despite, or perhaps because of, the hardships, poverty, and lack of opportunities that both faced. In this way Maya families demonstrated that family respect and understanding was essential for their survival as a people.

Economic Strategies

BECAUSE OF THE forced abandonment of their properties in Guatemala, the refugees became a people dispossessed, struggling for survival in an alien territory. They had to start all over again, to feed and sustain their families in exile. The land was not theirs, and they had no rights to resources such as firewood, edible greens, and small game animals. Poverty forced the earliest Maya refugees to participate in communal work directed by Mexican villagers to have access to basic goods and necessities. Such extreme misery provoked some refugees to risk their lives and go back to their homeland inside Guatemala to rescue some of the stored corn and beans they had abandoned. If their milpas were close to the Mexican border, men traveled at night and managed to return with some food for their starving families. This adventure was risky because the civil patrols appropriated the abandoned cornfields for themselves and would kill the refugees if they were caught smuggling corn from their own milpas. The lack of food forced some refugees to survive by eating wild roots and plants until international solidarity groups and the Mexican government through COMAR came to their aid.

The economic strategy of most Mayas in Guatemala was the production of corn and other staples grown in the milpa. According to their tradition, the rich man was the one who worked the land and could harvest a good amount of corn. The man who did not harvest enough corn was thought to be lazy

An old man shelling corn at Villa Cocalito

because he let his family suffer. As land available for farming declined in the twentieth century, this value of corn cultivation and the concept of wealth that it symbolized has become less meaningful. The small pieces of land did not produce enough corn, and drought could diminish the yield even further. Maya corn farmers had to find other economic strategies to compensate for the failure of a good harvest. Both the limited means of production and the ongoing uncompensated labor that was forced from the indigenous communities have perpetuated a cycle of poverty.

Before exile, Q'anjob'al men who lacked land were likely to engage in long-distance trade.[10] They were well known for venturing to distant places, even as far as the United States, a country they have come to since 1950 in search of work. Stories about such early travels of Mayas to the United States for economic reasons have circulated in the Kuchumatan highlands for generations.[11]

Other Maya ethnic groups have been more localized in their activities, because their small plots of land are still productive.

By limiting their production to one crop and engaging in economic exchanges, the Maya ethnic groups of this region were able to assure their mutual welfare and survival. Each group produced its traditional crops and did not encroach on the production of other communities, so that all might survive. Thus Jakaltek people grew corn, beans, and coffee, which was sold to surrounding villages, while the Mam of Todos Santos specialized in potatoes. And the Q'anjob'al sold pottery, ropes, and timber.[12]

Since the 1960s Mayas, even in the Kuchumatan highlands, have become part of a more global economy and the handcrafts of some Maya groups have been replaced by industrial products. Two very early imports into the region were plastic ware, which replaced Maya pottery, and plastic rope, which replaced rope of natural fibers. In these areas the small economic production of Maya families has been taken over by the encroaching forces of capitalism, thus narrowing the range of strategies for survival. Adding these changes to the impact of the repressive counter-insurgency war meant that a core Mayan value, economic self-sufficiency, was badly shaken.

When the refugees arrived in Mexico in 1982, they immediately started to produce what was basic to their survival. For example, in Rancho Tejas, according to Kaxh Pasil, a market day was established every Sunday at which all types of goods were traded and exchanged in the camp. At that time both Guatemalan and Mexican currencies were used and economic life began to be reorganized. Q'anjob'al men and women were the main participants in these business activities, and they went to Comitán or other Mexican villages and bought soft drinks, soap, candles, medicine, and other items that were needed in the camps. The merchants did not make much money, as is true of Maya merchants in general, but they did help the refugees acquire what they needed most.[13]

The refugees built communal storehouses and organized themselves by ethnic groups, selecting a few leaders for each group to distribute food and organize communal work in the camps. In some cases the communal work was directed by the Mexican villagers who needed the labor of the refugees.

The distribution of donated food sometimes created conflicts because of the economic circumstances of the beneficiaries. Those refugees who had the chance to harvest some of their corn at night inside Guatemala were better off than others who came from more distant places in the interior of Guatemala, or those who lost everything because the army burned their houses and their milpas. Thus the refugees decided that everybody should receive food proportionately according to their needs. "The refugees came to the conclusion that `equal distribution was not the just procedure,' and they decided to give to everybody according to their needs, thus avoiding a false egalitarianism" (Diócesis de San Cristóbal 1986: 5).

In the relocated camps in Campeche and Quintana Roo, new means of economic survival were developed. Because of the shortage of land for cultivation, refugees had to work and depend collectively on the production of corn for their subsistence. Refugee training for self-sufficiency was part of the overall plan for these Yucatán settlements as developed by COMAR and other relief organizations. "But [the] self-sufficiency strategy [was] not restricted to agriculture. Projects to generate income inside the settlements, through modest manufacturing and artisanal activities as well as paid labor in the surrounding areas are important. Carpentry, tailoring, and baking projects have all been set up and are now providing the refugees with new skills. But it will take time. `We are peasants and our tool is the machete,' said Feliciano, a refugee representative at Maya Tecun" (Van Praag 1986: 29).

Guatemalan refugees have been eager to become self-sufficient, and they have managed their subsistence by engaging in all types of work available to them. Some refugees have even come in contact with their ancient Maya heritage by working in excavation projects at the ruins of Edzna in Campeche. Van Praag described one such project in 1986: "With an initial grant of $30,000 from UNHCR, work began this September on the excavation of one side of the staircase bordering the central forum, where an estimated 5,000 people could sit and watch tournaments and games. Fifteen refugees are currently being employed in the first phase of the project. Each receives the equivalent of US $2.50 for an eight-hour day" (1986: 28).

By the summer of 1988 the refugees in Chiapas had developed a twofold economic strategy. Most economic activity involved the production of corn and textiles. Mayas in these camps continued the traditional techniques of cultivating corn, beans, and squash on land rented from Mexican peasants.

In the refugee camp of Las Maravillas, refugees paid 30,000 pesos (equivalent to US$10 in 1988) per hectare of land where they cultivated their own corn. But when they finished working on their own plots they then had to work for the Mexicans, picking coffee beans for which they received 2,000 or 3,000 pesos a day (equivalent to about US$1). In the majority of cases refugees also contributed to the communal work directed by the Mexicans to ensure their continued welcome in the Mexican villages and to have access to firewood, essential for cooking their food. If they disobeyed the calls for communal work, they were penalized with a fine by the local Mexican authority.

The refugees bought their clothes, hats, and sandals once a year, after they had accumulated some money or during the fiesta of the patron saint of the Mexican community. Otherwise their life was restricted to the camp where they could not spend money on luxuries but saved it to buy food or other necessities on market day.

The second economic strategy was to live in extended families; married sons and daughters lived with their spouses and children in the dwelling of one set of parents. Multifamily compounds contributed to the household's food. As communal labor was assessed against households, this strategy also offered a larger pool of adult men to take turns working in the camps or with the Mexicans to build houses, roads, and other community infrastructure. The Maya mutualistic tradition and the communal way of survival were strongly developed in the camps. Refugees built their own clinics, chapels, roads, houses, schools, grain storage facilities, and gardens.

Once in the refugee camps, Maya refugees tried to strengthen their weakened economy by reactivating some of their traditional economic strategies. Ethnic groups learned each other's crafts; they shared techniques and knowledge of artisan production to increase their options for economic survival. Everybody in the camp undertook some type of traditional small-scale production. They trained themselves as weavers, sandal and hat makers, bakers, carpenters, sawyers, or potters to earn money to complement the aid received from COMAR.

Raising pigs was another economic strategy that continued in the camps. If a tortilla fell on the dirt floor, it was saved for the pig, which was fattened on household scraps and what it could get rooting about the village and then sold in the market after a few months. It was a slow way to accumulate income, but it helped.

In most of the camps, but especially in the small ones such as Las Maravillas, Cocalito, El Raizal, and Nicolás Bravo, women raised chickens and turkeys. This was a household rather than a communal strategy in most places, but the extended family owning one of these poultry houses could improve their diet and also make some money by selling eggs, chickens, and turkeys to Mexican and refugee customers.

The refugees of Las Maravillas camp who rented land in the Marqués de Comillas region produced very good corn because their land was very rich and productive all year long. In other regions the refugees were more dependent on seasonal rains, as had been the case in Guatemala. In some places the refugees learned irrigation techniques from Mexican peasants. This was particularly true in the regions around Colón, Aquespala, and Comalapa where the refugees received permission to use community canals to irrigate their small plots.

In the refugee camps of the arid region of Pujiltik two ethnic groups have helped each other to survive. The Mam-Mayas depended primarily on the production of women's weaving. The other group, ladinoized refugees from Santa Ana Huista, depended almost completely on wage labor as they did when they were in Guatemala. In Mexico both groups lived on a big sugarcane plantation in the central valley of southern Chiapas, and they depended on the seasonal work in the annual sugarcane harvest. From November to April there was enough work in the zafra for the refugees, but most of the time, when the seasonal work ended, they were left without jobs and they had to wait for the next season. The refugees in these camps were limited in the size and type of construction they could undertake because of the lack of wood. The whole area was cultivated with sugarcane, and the refugees had to organize themselves and contribute collectively to buy truckloads of firewood that they ordered from distant places in the highlands of Chiapas. The Mexican plantation owners told the refugees that they should remain in their camps and be ready to work when they were needed. Here there was occasional off-season work in construction. Wealthy Mexicans were eager to take advantage of the low-wage workforce to construct their own houses of cement blocks.

By sharing the same camps this ladino group learned how to weave from traditional Mam weavers.[14] A refugee in charge of selling the weaving in this camp said that the women's production should be priced according to the hours spent working on each piece, a wage labor concept applied to handicraft production. This was the first time that I heard serious concern about the time spent in weaving production. Until then Maya weavers had not been able to set prices according to the labor-intensiveness of their craft.

Pricing was also a concern among weavers in Guatemala. Middlemen, either individuals or groups, bought a woman's woven pieces for resale elsewhere so that the weaver would never know the actual price for which her craft was sold in the capital or in the international market. Women's artistic production has long been undervalued, but they continued producing and carrying on the backstrap loom tradition of the ancient Maya. In the camps the refugees have learned to think differently about economic issues and have acquired mechanisms of economic and cultural survival that will allow them to preserve their traditions in a stronger way in Guatemala when they return.

Education

THE VIOLENCE THAT disrupted the refugees' lives also made them more aware of the importance of education for their children. It became a valued tool in the struggle for survival in an ever-changing world. Mayas want their children to acquire what had before been the sole property of the privileged ladinos, a good education. In this way the indigenous people can avoid being excluded, deceived, and abused in almost all aspects of Guatemalan national life as has been the case until now.

For Maya communities in Guatemala access to education has been difficult for several reasons. First, most communities are very isolated. Before 1950 almost all the communities of the Kuchumatan highlands were without school buildings and lacked opportunities for education. There were no roads, and the assigned teachers for the few schools available were ladinos from the cities who rarely showed up to teach but rather stayed at home and still received their monthly checks. Second, the school-teachers in larger towns in the Kuchumatan highlands did not know Maya languages. They taught Spanish to the first-graders through force and corporal punishment (a process known as *castellanización*). Because of the constant punishment received for speaking in the only language they knew, Maya children avoided going to school. And third, the extreme poverty of many Maya families made it necessary for children to accompany their parents wherever they migrated in search of work, thus eliminating any chance for education.

Some Maya elders did not consider Western education the best education a young Maya could receive. They complained that young Mayas who attended distant schools to be educated had become abusive, aggressive, and disrespectful. They asked what was the idea of education, if it was not for inculcating respect for our parents, the elders, the community, nature, and the supernatural world? In other words, if a person was educated, he or she must show the respect for life that is the essence of education. Recently the elders have said, "It seems that the ones who call themselves educated are the ones who are destroying the world and do not have respect for nature or even people's lives."

In fact, Maya people, as native people elsewhere in the world, have been very respectful of life in all its forms on earth. And this respect for life began with the traditional Maya way of transmitting knowledge through the oral tradition. In this way Maya people educated their children and emphasized respect as the cornerstone of social life. Unfortunately, some Maya values were abandoned because of the general ladino misunderstanding of Maya culture. For instance, in some communities the Ahb'eh, the Maya priests in the Kuchumatan highlands who are the keepers of the ancient Maya calendar, were called *brujos* (witches), and respect for them and their knowledge dwindled. With this mislabeling and its attendant stigmatization, how could children learn from those people whom they were taught to fear? In recent times, as Mayas became more aware of their lack of opportunities, there was a strong desire to share in the national life as Guatemalans, but this desire had to confront governmental racism and repression. Referring to this situation in the Guatemalan highlands, Douglas E. Britnall wrote, "In villages across the highlands, locals [ladinos] who had seen their position eroded by the new Indian economic success, education, and organization found their opportunity to strike back and reassert their dominance, now backed by the national elite, army and government" (1983: 16). The Mayas' desire for betterment of their lives was met with violence, and they were accused of being "subversives." The quest for access to the dominant culture was seen as subversion.

Nevertheless, more and more Maya children in Guatemala attended national schools in the 1980s. Because Maya culture was not emphasized in the curriculum, their traditional ways of knowing and understanding life diminished. For example, the primary-level social studies textbooks were obsolete and inadequate. The content of the curriculum provided neither useful knowledge nor preparation for the needs of people who have a different worldview and who explain the natural and supernatural world on different epistemological grounds. None of these concepts were even contemplated in the national school system into which Mayas were forced to assimilate. It was only with access to higher education that Maya students were able to understand and deconstruct the ideological forms of present-day Guatemalan education, which obliterated their Maya heritage. But this stage of higher education was unattainable for most poor Maya families.

In 1982 the army brought with it a total disrespect for education in poor Maya villages. Soldiers tortured and killed many teachers and used the classrooms as their torture chambers (Montejo 1987). As reported by one villager, "They killed a teacher who lived very near to us. Her father was blind. She was killed, machinegunned. Other friends were killed in different ways. Some were killed by chopping off their heads" (Anderson and Garlock 1988: 60). The soldiers targeted schoolteachers and priests as "intellectual" subversives who supported their Maya friends.

In Jacaltenango on January 1, 1981, the army killed a promising young schoolteacher, my brother, in the central park of the town during the patron saint's festival. Thousands of people witnessed the crime and condemned the army's brutality against the indigenous population. Other schoolteachers were disappeared when they went to cash their checks at the banks in the city of Huehuetenango. Another schoolteacher, a poet named Manuel, was kidnapped in 1982; his body has never been found. Hundreds of other cases exist in which schoolteachers were targeted by the army. Many families abandoned their villages and took their children out of school so that the schools were deserted. The school in La Laguna was abandoned in 1982, and the doorless building was invaded by pigs, donkeys, and other animals.

Repression deprived the native population of their children's opportunity for an education. While the children of the rich could be educated in good schools or abroad, Maya children were persecuted along with their parents and chased into the mountains where they have tried to find refuge or security. Thousands of children who were registered in school crossed the border into Mexico with their parents. And without education Maya children could have no other occupation than that of their parents, campesinos working in the milpas.

The refugees living in the camps in Mexico saw this time of exile as one in which their children could acquire some education, and they have consciously and tenaciously pursued whatever opportunities arose. Each camp had a school that was built communally. When several ethnic groups shared the same camp, they shared the same school and participated equally in communal work to improve their camp and its school. "Education has become a priority for refugees in Mexico. Each of the border camps has its own schoolhouse and teacher, although the Mexican government provides no help. The refugees explain that education is a high priority because, 'We don't want our children to be taken advantage of, like we were. It is important for them to learn Spanish so they can defend themselves'" (Bazzy 1986: 46).

Education for the children became the priority of the refugees. In La Gloria young Q'anjob'al and Chuj men helped the community by teaching hundreds of school-aged children who had to abandon their schools in Guatemala. In 1989 there were no school buildings, so classes were held in the shade of trees on the outskirts of the refugee camp. Later, with the help of the Diocese of San Cristóbal and COMAR, the refugees were able to build huts for classrooms and obtain salaries for their teachers and funds for school supplies. The education offered by native schoolteachers was more centered on Maya culture and history. There was some dissention at the beginning: some refugees argued that because they were in Mexican territory, their children should be taught the Mexican curriculum; others argued that their children should learn about their own country, so when they returned they would be prepared with a knowledge of their culture and history. Finally there was a consensus that the children would study Guatemalan culture and history and also learn about Mexico, the country that gave them refuge. There was a growing consciousness about their situation as Guatemalans exiled from their ancient lands. Schoolchildren were not taught about the wonders of the conquest as they would have been in Guatemala but rather, along with the adults, began to analyze the effects of that conquest on their lives.

Adults did not receive systematic education in the camps but had opportunities to learn skills as artisans, health promoters, and administrators. Some became carpenters, others foot-loom weavers. Some took active positions in the camp cooperatives and learned the skills necessary for those roles. Others were trained to become educational promoters to aid their communities. Later, under the leadership of the CCPP, adults learned about political matters and developed organizational strategies, recognizing that it was essential for them to understand the politics of exile as they negotiated their return with COMAR, CEAR, and the Guatemalan government.

There was also a mutual sharing of the Maya culture. A main concern was to teach children traditional artistic expressions such as weaving, pottery, and other handicrafts and traditional Maya values. "Through the daily examples of elders, children [were] taught that community responsibility is more important than individual pursuit, a perception which provide[d] a measure of cohesiveness as they wrestle[d] with uprooted aspects of their lives" (Boothby 1986: 48).

The refugees ran their own schools. They decided what material to use and how to organize the educational program. There were a few professionally trained schoolteachers in some camps, so young men and women, those who had middle or high school educations, taught reading and writing to the refugee children. According to Manz,

In Campeche where the refugees themselves run the schools, close to 100 people work as educational promoters (teachers with nonprofessional training). . . . Educational promoters receive a salary for two weeks of every month they teach; the other two weeks are considered to be their contribution to the community and exempts them from community agricultural work. Educational promoters are paid through COMAR. In early 1986 they received 12,000 pesos for their two weeks paid work each month. (1988a: 164–65)

The children of refugees who chose to live in Mexican communities have been integrated into Mexican schools, and they receive the same education as Mexican children. This strategy of survival in larger Mexican towns has distanced the children from their ethnic background. In addition, to avoid the scrutiny of Mexican immigration authorities, Maya children have been restricted from practicing their traditional way of life. They must act like ladinos to attend school and secure any permanence of residence (Boothby 1988).

From the beginning the Catholic Diocese of San Cristóbal has been especially helpful to refugees in the education of their children. In the refugee camp of Guadalupe Victoria, the church of Motozintla created a school for refugees during the years 1982–84 financed by Danish solidarity groups. Two trained schoolteachers, refugees themselves, worked with some eighty

Maya children mainly from the Q'anjob'al, Jakaltek, and Mam ethnic groups. The children shared the same school and had the opportunity to hear the different sounds of their languages and observe some similarities in their cultural traditions. They were also able to share the fears and nightmares of their common experience of the violence in Guatemala and the flight into exile.

According to Kaxh Pasil, who was a schoolteacher, the outstanding refugee students were later sent to the Mexican school in Guadalupe Victoria and performed very well academically. This caused the Mexican parents to believe that the teachers were spending more time with the Guatemalan pupils than with their children. A group of Mexican parents asked the Mexican teachers not to accept the Guatemalan children as students, "if they did not want to lose their jobs." The Mexican teachers stopped admitting Guatemalan children. The ban on refugee children remained in place until 1984, when the camp was dismantled as a result of the relocation to Campeche and Quintana Roo. In this case most refugees at Guadalupe Victoria avoided the relocation by splitting into small family groups that moved to other places.

Although most children of parents living in registered refugee camps in southern Mexico have managed to attend school, thousands of other children whose parents preferred to live outside registered camps have not had the opportunity to attend school. Small groups of families were dispersed all along the southern Mexican border and did not receive help from COMAR or education for their children. Unfortunately, these children had been in school in Guatemala in 1982. Now adolescents, any education they have received has been obtained solely from their parents.

Not all schools were well built or well supplied. Indeed, many suffered from a lack of essential equipment for teaching. During my 1988 visit I observed that some of the little huts that refugees had constructed for use as schools had been neglected. The children lacked basic school supplies such as paper, notebooks, and pencils, and their education was conducted under very difficult conditions.

Where there were no professionally trained schoolteachers among the refugees, they selected education promoters who were then trained by COMAR and the Catholic church. Their major goal, as one promoter told me, "is the preparation of the children for the future. Our children are our wealth in the camps and we should give them the preparation that they need in order to have a better life than the one that we have offered them until now."

In the refugee camp of Pujiltik the ladinoized refugees from Huista sent their children to the Mexican federal schools and were satisfied with the education their children were receiving. A representante of this camp told me in 1988,

> After school, our children used to go to the houses of Mexican families to watch television, but since the "streets" are muddy, the children dirtied the floor of the Mexican houses and then the refugee children were pushed out. Immediately they would go to another house and the same thing happened. Then we decided to buy a television set communally, and we placed it in one of our conference rooms. Since then our children have watched the programs they like, and we the adults have watched the news broadcast from Guatemala, so we can discuss the news among us and talk about it with our children.

In this way the refugees kept in touch with the outside world, especially with political events inside Guatemala.

While the refugees in Mexico struggled to educate their children, those Maya refugee families that decided to return to their homelands were often forced to relocate in model villages, where most of their actions and movements were controlled by the army and civil patrol groups working in the villages as intelligence sources. Some of the model villages, those specified by the army as reeducation centers, were no more than concentration camps. There children suffered the most; they were indoctrinated and alienated from their Maya values and traditions. The army forced the refugees to identify themselves as subversives and as bad Guatemalans who made war against their mother nation. Christine Krueger described an *acto cívico* (civic act) in the Saraxoch model village in northern Guatemala:

> During the acto, they pledged to the flag; sang the national anthem, the hymn to the Guatemalan soldier, the hymn to the civil patrol; all with straight backs, eyes forward, arms in salute at their hearts, except for the women with small babies in their arms. . . . They responded with crisp shouts when the leader standing before the group denounced publicly the errors they had made taking up arms against their mother Guatemala. (1986: 43)

It was the fear of such an education for themselves and their children that kept many families from returning to Guatemala.

Today it is crucial that the education of Maya children incorporate an understanding of their ethnic identity and heritage so that Maya culture will continue to live. It is a difficult task for the parents to teach Maya culture and traditions to their children under conditions of exile. For refugees who live in distant industrialized nations, this task is even more difficult because of the alien cultural context in which their children are developing. Refugee children in the United States, Canada, and Europe constantly question the circumstances that forced them to come to a very different culture. Maya children in southern Florida have adapted themselves to their new life and educational opportunities better than the adults have, but their future as Mayas is uncertain because of the seductiveness of the dominant culture. To maintain contact with Maya culture, some refugee children have learned to play the marimba, the Guatemalan national instrument, and also about the social conditions in Guatemala.[15]

One day Guatemalan Mayas and non-Mayas in exile will return to their homeland to reconstruct their lives. If the

Eurocentric and racist view of the dominant classes and the ladinos toward the Mayan population truly changes, and if there are
appropriate and culturally sensitive educational opportunities for
all Guatemalan children, there may be hope for constructing a
pluralistic and democratic national culture for all Guatemalans.

9

ETHNIC RELATIONS
AND CULTURAL REVIVAL IN
THE REFUGEE CAMPS

GUATEMALA IS A multicultural nation where the Maya population is the majority. Nevertheless, the Maya have remained powerless because the ladinos and a small white elite have historically controlled the country with a politics of violence, using humiliation and discrimination against the native population (Cojtí Cuxil 1991; Sam Colop 1991). Since the Spanish conquest they have promoted cultural disintegration of the Mayas, especially through the use of forced labor. During those times in Guatemalan history when that labor was most needed, the Mayas have suffered the most. The modernization projects directed by the Liberal government of the dictator Justo Rufino Barrios in the 1870s was one such time; road building and infrastructure construction under Jorge Ubico in the 1930s was another. The repression of the indigenous population in the highlands of Guatemala can be seen as the modern continuation of the sociopolitical, religious, economic, and cultural domination of the Guatemalan ruling class (Carmack 1988; Smith 1990; Warren 1978).

This conflict between the dominant classes and the Mayas is the core of the problem of ethnic relations in Guatemala. The present efforts to search for peace and social justice by a number of Maya and non-Maya organizations in Guatemala are part of the solution. In this chapter I discuss the conflicts among ethnic groups both in Guatemala and in the refugee camps and examine some resolutions of these conflicts that are in process. Ethnic conflict between Mayas and ladinos became more pervasive in 1982 when the military counterinsurgency war intensified.

Mayanness: How Mayans View Themselves

THE MAYA LINGUISTIC communities—or Maya nations, to use the terminology of North American indigenous groups—are the inheritors of the ancient Maya civilization that flourished during the Classic Maya period from 250 B.C. to A.D. 900 (Campbell and Kaufman 1985; LaFarge and Byers 1931). Each of these first nations speaks a different Maya language, but most linguists believe that all are ultimately related to an ancient mother tongue, the proto-Maya language (England 1992; see map on page 000). That is, different Maya linguistic communities share a common underlying Maya language stratum, worldview, and culture. Each Maya nation has maintained its traditions and respect for its language as it changed over time. With the Spanish conquest, the Maya groups, already greatly differentiated, subdivided further, and each ethnic group developed mechanisms of cultural survival that depended on its ecological resources and geographic location. Maya groups became more corporate (Wolf 1957), and internal mechanisms of cultural construction and transformation began to operate on different scales. In some cases Maya communities changed at great speed and were absorbed into the ladino culture, especially during the development of the hacienda system in the 1800s. In the Kuchumatan highlands these communities included San Antonio Huista, Santa Ana Huista, Nentón, La Democracia, and Cuilco. Other Maya communities remained closed and resisted total integration and absorption by the Wes or Kaxhlan (ladino or Spanish culture), such as Todos Santos Kuchumatan, Jacaltenango, Concepción Huista, San Mateo Ixtatán, Santa Eulalia, San Miguel Acatán, San Ildefonso Ixtahuacán, and Santiago Chimaltenango.

Motivated by the need for cultural distinctiveness, each community had developed a separate view of itself. Consequently, this uniqueness was expressed in their sacred myths of origin and physical location on earth. For example, the Tzotzil Mayas of San Juan Chamula argue that they have been placed at the center of earth, or Smixik Banamil (Gossen 1974). Others, according to their myths of origin, were placed in similarly privileged positions, such as the Jakalteks, who were at the center of the sky or universe, or Smuxuk Kanh.

Mayas have their own concept of otherness and have maintained images or stereotypes of other Maya or non-Maya ethnic groups. As they see themselves at the center of the earth or heaven, as explained in their cosmology and worldview, Maya groups have classified more distant groups as ranging from less Maya to more dangerous in behavior. For example, for the Jakalteks, Mayas must be clean and follow the paths of the ancestors, who were virtuous and hospitable. Thus, for the Jakalteks, the behavior of the residents in the surrounding towns or communities is not only different but also less desirable. The Jakalteks consider the Q'anjob'al at the north of the Jakaltek region to be less hospitable, more dangerous, and even polygamous. Similarly, the Lacandón Maya who inhabit the Lacandón rain forest are considered wild people who hide from outsiders. "Tom Lakanton hach" (Don't be a Lacandón) a person would tell a child if he or she hides from visitors. The Chamula (Tzotzil) are thought to be dirty, because they have long hair and do not bathe. A person who does not care for his physical image is reminded, "Don't be a Chamula, cut your hair." Cultural ethnocentrism was expressed especially strongly when Maya groups became closed corporate communities. These stereotypes were strengthened during the colonial period when Mayas were forced to remain concentrated in Indian towns (*reducciones*) and thus the links to and knowledge of other surrounding Maya cultures became weaker. Despite the reductionist system that controlled their lives through the last five hundred years, modern Mayas are in the process of understanding that they shared a common culture, as exemplified by their shared calendrical rituals, cyclical ceremonies, and languages (Cojtí Cuxil 1991; Rodríguez Guaján 1989).

Mayas have specific identities that they accept as theirs. In creating these identities, Mayas find it preferable to call themselves by the names of their linguistic communities (I am a Jakaltek, a K'iche', a Q'anjob'al, a Mam, an Ixil, etc.). Then the individual identifies with the aggregate of being a Guatemalan Maya. Among the general Maya population it is not common to hear a person say, "Soy indio" (I am an Indian). *Indio* has been used, on the one hand, as a pejorative by non-Mayas and, on the other, by some Maya intellectuals as a whip for political reaffirmation of the "Indian" identity. Nevertheless, as descendants of a great Maya civilization, we have an identity for ourselves as a Maya nation, and we do not need to maintain the stereotypes and images imposed on us by the invaders. I personally prefer to use the term "Maya" to speak of the native people of the Mayab'. But the use of this term is optional, depending on the ideology that guides the political struggle in which those who work for Maya culture are engaged (Cojtí Cuxil 1991; Adams 1990). Nevertheless, I suggest that "Maya" should be used as the central identity of the people of the Mayab'. We must redefine ourselves through Maya ideology and politics if we are to understand Maya culture and promote it for the future. One major step in this process is to get rid of the denigrating categories that distort our modern Maya images.

To call ourselves "Mayas" is a political act, since Mayas have been called *indios*, *naturales*, or *primitivos* by politicians, anthropologists, missionaries, and other non-Mayas. It is interesting to note that some modern Mayas from the most isolated communities are now calling themselves "Mayas" and are proud of retaking such an empowering identity. "Maya" was used in the past by the indigenous people of the Mayab' to name themselves. For example, the use of the name "Maya" was recorded on Columbus's fourth voyage (1503–4). Columbus's crew intercepted a canoe and "the natives in it gave him to understand that they were merchants, and came from a land called MAIA" (Brinton 1969: 10). In native and nonnative documents of the postconquest, the term "Maya" was widely used.

> *The natives of all this region called themselves* Maya uinic, Maya men, *or* ah Mayaa, *those of Maya; their language was* Maya than, *the Maya speech; a native woman was* Maya ch'uplal; *and their ancient capital was* Maya pan, *the Maya banner, for there of old was set up the standard of the nation, the elaborately worked banner of brilliant feathers, which, in peace and in war, marked the rallying point of the Confederacy.* (Brinton 1969: 11–12)

In this historical context, modern Mayas view themselves as inheritors of the great Maya culture and are proud of calling themselves Maya. With this consciousness of being Maya and not just "Indians," modern Mayas will contribute to the awakening of the Maya nation, to ensure its life for the future. I believe that by renaming ourselves with historically established Maya names, we will begin to overcome domination and control imposed by those who insist on considering us inferior. Until now the power of naming has been in the hands of outsiders, and of course, the one who names is the one who takes control. This must change for us if our Maya culture is to flourish again in the future *katuns* (prophetic and calendrical time cycles of twenty years). It is not for being "Mayas" that the dominant classes have persecuted and killed us since Columbus but for being placed in the denigrating category "indios."

Indians as Subversives: Dangerous Identities

HISTORICALLY ALL MAYA ethnic groups of Guatemala have suffered the same oppression throughout the past five centuries of Western domination. But in spite of their marginalization, each Maya group has contributed to the development of the nation-state. Guatemala draws its distinctiveness from using Maya symbols to create a "national identity" (Anderson 1988). Maya symbols have dominated the allegoric representations of nationality, especially in the image of Guatemala projected to the international community. Many organizations, both Guatemalan and international, profit from the exploitation of Maya culture.[2] "[In] Guatemala, everybody is Indian when the occasion is right," wrote Carol Hendrickson. "Non-Indians from the national level down equate 'Indian' with 'Guatemalan' in expressions of Guatemalan national identity. . . . [Thus] by proclaiming ties to a rich Mayan heritage, Guatemalans are united and shown to be different from every other people on earth" (1985: 22). International recognition of Maya culture as one of the world's great traditions is dignifying for Mayas themselves, but the discrimination, repression, and genocide to which it also condemns them in their own nation is insupportable.

Before the violence of 1982 people from different Maya communities and languages could travel for any purpose to other Maya communities. But with the advent of violence in the Kuchumatan highlands, ethnic groups began to isolate themselves and to turn away Maya and non-Maya people from outside their community. Outsiders were suspect because the army used indigenous people to spy on Maya communities. In this way freedom of movement was restricted (Montejo 1987). People also became suspicious when ladino merchants came to town suddenly and set up businesses or training centers for young people in the martial arts. These outsiders were suspected of being "ears" for the army and the Guatemalan government.

If the mistrust of people from a different town or ethnic group eroded the traditional Maya sense of kinship, the formation of the civil patrols played an even more drastic role in destroying solidarity among villagers and between communities. The most elemental human rights and the Maya ideal of hospitality gave way to unspeakable behavior and treatment of the people in Maya communities. The indigenous people were condemned to die, and when they were dead, the military officers would say, "Don't bury those dogs, those pigs; they are guerrillas. Let the buzzards take care of their fucking bodies." This way of thinking shocked the Maya people who were accustomed to burying their dead with rituals and great respect. Under the command of the army, the people were prevented from expressing sorrow, even for the death of their own relatives. This was an attempt to destroy the dignity and humanity of Maya communities. Because of the insistence of the army that each civil patrol give them captives as proof of having obeyed military orders, the villagers generally had to produce undocumented people from other ethnic groups so that they could avoid reprisal (Montejo 1987). These civil patrol duties, carried out under army control, widened the existing gap between different ethnic groups. The army thought that certain ethnic groups were more likely to be guerrilla collaborators and took special control over those villages with the help of the civil patrols and paramilitary groups.

In 1982, during Ríos Montt's short presidency, the cultural traditions of the Maya seem to have been damaged to the core. Maya culture was attacked from every possible angle, and the natives were silenced and separated from their ancient roots. In this context "the first legacy of *la violencia* was silence" (Warren 1993: 32). The elders had earlier protested the destruction of Maya culture by the catechists of Catholic Action but now were forced into silence in the face of the civil patrols (Wilson 1991). There was fear of a demise of the Maya culture, as predicted and anticipated by the army.

As noted above, the army and most of ladino Guatemala equated "Indians" with subversives. The genocide of thousands of Guatemalans, Mayas and non-Mayas alike, was justified as a religious war against the evil of communism. While the army carried out the killing of thousands of innocent Mayas and poor peasants, they argued that they were killing guerrillas. Although the destruction was generalized among the Guatemalan population, Mayas were more affected in terms of both numbers and cultural destruction. As Chilin Hultaxh related,

> Properly speaking about the war itself, it was unleashed in all its savagery against the indigenous population. Then [the army] gave preference to the "mestizo" population, which we commonly call ladinos. They were given preferential treatment, because in Guatemala racism is still very strong. There is racial discrimination against the indigenous people. The "Indians" have been considered within army circles as an infamous race, ignorant people not capable of assimilating the new technology, that we have to be always in the fields and doing the hard work with little pay.

Refugee: A New Category of Social Identity

SINCE WORLD WAR II the increase in the number of refugees around the world has been startling (Edwards 1988; Ferris 1987; Haines 1989; Loescher and Monahan 1989). The displacement of people from their homelands has demonstrated the difficulties that the modern nation-state creates by imposing its political ideology on ethnic minorities (Worsley 1984). "The twentieth century has witnessed many transformations in the organization of peoples and nations, and not the least of these is the creation of a new category of social identity: the refugee" (Edwards 1988: 313).

The social identity "refugee" is not a desirable one, as it is imposed on those who have been persecuted for political, religious, or ethnic reasons and have abandoned their homelands forcibly because of war, ethnic strife, economic hardship, or even their own government. When the Guatemalan Mayas crossed the border into Mexico, they became something else: refugees. As refugees they have become more politicized. Under this premise we can agree with Francesco Pellizzi that the condition of refuge "often contributes to the creation of an ethnic identity" (1988: 166). Refugees are engaged in a continuous struggle to maintain their identity and to avoid being assimilated completely into the host culture, in this case, to become Mexicanized. This struggle was more intense for the adults and those born in Guatemala who were old enough to remember their homeland than for those who were raised in the refugee camps. For the youngsters, life in the refugee camp has been "normal," for their contacts have been limited to Mexican peasant communities and towns close to the Guatemala-Mexico border. The complaint of many refugee parents concerning repatriation to Guatemala is that "the young boys and girls do not want to go back to Guatemala. They argue that they already know life in Mexico and have their own social relations with people in other camps or communities. So they prefer to stay, instead of going back to a place that they do not know or that they have heard to be 'unsafe' and dangerous" (pers. com. January 1993).

Because of the restrictiveness of the refugee camps, refugees also have been seen as "prisoners" (Pellizzi 1988). Certainly the refugees were like prisoners at the beginning of camp life (1981–89). During this period their movement was restricted, and they decided not to use their traditional dress and language so as to avoid being recognized as illegal aliens by Mexican immigration authorities. They were also mobilized and relocated against their will several times, which makes the "prisoner" analogy more pertinent. But as the refugees became more politicized, they developed organizations that fought for their rights.

The earliest and strongest of these organizations was the CCPP. The impetus for organizing came from refugees in sympathy with the guerrilla organizations in Guatemala. One original purpose was to provide a consistent voice to the outside world—to the Mexican and international media, to human rights and solidarity groups—so that the refugees as a group had a voice in the world arena. Ultimately the CCPP became the official refugee negotiator for the return.

Another major organization was the women's group, Mama Maquín. The men who were active in the CCPP did not always recognize the specific problems of the women refugees so women organized Mama Maquín to address education, skill training, literacy, and leadership training. Led by the more political women refugees and aided by a number of international solidarity organizations, Mama Maquín attempted to reach all refugee women through camp meetings and camp representatives.

The third, but less politicizing, force came from the Catholic church, which organized catechists in the camps and maintained the Catholic structure and rituals. The role of the Diocese of San Cristóbal in meeting basic food and health needs gave it great credibility with the refugees, although catechists, especially those working in multiethnic camps, did not generally have leadership positions.

Because of the Mexican government's concern for "political exiles" and human rights issues, the refugees, by calling themselves political refugees, were provided more freedom of space and movement outside the camps, at least until the first wave of *retornados* (returnees) on January 20, 1993.

The refugee status is then a liminal one. In this condition of statelessness, refugees are seen as dangerous and as a threat to the nation-state system. There is also a tendency to pathologize the uprooted refugee. For example, Lisa Malkki (1992) states that after World War II scholars and policy makers often defined refugees as a politicomoral problem. It is in this context that the refugee has become a new object or field of study. Nevertheless,

> the more contemporary field of "refugee studies" is quite different in spirit from the postwar literature. However, it shares with earlier texts the premise that refugees are necessarily "a problem." They are not ordinary people, but represent, rather, an anomaly requiring specialized corrective and therapeutic interventions. It is striking how often the abundant literature claiming refugees as its object of study locates "the problem" not in the political conditions or processes that produce massive territorial displacements of people, but, rather, within the bodies and minds (even souls) of people categorized as refugees. (Malkki 1992: 33)

The Guatemalan refugees in Mexico have also had to cope with an anomalous social identity. Mayas have been able to depoliticize the dangerous identities imposed on them by reviving their Maya cultural traditions in the camps, which shows the world at large that they are not dangerous criminals or pathologically ill. But the refugee status is also problematic for several other reasons. First, the land on which they are settled is not theirs, and they want to return to the land where their placentas were buried, according to their tradition of symbolically rooting them to their homeland. They can work and live in Mexico, but the land is not theirs. Uncertainty is the most difficult part of living as refugees. Second, social relations with the Mexicans have often been unequal and abusive, as many Mexican peasants, especially those without Maya roots, have treated the Maya refugees as inferiors. According to Manuel Santos, a Jakaltek Maya refugee composer and singer in the camps,

The Mexicans call us names, and when they shout at us the word *refugiado* [refugee], they use it in a racist way, as if we were inferior or a category of people that has to be treated badly. I know that we are "refugiados" and that this term is used widely, but when the Mexicans use it to name us, they inject it with other meanings, transforming it into an insult.[4]

Something similar happened to the Q'anjob'al, Jakaltek, and Akatek Mayan refugees in Florida.[5] As most of the Maya immigrants to the United States work on farms, they have had to compete for the same jobs with other immigrants primarily from Mexico, Haiti, the Dominican Republic, and Jamaica. Guatemalan Maya farmworkers are at the bottom of the scale in the struggle for identity. For example, Mexican migrant workers call the Q'anjob'al Mayas "Guatemalitos" or "Chakuates," both of which have racist connotations.[6] Mayas are seen as inferior by other immigrants, even though they do the same hard work. But Mayas have not remained passive; they have created names for those who would discriminate against them. The difference is that they use those names in their Maya languages, thus having a weapon by which they exteriorize their anger and laugh at those who discriminate against them. They have also managed to re-create their Maya communities in Florida and continue their cultural traditions and the religious celebrations honoring their patron saint, San Miguel.

"Refugee" as a social category has thus been made problematical, and refugees have struggled to create new identities for themselves that are more advantageous according to their social and political situations. In the refugee camps in Mexico, despite the different identities imposed on the refugees, their own project of renaming themselves "Mayas" has become essential in their struggle to maintain their link and identity with their homelands—past, present, and future.

The use of the term "Maya" was widespread in the refugee camps. It was used in the names of two major cultural organizations, Maya-Honh and Ah Mayab' (We the Original People of the Maya Land). Both groups traveled to various refugee camps, singing, reading poetry, and telling stories and stressing that the refugees are Mayas because their roots come from the ancient Maya civilization. In the Jakaltek-speaking areas, the refugees used the book *El Q'anil* to retell the stories of their origin and their ancestors. A Q'anjob'al refugee, when asked what the term "Maya" meant, responded, "Chi yala tato hey ko ti', tato yik'alto heb'naj payvinaj jeyi, tato ah tx'otx'onh" (It means that we have our language, that we are descendants of the ancient ones, and that we are from the land). Mayanness was also reinforced by the camp schoolteachers, who stressed to their students that they were Mayas from Guatemala, a country to which they would return some day.

The alternative term "campesino" was used in the highlands before exile, and it continued to be used in the camps. Campesinos are people who make their living working the milpa, the land. This term, used to identify people by their mode of production, has roots in the ladino and leftist political dialectic of organizing workers and is so used because there are also ladino campesinos. It is thus a class-based concept. Many refugees will say, "I am a Maya campesino." But the label "campesino" is superficial and does not hold the powerful and deep identity that "Maya" does. It speaks only to the type of work they do. A man could become a mason or a merchant, but he would remain a Maya. And in the camps many cannot be campesinos because there is no land to farm.

But the refugees are, above all, victims: men, women, and children uprooted from their homelands, who have found refuge in a hostile territory where they are unwelcome and treated with suspicion. As Elie Wiesel has written, "There is some honor attached to the name [refugee]. To be a refugee from Nazi Germany or communist Stalinist Russia was an honor, a privilege. It still is" (1983: 17). In the same way Guatemalan Maya refugees have managed to escape from the bloody army of

Guatemala, and as survivors of that holocaust they also are entitled to respect. Unfortunately, the genocide suffered by the Mayas has largely remained unknown, not only to the world but also to the rest of Guatemala.

The Culture of Resistance in the Refugee Camps

THE REVITALIZATION OF Maya culture through songs and poetry is a form of cultural resistance in the refugee camps. The different forms of resistance against neocolonial domination are "expressed in the current struggle [of indigenous people] in recuperating their legitimate political, economic, and sociocultural rights" (Sam Colop 1991: 36–37; see also Scott 1985).

From this perspective, the Mayas in the refugee camps succeeded in establishing a positive self-image and redefining themselves as a group. Their lives were transformed in many ways, and because of their status as refugees, they learned new skills and techniques to survive. After more than a decade in exile the refugees understood better the sociocultural, political, and economic circumstances that motivated their exile, and they have resisted a destructive assimilation and the erosion of their cultural traditions.

The refugees managed to adapt (sometimes very painfully) to the restrictions and limitations of the refugee camps. As in the past, the Mayas demonstrated the ability to develop strategies of accommodation to adverse situations and to reconstruct or replicate their communities, under the most oppressive circumstances, using elements that they appropriated from other cultures. "The fact that adaptation and not total disintegration was the Maya response to conquest can be accounted for partly by their own resources, which included a cognitive framework for assimilating conquest and a set of strategies for accommodation, developed during a long pre-Hispanic history of foreign domination" (Farriss 1984: 9).

Maya people know that a culture that lacks the ability to adapt in alien territory to threatening outside forces will die or be defeated (Farriss 1984). Mayas have lived for more than a decade in exile without property or many material possessions, but they have survived as a "community" thanks to their skills in weaving, communal work, and organization and in developing other types of economic production. In some cases they have accepted Mexican elements into their cultural traditions, and as a result a reelaboration and cultural transformation has occurred.

But the refugees have not been completely isolated from the mother culture of their Guatemalan communities. There has been cultural continuity with their own traditions as well as new contacts with other Maya cultural traditions. From this cultural sharing in the camps, new forms of artistic expression have been developed by the refugees that can be called the "culture of resistance." This culture of resistance is rooted in the work of artistic groups that have recovered their native musical instruments and traditional dance costumes from Guatemala and dedicated themselves to expressing the reasons for their exile and their feelings about it in their songs, poetry, and theater.

The revival of these aspects of the Maya culture is of vital importance. Traditionally after a major catastrophe Mayas have reworked their culture through indigenous art and literature. During the violence that affected Maya culture in the early 1980s, dozens—if not hundreds—of marimba players, native organizers of traditional dances, and storytellers were killed. During the years of repression of native communities, especially in 1982–83, even the marimba was silenced. The traditional festivals were canceled, and the vivid community life was overshadowed by death and destruction. Worst of all, the indigenous people were also silenced; it was impossible to openly criticize the destruction of their lives and their culture. In addition, outside religious organizations (mainly fundamentalist Protestant and based in the United States) arrived in Maya villages to criticize the traditional Maya way of life. They employed a strategy previously used by Catholic Action in the 1950s and 1960s, before the intensificiation of army repression in the Kuchumatan highlands, and preached against the religious festivals, dances, and music as an expression and continuation of their "paganism." They argued that the marimba and the guitars were instruments of the devil. It was necessary for Mayas to bury and destroy such objects, they said, because their traditional practices had attracted this horrible reign of death and destruction.

During the massacres in the Kuchumatan highlands, some indigenous people managed to escape with their marimbas and guitars; others hid their instruments and returned for them later. So in the refugee camps there has been a strong revival of native artistic expression. For example, several musical groups have created new songs in Maya languages and have entertained the refugees in camps along the Mexican border. In the United States, Canada, and Central America, marimba groups have been promoting Maya cultural traditions and denouncing the violations of human rights in Guatemala.

In July 1992 I visited refugee camps in the Comalapa and Comitán border regions and met with several Mayas who wanted to save, promote, and revitalize Maya culture. As we discussed the values of the Maya tradition, they recognized the need to participate actively in the process of cultural revitalization. They organized themselves into an indigenous association to promote Maya culture and named it Ah Mayab'.[7] In a newsletter to publicize their activities, Ah Mayab' stated,

> As Mayans, we recognize that we are called upon to continue the cultural heritage of our ancestors and promote it for future generations. Thus, we are pained to see the tears of our elders who have witnessed for centuries the destruction of our cultural values. We cannot permit the total destruction of this great civilization; therefore we wish to reaffirm and revive our cultural identity, making it flourish amidst an atmosphere of extreme anxiety. And so we stand after five hundred years, a

wise and dynamic people, intensely participating in the process of rewriting our own histories. Also, as inheritors of the Mayan culture, we realize that our people have a worldview different from European cultures. In this right, we want our traditions, ways of thinking and indigenous philosophies to be respected. We seek the brotherhood and sisterhood and solidarity of all peoples to live in peace: not only with people, but in harmony with nature as well.

Then Ah Mayab' presented a brief history of how the association originated in the refugee camps.

In the refugee camps, silence reigned and hung over us like an ominous cloud. In our longing, we could see from afar our majestic mountain ranges. Little by little, we began to hear again the weeping of the violin, the echo of the drum, and interwoven in the music were memories of home. Then our hearts rejoiced and our minds were inspired, as our poets, musicians and writers began to write and sing about the sorrows and joys of our peoples. In the camps, we despaired of not being able to wear our multicolored dress for fear of being deported. We spoke our Mayan languages in private for fear of being discriminated against. We were in danger of losing our rainbow-colored identity. But our Mayan artists, such as the group Maya-Honh, kept on singing and bringing hope to the camps. (Ah Mayab' 1992)

In 1989 I went to Nicolás Bravo, located in the Comalapa region of southern Mexico, and met the members of Maya-Honh. The group is mainly composed of Jakaltek Mayas and is perhaps the best-known group of singers in the Maya language in the Jakaltek region of the Kuchumatan. With the destruction of the Jakaltek Maya communities close to the Mexican border, this group took its musical instruments and crossed the border with thousands of other Mayas in August 1982. It has been successful in expressing in song a social critique of the Guatemalan political turmoil and has promoted solidarity among the ethnic groups coexisting in the refugee camps. Their songs have been widely heard in the refugee camps. Their impact has been strengthened because the songs are based on the common experience of the Maya people, the massacres and abandonment of their villages, and because they write and sing in Jakaltek and Q'anjob'al, the native languages of most of the refugees.

Maya-Honh has brought solace and amusement to the suffering refugees, thus creating a sociocultural network that has strengthened solidarity. Their songs have been broadcast by Radio Comitán and Radio Margaritas, the latter dedicated to promoting the indigenous culture of the Tojolab'al Mayas of the Mexico-Guatemala border. Inside Guatemala these broadcasts have reached the Maya communities from which the musicians came. And Q'anjob'al and Jakaltek refugees have taped their songs, especially those referring to the camps where interethnic marriages or romances have occurred. Some Mexican Mayas have also learned the songs and participated in the dances or musical groups of the refugees, as in Rancho Tejas or in the Mexican communities of Colón and Guadalupe Victoria. Mexicans have also been attracted to the cultural expressiveness of the refugees, which has promoted friendship and mutual enjoyment. Artistic groups such as Maya-Honh seek to maintain social solidarity and to express the collective memories of their persecution in their motherland and their trials and tribulations in an alien territory.

Conclusion

IN THE CAMPS in southern Mexico, the refugees have reinforced their communal way of life, and this practice has been expressed in their communal projects and the structure of the refugee camps. The Mexican people have been very helpful in allowing the Guatemalan refugees to develop new approaches to survival and resistance. Ethnic relations were strained at the beginning, especially between Mexican peasants and Maya refugees, and in some cases they continued to be conflictive. But when most Mexican peasants and hosts recognized the circumstances that caused Mayas to abandon their homelands, attitudes of mutual respect and understanding were initiated.

Despite the early conflicts of the refugees with Mexican immigration authorities and the forced relocation to the Yucatán peninsula, Maya refugees recognized that the Mexican government had historically treated the Mexican Maya and other Mexican indigenous people better than the Guatemalan government did. The Mexican government showed more appreciation for and provided more support to its indigenous communities, as compared to the violent treatment of the Guatemalan Maya by their own government.

Cultural sharing was evident in established refugee camps. But refugees who chose to live in Mexican towns and cities had other problems in their social relations with Mexican mestizos. For those refugees, the maintenance of cultural traditions and the enforcement of ethnic identity was more difficult. Their children assimilated more because their parents were unwilling to talk to them in the Maya language or to speak about their culture for fear of being identified as illegal aliens. In official refugee camps, however, schools emphasize Maya cultural values. This knowledge of the past and the historical relationship between Maya linguistic regions of the Mayab' creates a new understanding of what it means to be Maya, which in turn reinforces the links of modern Mayas to the land and their ancient traditions.

Another major process of ethnic relations operating among Maya refugees is the challenge to the traditional and rigid endogamy. In past decades it was uncommon for a Jakaltek to marry someone outside the Jakaltek ethnic boundaries. Each Maya group maintained its strategies of cultural distinctiveness and avoided mixing with outsiders. Each group, of course, obeyed its own systems of family structure, lineages, and land tenure (Casaverde 1976; Davis 1988b). But in the refugee camps the shared communal work and strong solidarity opened the door for mixed marriages among ethnic groups. For example, some Jakalteks have married Q'anjob'al women, Mames have married Mexicans, and Chujes have married Q'anjob'ales or Jakalteks. With the undermining of restrictions imposed by traditional endogamous marriage rules in Maya communities has come a recognition of their "equal value" as humans and Mayas.

Intermarriage has also promoted closer relationships and ruptured the ethnic barriers and ethnocentric views of the other. In the long run there is the possibility of a Maya integration, which would give birth to a unity of Maya ethnic groups and establish the basis for a stronger Maya national identity. It has become obvious that governmental repression has not achieved its desired goal of eliminating the Maya cultural tradition expressed in modern Maya communities. Instead a dialectical process is operating in which the unity and solidarity of all the people of the Mayab' is being promoted as a response to the attempted genocide against the Guatemalan Maya population. "Thus we see that Indians, as a result of consciousness raising in the past decade, combined with their suffering, have experienced a dramatic awakening. . . . Now, when Indians come in contact with other Indians, regardless of language, in the words of a Mam Indian, 'we feel more human warmth, we feel closer, more fraternal'" (Manz 1988c: 89).

A common understanding has arisen among indigenous people, a solidarity that has revived the sense of belonging to a common Maya heritage.[8] In the refugee camps religious activities and rituals united the people, and there has been a mutual learning of the other's language and traditions. Of course, ethnic relations in the camps have not been entirely harmonious. In some camps refugees have been able to manage their differences and solve their common problems; in bigger camps the tendency has been to split into smaller camps to avoid major conflicts. The latter was the case in La Gloria and Cieneguitas, where internal conflicts concerning political leadership caused splits. For the most part there is a strong respect for family and for neighbors in the camps. Exile has showed the refugees that in Guatemala many dysfunctional behaviors such as drinking, spousal abuse, and ethnic tensions were rooted in the system of oppression and marginalization under which the Mayas lived. In the refugee camps there has been a reevaluation of the past that has brought changes in attitudes.

The major transformations can be summarized as follows: the refugees have become politicized as they have questioned their social relations Guatemala; they have grown proud and conscious of their Mayanness and their cultural ethnicity; they have developed a better understanding of the politics of national life and their relations to the ladino culture as another component of the Guatemalan nation; the refugees' worldview has been expanded during their exile, especially as they have shared their knowledge and productive techniques with their Mexican hosts; and finally, there is interest among the more politicized refugees in understanding their relationship to a greater underlying Maya tradition that gives them a Maya identity. All of these transformations have given them a better way of thinking and conducting their lives in exile.

Meanwhile the Mexican Mayas have also learned more about the history of Guatemala and the refugees; they have come to understand that the distance between all Maya people is not unbridgeable, so there will be possibilities for wider cultural contact among Mayas in the future. The Mayan-Honh and Ah Mayab' have been very effective in contributing to this transformation. These musical groups created songs of suffering, exile, hope, and return and shared them in the camps and in the larger Mexican and Guatemalan Maya communities.

10

SONGS AND POETRY
FROM THE CAMPS

Songs

THE EXPRESSION OF thoughts and feelings in songs composed and sung in Mayan flourished in the camps. The lyrics grew out of the refugees' longing for home, grief over all they had lost, and responses to their current lives. The tunes were composed by the authors or singers and were based on simple Maya melodies, relatively uncomplicated in structure and rhythm. Most of the time the composition, arrangement, or lyrics were the work of an individual artist. When the lyrics were completed the writer would take them to the group, which would practice them until it was ready for performance in public. In this way songs were written by individuals or were the result of collaborative efforts of groups of refugees or musicians. Among the songs composed by Maya-Honh, "María Q'anjob'al" is one of the most popular. It was written by José and Alfonso Rojas, Jakaltek refugees at Nicolás Bravo, for a Q'anjob'al Maya girl living in La Cieneguita. The song expresses feelings of love unfettered by the usual ethnic barriers that existed in Guatemala.

MARÍA Q'ANJOB'AL

As I sing this song
I give you my heart,
remembering those times
when I also lived in this place,
remembering those times
when I also lived in this place.

I came to know many friends
and the people of this place,
and that is how I knew that Cieneguita
it is the cradle of love,
and that is how I knew that Cieneguita
it is the cradle of love.

During the year 'eighty-four,
I thought the camp a garden
where there were many flowers,
and one of those I cut for myself,
where there were many flowers,
and one of those I cut for myself.

That beautiful flower I had chosen
unknown to me was her name,
but very soon someone told me
that María was her name,
but very soon someone told me
that María was her name.

Oh, how pretty you are, María!
what a soft and nice perfume,
I will take you to Jacaltenango
the town where I was born

I will take you to Jacaltenango
the town where I was born.

Ay, María of my life,
when you went to wash clothes
in the Morelia River
I gave you all my love,
in the Morelia River
I gave you all my love.

The trumpeter and the mockingbird
were witnesses to our love
so at the foot of a cypress tree
you said that good is for good.
so at the foot of the cypress tree
you said that good is for good.

With your hair blown by the wind
we returned slowly together
and when we reached the road,
I gave you a tenderest kiss.
and when we reached the road
I gave you a tenderest kiss.

This Jakaltek must say now good-bye
to María, the Q'anjob'al girl,
she is a flower from Cieneguita.
whom I will remember forever,
she is a flower from Cieneguita,
whom I will remember forever.

Maya-Honh has also composed songs of the refugees' sadness and pain. In 1985 a young boy was drowned in the Grijalva River at the edge of the Nicolás Bravo refugee camp. The father's lament at the death of his son inspired José Rojas to write the following song.

MARTINCITO

As I start to sing my song
I ask your permission first,
because this is my sad story
that I want to tell you now.

Martín, was the name of my son
and he was fourteen years old.
He died in the year 'eighty-five
on the thirty-first of July.

But what hurts me the most, brothers,
is that my son was drowned
in the Grijalva River
of the colony of Nicolás.

I plead with you, oh, my God,
that you give me patience,
that you take to yourself my son Martín
whom I buried after the fourth day.

I just brought my little son
to seek refuge in this place.
But bad luck has struck me,
to lose the life of Martín.

With this, I tell you,
I, Miguel Francisco, who suffers so
with my eyes full of tears,
always will I remember Martín.

In December 1992 I visited the refugee camps again. At the Cocalito camp a new musical group was organizing and writing songs in Mayan about their exodus and life in the camps. Some of the songs also talked about the massacres in Guatemala that forced them out of their homelands. The following song was written by refugees from Villa Cocalito and honors the sixteen men killed by the army in El Limonar on January 6, 1982.

HEB' YA' WAJLANH-WANH

Che ya' niman k'ulal jinh-an
xhko b'itnhenotoj ni'an son ti' an
haxkam mach xhk'aytoj yinh ko k'ul-an
tzet xu skamtoq heb' ya' wajlanh-wanh.

Hune swaj tz'ayik enero-al
b'ay xpotx'lax heb' ya jet konhob'
ay heb' ya' aykoj yinh stzoti' komam dyos
yet x-apni hune xtx'ojal tu'.

Okojonh tzujnoj yinh tzet xu heb' ya' ti'
xhko txumuloj hune' sk'ulch'anil
tzet jekoj sat yib'anh q'inal ti'
haktu' chu jilnoj naj sk'ulch'anil.

Members of Ah Mayab' rehearsing for a performance in Villa Cocalito

Hune' swaj tz'ayik enero-al tu'
hununonh mach xhk'aitoj yinh ko k'ul
tzet xu ko poh-nikantoj ko b'a
ayonh joktoj, ayonh jelkantij.

Haktu' b'ay chonh taq'likanan
kaw niman che yute he k'ul jinhan
xhko b'itnhentoj ni'an son ti'an
komo yinh janma xhpitzk'atijan.

Haktu' b'ay xhtanhkan ni'an son ti'
yalb'anil heb' ya' wajlanh-wahn
mach xhk'ay he k'ul mak xhb'itnhentoj ni'an son ti'
ah Limonar heb'o' xhb'itnhentoj.

THE SIXTEEN MEN

Have patience with us all
as we sing this song
because we cannot forget
how the sixteen men were killed.

It was on the sixth of January
when the massacre of our people occurred.
They were praying and singing to God
when this evil befell them.

Let's understand what happened to them
so we may see the truth,
and from this we may realize
that we should live in a better way.

That is why that day January sixth
none of us can ever forget;
how we all became dispersed
as we took different paths to save our lives.

This is how we end our song
have patience with us all,
as we have sung this song
since we must sing it from our heart.

This is how we conclude this song
in memory of the sixteen men,
and remember too, those singing to you
from Limonar, the singers of this song.

In August 1992 I met Manuel Santos, a twenty-year-old Jakaltek who had written many songs in the refugee camp of Nuevo Nicolás. On the occasion of the five hundred years of indigenous resistance he wrote and sang the following song.

The Five Hundred Years

Five hundred years ago
my ancestors had a dove,
it was beautiful, and a happy one.
Every morning it sang for them
and with its melodious song
made them laugh and laugh.

But, then, someone came and shot at it,
wounded it flew, wounded it flew away.
But, then, someone came and shot at it
wounded it flew, wounded it flew away.

My ancestors became mute when it flew away
with its wounds bleeding without stopping.
My ancestors cried when it never came back
and my ancestors died without seeing it again.
Ay! without seeing it again!

They lost their freedom, and it didn't return
because the one who shot it never abandoned the land.

The sky also changed its colors when it flew away
and its blood fell as if saying, "Good-bye."

My ancestors became mute when it flew away
with its wounds bleeding without stopping.
My ancestors cried when it never came back
and my ancestors died without seeing it again.
Ay! without seeing it again!

Poetry and Prose

THE POETS AND writers in the refugee camps were the least-known artists, as their work was rarely performed in public and was not a collaborative effort. Pascual Juan Sebastián wrote poems without having the opportunity to share them with anyone. Similarly, the Jakaltek Maya poet Antonio L. Cota García spent a great deal of time writing poems and stories, none of which was published for a local audience. I stayed in touch with Cota and was able to assist in his participation in the symposium "Native American Festival of Poets and Writers: Returning the Gift," which was held at the University of Oklahoma in July 1992.

The Guatemalan army attack on the El Chupadero camp on April 30, 1982, was the basis for the following poem by Pascual Juan Sebastián, a Chuj Maya poet and schoolteacher at La Gloria camp.

"THE NIGHT OF APRIL 30, 1984"

On that sad and silent night
of April the 30th, 1984,
a fresh and quiet breeze
was blowing through the camp,
and only the monotonous
chirping of the crickets

broke the silence
of the dark night.

Eyelids were closed
in a deep sleep,
and hearts beat
with an immense fear
when the echo of the mountains
repeated furiously
the explosion of the firing guns
against thousands of refugees.

It was two o'clock in the morning
the most sad and terrible hour
of our history,
the bitterest night.

Then, through thorns,
bushes and barbed wires,
and in the darkness of the night
we ran to defend ourselves
from the bullets
of those criminals,
who even outside the border
of our loved country
continued to persecute us.

The blood that was spilled
from the seven who died
will never be forgotten
because with pain in our hearts
now and forever we will remember
that night of bitterness
on April 30th, 1984.

The following poem by Cota, even in translation, displays his considerable talent.

"THE OIL LAMP"

It is ten o'clock at night
Saturday, May 14, 1988.
Barely, an oil lamp, blackened
by its long use, gives me its light,
and it is similar to my age and the pains
that consume my weakened body,
tied to the history
of refuge in Mexico.

Arrow without rest
wind without destiny.
My desk?
Just an old flat-bottomed wooden washtub
cracked at the bottom
like the history of my country,
split in two, split in two,
where the voice
is only a voice which nobody hears,
and the ears deaf to voices,
hearing as weak as the same oil lamp
that hardly gives me its light.

The palace where we live?
everybody fits in it,
and makes us laugh.
Its size, four square meters
and inside everybody fits
and we still welcome everyone.
It is incredible! someone would say:
How can so many live with so little
and so few with too much?

The oil lamp has survived seven years
while the history is split in two

but its halves move in tandem
attending with loyalty its mission
to walk always with you.
How many would dislike its presence?
How many arms would raise against its innocence
as if in reality, the oil lamp
would be responsible for the impertinence
of illuminating even the one that dislikes its light.

But, if they would know
that its light is the nested future,
if they would know that its heat
is love that overflows,
Then, my oil lamp and my old age
would be well accepted.
. . . But no!

We are intruders who do not take anything,
we are strangers who invade them by fear,
we are old threads of an ancient glory
that cause shame to those who don't know our history
and admiration for those that value our culture.

And this is how our lives are consumed
within the livelihood of our experience,
and even if so many condemn our presence
the oil lamp will continue with its dim light
and on the cracked bottom of the old wooden washtub
we will continue night after night, our duty
of writing down the history of our people in exile.

Maya culture has been constantly revived and revitalized throughout the long history of oppression against the Maya people. It appears that extreme violence against Maya communities has prompted artists and writers to chronicle the events. This revitalization of Maya culture is a collective effort and reinforces pride in being Maya. Mayas are now inscribing their footprints and their history for the future and securing their place, where they will have a stronger voice and presence in a reconstructed, multicultural Guatemala.

The following is a song of protest and hope called "Sb'it Refugiado" (The Song of Refugee) composed by a Jakaltek Maya, Mat Leonh (Mateo Castillo), and written in Popb'al Ti' in the refugee camp of Nicolás Bravo in 1988.

"Sb'it Refugiado"

Kaw niman che yute he k'ul winhan
xwalnoj hin b'isk'ulal te yet
Kaw xhtz'akanoj hin k'ul winhan
xhtit yul hin k'ulan tz'et xwa'lean
Kaw xhtz'akanoj hin k'ul winhan
xhtit yul hin k'ulan tz'et xwa'lean.

Yet kin eltij b'eteti'an
kaw b'isk'ulal wekanojan
kochnhe matxa chin meltzohojan
sat hin tx'otx'al b'ay xkin pitzk'a han.
Kochnhe matxa chin meltzohojan
sat hin tx'otx'al b'ay xkin pitzk'a han.

Matoj tzet yuxin xkin el-han
yu hantaq wet anmahil xkaman
yinh tu' xkin hok hin txumulujan
tato meb'a-honh kamb'chal jeyih
yinh tu' xkin hok hin txumulujan
tato meb'a-honh kamb'chal jeyih.

Oxhimih che txumu' tzet xhwalan
ko watx'enkoj ko b'a yin sk'ulal
kat xin jalni tet juninal

tzet chu skolnoj sb'a tet naj xtx'ojal.
kat xin jalni tet juninal
tzet chu skolnoj sb'a tet naj xtx'ojal.

Yaja' wal yinh hin meltzoan
xhtik'a apnoj stz'ayikalil
komo wal naj st'inhanil ti'
sat yib'anh q'inal xhkankan naj.
komo wal naq st'inhanil ti'
sat yib'anh q'inal xhkankan naj.

Haktu' chu hin taq'likanan
niman che yute he k'ul winhan
tato k'ul mato tx'oj xhwalan
yaja' ya' yekoj yinh wanma han.
Tato k'ul mato tx'oj xhwalan
yaja' ya' yekoj yinh wanma han.

"THE SONG OF THE REFUGEE"

Have patience all of you, with me,
for telling you today my sadness
because I suffered so . . .
remembering what has happened to me,
because I suffered so . . .
remembering what has happened to me.

When we took refuge in this place
oh, how sad we felt!
It seems that we are not going to return
to the land where we were born.
It seems that we are not going to return
to the land where we were born.

We have fled for no other reason
than for all the people who have died.
And this is what makes us think,

that if we are poor, we are condemned to die.
And this is what makes us think,
that if we are poor, we are condemned to die.

I wish you would understand what I am saying
and change our ways for the common good
and then, teach our children
how to protect themselves against the world's evil.
And then, teach our children
how to protect themselves against the world's evil.

But when, when will we return?
In the future will come the day.
Because the truth and the justice
in life remain and do not die.
Because the truth and the justice
in life remain and do not die.

Thus it is that I leave you.
Please have much patience with me,
I hope I have expressed myself clearly
Because this is a great pain in my heart.
I hope I have expressed myself clearly
Because this is a great pain in my heart.

During my 1992 visit I discovered that a new musical group had been organized by the Ah Mayab' cultural association. Like Maya-Honh, this group has also been invited to sing in refugee camps as well as to entertain in Maya communities of the Kuchumatan inside Guatemala.

The songs and music that both groups have composed are now also played by marimbas in Guatemalan communities of the Kuchumatan highlands. In this way the brotherhood and friendship between refugees and residents of the communities who remained in the Kuchumatan are being rebuilt. "In Concepción Huista, the people loved our songs in the Maya language," a member of Maya-Honh said. "In that community, the civil patrol was still operating, but since we were invited by the mayor, we accepted the invitation. As we sang, the civil patrollers placed their rifles and clubs on the floor and listened to our songs with enjoyment. Then, after we finished, they came to us and said, "Paxanwejiktij wuxhtaj, nantik'a slow je sat ko tx'otx'al" (Come back brothers, it is always different to live in our own homeland).

11

RETURNING HOME

Peace, which is the highest desire of the Guatemalans, is indispensable for a definitive solution of the problem. While the war continues there will be more refugees. Repatriation will have a successful result only if in Guatemala there is peace as the fruit of social justice. Without peace, the refugees who would return will only enlarge the long list of the persecuted and the thousands of internal refugees.

Guatemalan Church in Exile,
Guatemala: Refugiados y repatriación

THE RETURN HOME has required planning, actions, and agreements on three fronts: the policies and actions (or inactions) of the Guatemalan government, the maneuvering of the international agencies and the government of Mexico, and the organization and work of the refugees themselves.

Guatemalan Policies

THE GUATEMALAN GOVERNMENT first attempted to solve the refugee problem unilaterally because the refugees had tarnished its international image. The presence of forty-six thousand refugees in southern Mexico was tangible proof of the continuing violation of human rights in Guatemala. To counter international criticism,

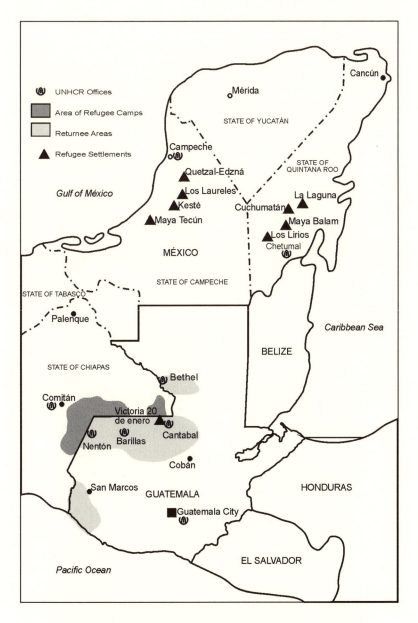

Location of refugee camps/settlements and returnee areas.
From Nolin Hanlon 1995. Map by Darren R. Stranger,
courtesy of Catherine L. Nolin Hanlon.

the army tried a number of mechanisms to get the refugees back to Guatemala. During the dictatorships of Ríos Montt and Mejía Victores, there were efforts to convince the refugees to be repatriated in model villages, army-controlled concentration camps within militarized regions. The army also built a large processing center in the department of Huehuetenango to receive the refugees as they returned. But most of the refugees denounced these efforts and preferred to stay in Mexico rather than return to Guatemala under the conditions the government imposed. Then the army offered "amnesty to the subversives," which included the refugees, but this measure also aroused suspicions, suspicions that were confirmed when General Mejía Victores denied the presence of refugees in Mexico, arguing that the United Nations and the Mexican government were feeding lazy Indians and guerrillas in the alleged refugee camps (Guatemalan Church in Exile 1987).

In January 1986 Vinicio Cerezo Arévalo became the first civilian president of Guatemala in twenty years. The army, which had ruled Guatemala since the coup of 1981, needed to end the international isolation that had limited foreign income through investments and multilateral loans. They allowed certain political parties to reconstitute themselves and ran elections in 1985. Cerezo, the Christian Democrat candidate, was elected in the fall of that year. Direct military control was replaced by military control wearing civilian clothes. Cerezo's presidency created another hopeful space in which people thought that the violence would end and lives could return to normal. But Cerezo did not or could not challenge military power. When people began organizing political groups, restructuring trade unions, or leading protests about human rights the result was more political violence, and the secret death squads linked to the army resurfaced. This violence persisted throughout Cerezo's presidency and indicated to the refugees in Mexico that their safety could not be assured in Guatemala.

When Cerezo assumed the presidency, he continued the

military's repatriation programs. To induce refugees to return and to facilitate the process, he created a governmental commission, the Special Commission to Aid the Repatriated (CEAR), in September 1986. The Cerezo government and CEAR tried to convince refugees to return. They set up facilities and programs and worked with a trickle of individual repatriates. Every year they predicted that there would be a great rush of returning refugees, but the refugees' answer was,

> *Knowing what happened to the ones who have returned, we don't want to return in the same conditions as our brothers were received, without the recognition of their rights to live in their homelands as free citizens. . . . Our return will not be possible until the situation in Guatemala has changed, and when we are given guarantees for our lives and the recognition of our rights as Guatemalans.* (*Guatemalan Church in Exile* 1987: 26)

The government sent the *alcaldes*, the mayors of the municipios from which the refugees originated, to the camps to discuss repatriation. These civilian authorities went to the refugee camps in March 1987 to talk their fellow villagers into returning home. But they could not assure the refugees that the government would give them the necessary protection for their survival. Even the First Lady, Raquel Blandón de Cerezo, visited the camps, and attempted to convince the refugees to go back home, but the refugees answered, "While the repression, killings, disappearances, and forced military service continue, and until the civil patrols and the model villages are dismantled, we will not live in peace" (Guatemalan Church in Exile 1987: 42).

Despite these negative responses from the refugees, the three major agencies, CEAR, COMAR, and UNHCR, signed an agreement in January 1987 that contained a plan for the repatriation of refugees. The UNHCR then opened an office in Guatemala to facilitate this work.

Throughout the 1980s a small number of individual families made the decision to return home.[1] Once CEAR was formed in 1986, it took over the management of repatriation. CEAR representatives met the returning refugees at the border under the supervision of UNHCR and COMAR officials. The refugees were then taken to the reception center in Huehuetenango where they could rest and receive medical attention. Their refugee identification cards were exchanged for repatriation cards, which functioned as Guatemalan identity cards but were clearly marked "repatriate." Each person or family was given a three-month food supply, basic tools, twenty sheets of zinc sheet roofing, and a small amount of cash. Each person or family also received transportation to their home community or the village to which they were assigned. They were also promised two additional rations of food, making a total of nine months' support from CEAR. This latter delivery of supplies did not always arrive (WOLA 1989: 16–17).

Several factors in this process caused tension for the repatriates. First, their status in their home community was uncertain. They were not welcomed home with open arms. There was a continuing suspicion that the former refugees would be trouble for the community. Old slights, wounds, and divisions remained intact. The repatriates, with their three-month supply of food, roofing tin, and tools, seemed privileged to those in the village who received nothing from the government. This local and very clear inequity caused resentment against the refugees. And above all, land was an issue. In most areas of conflict the army had declared the lands abandoned and had resettled the communities with people, usually ladinos, who were willing to side with the military and perform their civil patrol duties. These newcomers received titles to the land from the National Institute for Agrarian Transformation (INTA), often over the objections of CEAR. When the repatriates returned to their home villages they found their land occupied by others. Because of the conflicts between INTA and CEAR, land disputes were difficult to resolve and government policy on land for repatriates was unenforceable. The general shortage of *minifundia* lands for family subsistence is the basis for many ongoing and persistent problems in the process of repatriation (WOLA 1989: 30–31).[2]

Second, the government agencies that constituted CEAR included several representatives of the Ministry of Defense. Army representatives sit in on all meetings of CEAR, even at the local levels. The army S-5 (Civilian Affairs) unit has played the most prominent role and "orients the repatriates and accompanies them to their village . . . to give them confidence and security, because if they go all alone they go crazy" (S-5 officer, quoted in WOLA 1989: 20).

The third, and most important, factor was the security of their persons in a country where the dominant institution still considered them subversives. Through 1987 the army continued to issue statements questioning repatriation, recommending that all repatriates be sent to military-controlled reservations or linking repatriation to a rise in terrorism. Although the army's public message changed after 1987 to one of support for the process, their position seemed ambiguous at best. They continued to see the refugees as the pawns of groups trying to "impose conditions on the Guatemalan state" and to claim that a large-scale return would mean the infiltration of guerrilla forces (WOLA 1989: 24–25).

Individual decisions to return were not easy to make. Several criteria seem to have been considered. The first related to the ability of the potential repatriate to receive useful information from inside Guatemala. If the person or family was able to get information from Guatemala, if they trusted that information, and if that information indicated a reasonable chance of personal security, they would be more favorably inclined. The second related to their desire to recover family lands or lands they had worked for a long time. If their information indicated that their lands might be in jeopardy or that they were still free of outside settlers, this information would also incline them favorably toward repatriation. This return to the land would also strengthen their sense of themselves as Guatemalans.

The third criteria related to the refugees' religious attitudes. Protestants, particularly of the two major sects in the Kuchumatan highlands, were more likely to return than were Catholics. Guatemala saw the proliferation of many Protestant religious sects during the decade 1982–92 (Stoll 1988). Pastors from some of these groups arrived at the refugee camps to preach to people and convince them to return. They preached that God had sent Ríos Montt as their savior and that they should recognize the divine will of God and return home (Guatemalan Church in Exile 1987). Protestant fundamentalist religious organizations such as the Central American Religious Mission and the Jehovah's Witnesses (Testigos de Jehová) promoted the repatriation projects proposed by the government. Indeed, most of the refugees who were repatriated during the 1980s are members of these churches. One of these repatriates, a Jehovah's Witness, said, "The elders, superintendents of the District went to talk to the Guatemalan authorities and they have negotiated that nothing will happen to us, since we do not get involved in politics" (quoted in Hernández Castillo 1992: 101–2).

The last major consideration was the current conditions in Mexico, both in the camps and with regard to the Mexican government's refugee policies. The constant movement of camps, the division of people from one group into another, the cutting off of food and services to force the refugees to move to the Yucatán peninsula were all elements of Mexican policy that made refugees reconsider remaining in Mexico. But it is interesting that despite the Mexican government's policy of providing greater support and more services to the camps in Campeche and Quintana Roo, more refugees from those camps sought repatriation in the 1980s (WOLA 1989: 13–14).

International Policy

CONCERN ABOUT REFUGEES as a worldwide phenomenon has become a major issue in international forums and conferences. With wars in Nicaragua and El Salvador, the refugee situation throughout Central America took on staggering proportions in the 1980s. It is in the context of international discussions about the fate of Central America and all its refugees that internationally recognized standards for repatriation for Guatemalan refugees were first seriously discussed.

In the mid-1980s Costa Rica's President Oscar Arias led a series of discussions among representatives of the Central American governments, European envoys, and the U.S. State Department. These talks resulted in the Central American Peace Accord signed in Esquipulas, Guatemala, in August 1987 by the presidents of all Central American countries. The accord attempted to find regional solutions to problems of peace, democracy, and national reconciliation. The policy of the United States toward the region, while it spoke much of "democracy," had put its highest priorities on funding the militarization of these countries' internal conflicts. The accord tried to harness U.S. policy to seek solutions rather than to continue to polarize the situation (WOLA 1989: 1).

One part of the document spoke directly to the problem of refugees:

> The governments of Central America commit themselves to give urgent attention to the groups of refugees and displaced persons brought about by the regional crisis, through protection and assistance, particularly in areas of education, health, work and security, and whenever voluntary and individually expressed, to facilitate in the repatriation, resettlement and relocation [of those persons]. They also commit themselves to request assistance for Central American refugees and displaced persons from the international community, both directly

through bilateral or multilateral agreements, as well as through United Nations High Commissioner for Refugees and other organizations and agencies. (quoted in Manz 1988b: 2)

In this framework the Guatemala refugee problem was seen as part of larger issues. Refugee resettlement could occur only when other changes toward peace and national reconciliation were also taking place. Both money and planning were needed for the successful reincorporation of refugees into Guatemalan life. At the UNHCR meeting of May 1987 in Geneva, solutions to refugee problems in all of Central America were discussed, and the following points of agreement were reached.

1) That refugees have the right to return to their own country, their security guaranteed by international human rights and that country's constitution;

2) That governments should encourage voluntary repatriation without jeopardizing the rights of the refugees to assistance while they remained in exile;

3) That governments should recognize and implement the principle of voluntary and individually chosen repatriation;

4) That the refugees have a right to information on prevailing conditions in [their] native country and region, so that their decision should be based on free and informed choice.

5) That the refugees have the right to protection for the exercise of the option to return;

6) That the refugees should have the ability to choose freely the place of return, especially the place of their origin, their place of habitual residence, or those offered by the government;

7) That there must be sufficient guarantees of non-discrimination and full respect for the human rights of the refugees equal to those of their non-exiled compatriots. (WOLA 1989: 3)

At this and subsequent meetings the UNHCR and the European countries pledged financial support for repatriation efforts. Indeed, CEAR was funded originally with $445,000 from the UNHCR. Part of the inducement for the Central American countries to become signatories to this program was the money that accompanied it (WOLA 1989: 19).

Up to this point the only framework within which governments had discussed the refugee issue was that of individual voluntary return, called repatriation. Repatriation is something that happens to the refugees through the auspices of governmental and international agencies. The refugees have little to say about what is done or how it is carried out. They are transported to their home country and assisted in reintegrating themselves into their national life and local communities. Both the UNHCR and CEAR have strongly supported this mechanism for ending the exile. But life in Guatemala did not admit to easy reintegration: both violence and insecurity continued. And it fell to the refugees themselves to work out a different mechanism for going home (Nolin Hanlon 1995: 79).

The Refugees

IN 1987, AS a result of the repatriation agreement signed by COMAR, CEAR, and the UNHCR, the refugees in all the camps, Chiapas, Campeche, and Quintana Roo, elected representatives to an organization they called the Permanent Commissions of Representatives of Guatemalan Refugees in Mexico. This organization undertook the job of defining and drafting the refugees' position on returning to Guatemala. By March 1988 they were prepared to participate in discussions with the above agencies, but they faced strong opposition from the Guatemalan government, which linked their organization to the guerrillas and aggressively advanced their military-supervised repatriation program (Nolin Hanlon 1995: 204).

In January 1989 the CCPP proposed the idea of a "collective and organized return," stating that 70 percent of the official refugees supported this type of return as opposed to the government's program of repatriation. Finding no other arena open to them, CCPP members traveled to Guatemala in the spring to present their document to the National Dialogue, a forum convened by the National Reconciliation Commission itself created under the terms of the Central American Peace Accord. This document outlined those points of international law and the Guatemalan Constitution that should guide their return, and it put forth the refugees' six specific preconditions for participating in a return to Guatemala:

1) The return must be [a] voluntary, individual decision, undertaken in a collective and organized fashion, under secure conditions and dignity;

2) The right to free association and organization by the returnees must be recognized;

3) There must be international accompaniment for the return;

4) The returnees must have freedom of movement within Guatemala, along with free entry and departure from the country for the refugees and members of the CCPP;

5) The right to life and personal and community security must be guaranteed;

6) The refugees must have access to land. (U.S Committee for Refugees 1993: 11)

The Guatemalan government and international agencies saw the participation of the refugees as unnecessary. But the diplomatic procedures that left those affected by them without voice and participation created insecurity and suspicion among the refugees. So the refugees insisted on their active participation, and their work became an indispensable factor in the negotiations for their return. But even arranging talks between the government and the CCPP was a formidable and arduous task. It was not until 1991 that the government acquiesced to strong international pressure and began serious negotiations with the CCPP. In October of that year CEAR signed a joint agreement with the CCPP recognizing it as an official representative of the refugees and binding the government to establishing returns in 1992 (Nolin Hanlon 1995: 205).

The negotiations over the conditions for the return took another year, and in October 1992 the Basic Accord for Repatriation was signed by the government and the CCPP. The accord also established the International Consultant and Support Group for the Return (GRICAR), whose role was to mediate problems and verify that the conditions of the accord were met. By January 1993 an agreement was reached to facilitate the first collective return to the Ixcán, to a site called Polígono 14 (Nolin Hanlon 1995: 206).

Going Home

AFTER TEN YEARS of waiting to go home the day finally arrived for the first group of refugees. The almost 2,500 returnees were accompanied by 240 international observers, of whom I was one. The first date established for the return was January 13, 1993, so the refugees began to prepare for a massive mobilization. As the date approached a disagreement arose between CEAR and the CCPP on the logistics of the journey. The Guatemalan government did not want the refugees to return along the Pan-American Highway, the CCPP's choice, which had been agreed to in the document and signed by both parties. It became evident that the Guatemalan government did not want to permit the greater visibility for the refugees that this route entailed and suggested that they enter Guatemala through La Ruta de Ingenieros (Engineer's Road), an almost unknown road through the Petén region. Meanwhile thousands of refugees from Campeche and Quintana Roo began their journey by foot and by bus to reach

Comitán in Chiapas, where the returning refugees were scheduled to meet on January 12, 1993, to start their journey back to Guatemala the next day. In Comitán, 2,480 refugees from different ethnic groups were concentrated under the supervision of COMAR.

In the reception center in Comitán there were many children. Most of them had been born in Mexico, and they did not have a clear idea of their parents' country of origin. Similarly, those who went into exile with their parents at an early age were also extremely anxious to know more about their homeland. During a cultural activity in the reception center in Comitán, I asked a few six- and seven-year-olds where were they going, and they replied, "We are going far." Another said, "We are going to Guatemala, Mayan, Mayan." Then I asked, "Do you know Guatemala?" The children answered that they did not. "But how do you imagine it?" They tried to imagine Guatemala and said, "There are trees, thorns, rivers, stones, birds, people." While the children tried to imagine Guatemala, the adults tried to forget the horrible massacres that forced them into exile. They, too,

Going home, the caravan of buses and accompanying cars

tried to imagine a more peaceful country, where there would be respect for human rights.

Because of the complexity of the situation, the return scheduled for January 13 was postponed. On January 20 after Mass was celebrated, the refugees left Comitán in a caravan of seventy buses provided by COMAR, with other vehicles for the accompanying international teams. Their final destination was Polígono 14, an isolated region of Ixcán in the department of El Quiché in northern Guatemala. The refugees crossed the border into La Mesilla on the Pan-American Highway without incident, as Guatemalan immigration authorities had previously documented the refugees in Comitán to avoid problems and facilitate

A young Mam, wearing her identification badge,
at the Huehuetenango camp stop on the return

their journey. There were tears of joy when the refugees crossed into their country. This was the most emotional moment. Refugees had waited ten years to set foot in their homelands, and the children born in Mexico saw for the first time the grandeur of the Kuchumatan highlands, the land of their ancestors.

Unfortunately the returnees did not receive a welcome in Huehuetenango appropriate to the occasion. The CCPP protested the many restrictions imposed by the government and the presence of army personnel at the reception center. But at the next stop, Chimaltenango, the refugees were given an eloquent and awe-inspiring welcome. With marimba music, church bells, and firecrackers, the local people offered their support to the returning Guatemalans.

In Guatemala City the refugees were divided into three major groups and quartered in different locales before continuing their journey to the Ixcán region. In one of these reception centers, the Instituto Indígena Santiago, two little Q'anjob'al Maya girls, age four or five, were crying loudly, "Tonh pax b'et ko

Returnees being welcomed by marimbas

pat!" (Let's go back to our hut), pleading to go back to what they thought were their homes in the refugee camp in Campeche, Mexico. "They don't know where we are going, and they are too young to understand," their mother said in Q'anjob'al, while she tried to calm the crying girls.

By February 4 more than half of the retornados had arrived at their destination, Polígono 14. The final stage of the journey, from Cobán to Polígono 14, was the most difficult. The roads were in very bad condition, and it was necessary for the UNHCR to establish an air bridge from Cobán to Playa Grande to transport the more vulnerable of the refugee population. The whole process was difficult because there were many children and elderly people who needed attention during the entire journey of several weeks. Nevertheless, all the governmental and nongovernmental organizations involved in the process expressed their satisfaction with the general conditions of the return. In honor of their return the returnees named their new settlement Victoria 20 de enero.

Over the next three years other groups were mobilized for the return to Guatemala. The Guatemalan government approved a loan of four million quetzals for the second refugee group to buy a finca in the municipio of Nentón, Huehuetenango. This group was composed of Q'anjob'al, Jakaltek, and Mam Mayas who constructed their new community in Chaculá, a finca close to the Guatemala-Mexico border that contains a large Maya archaeological site. But, of course, none of these subsequent returnees received the marimba and fireworks welcome of the first group. Despite three years of individual repatriations and collective returns, as of this writing only about one-half of the refugees have left Mexico to take up residence in Guatemala. Two major issues impeding the process are the slowness with which the Guatemalan government addresses the problem of finding land for collective returns and their continuing preference for individual rather than collective repatriation (NCO-ORD 1996b: 13).

The community of Chaculá provides an example of certain problems faced by the refugees. It is a remote community where the residents have little contact with their old communities and, indeed, little contact with the outside world. The former refugees have purchased this land with a government loan, and they struggle to survive with little useful assistance from outside. The land in Chaculá is quite barren. Some current income is derived from timbering, an economic activity with potentially disastrous ecological consequences. A development project to aid the women of the community failed, and the status of a coffee-growing project is marginal. The Jakaltek-speaking community members of Chaculá now live in Nentón, a small ladino town with a large number of Q'anjob'al-speaking Mayas, and their newborn children are registered in this town. Currently the dirt road between Chaculá and Nentón is being repaired. Chaculá residents return to Jacaltenango only for the patron saint's yearly festival.

The situation for the returnees has also been fraught with problems. It has not always been possible for them to keep the military out of their settlements. The community of Xamán suffered from a military attack that left eleven dead and thirty wounded in October 1995. Although the survivors have pursued the matter in the Guatemalan courts, they have not received any justice, the court officers being subject to both intimidation and bribery. Government inaction against abusive civil patrollers and local authorities who attack returnees has been reported by Human Rights Watch/Americas in their report, "Return to Violence in Guatemala: Refugees, Civil Patrollers, and Impunity" (JRS/USA 1996: 14). In other instances mediation has been necessary to avoid conflict in communities where returnees and newcomers struggle over issues ranging from land to community control (NCOORD 1996b: 11).

It is evident that the Guatemalan refugees have become highly politicized and aware of their ability to mold the future.

Their understanding of the political situation and their deepening sense of their own history have made them new Guatemalans. The refugees are more aware of the political implications of their exile, and they continue to organize themselves and demand recognition as full Guatemalan citizens. Recently another coordinating group, the Coordination of Return and Resettlement Groups (CBBR), has emerged among the refugees remaining in the camps (NCOORD 1996a: 1). It will be difficult for the Guatemalan government to manipulate the refugees easily, as it has tried to do in the past. Despite the difficulties the refugees have insisted on going home to fight for their rights as Guatemalans. "Our placentas are buried in our homelands in Guatemala, and that is where we desire to go," Mayas have insisted.

12

FROM THE PRESENT
INTO THE FUTURE

THE REFUGEES CONTINUED to travel home in organized returns during 1994, 1995, and 1996. CEAR set a
minimum limit of fifty families per group if they were to
be eligible for the government land program, whose
implementation was always slow and cumbersome. This
minimum limit opened for other refugees the renewed
possibility of individual repatriation, and one group of
twenty-nine families returned in 1996 without permission from the government. But by no means have all the
refugees been accommodated in this process. More than
half of them still remain in Mexico.

For those refugees still in Mexico, the future is
uncertain. While the government of Mexico had provided refuge and hospitality for more than ten years, this
position began to change with the surprising emergence
of the Zapatista Army of National Liberation (EZLN) on
January 1, 1994. This Chiapan rebellion was fueled by
the poverty, discrimination, and marginalization faced by
the poor Mexican Mayas and their mestizo counterparts.

Some Mexicans in positions of power in Chiapas and in Mexico City blamed the insurrection on the refugees, whose "leftist" ideology had somehow rubbed off on the local population. The Mexican army moved into Chiapas to contain the rebels, and fighting took place in areas close to Guatemalan refugee camps. Chiapas became a militarized state, and the refugees once more became a distraction and a problem to the Mexican government.

More important, the Diocese of San Cristóbal de las Casas and its bishop, Samuel Ruíz García, were no longer able to provide the level of support and interface for the refugees that they had once given. The already overburdened Catholic church and the bishop took on the work of seeking security for the uninvolved civilian populations, giving aid to those displaced by the conflict and acting as negotiators between the government and the EZLN. In response the bishop became the target of death threats and hate campaigns (EPICA 1994: 22).

COMAR sought to hasten the return of the refugees by cutting off food supplies and threatening other actions, but CEAR could not hasten the Guatemalan government's land programs and the refugees were caught in the middle. Ultimately the conflict between the EZLN and the Mexican government reached a stalemate and food shipments were restored to the refugees, but the Mexican government has continued to apply other pressures to get the refugees to leave. In August 1996 Mexico offered permanent status to the thirty-two thousand refugees still in the country, citing their important contribution to the Mexican agricultural workforce. The refugees in Campeche and Quintana Roo would benefit from this program first, followed by those in Chiapas. The offer of permanent status was not open-ended, however, and refugees had only a limited time to make their decisions. At almost the same time, the Guatemalan government's National Peace Fund (FONAPAZ) director, Alvaro Colóm, announced that it was running short of funds to provide land for returning refugees and could at best support only two thousand additional families before the funds were gone (CERIGUA 1996: 3).

So for the refugees still in Mexico options are disappearing and time is running out. They can repatriate individually, they can hope to be accommodated in one of the remaining group returns, or they can become Mexicans. Recent studies predict that at least seven thousand Guatemalan refugees in Mexico will accept this option.

For the retornados, those who have returned, life is still fraught with difficulties and conflicts. These conflicts are evident between the army or former civil patrol groups and the returnees, between the returnees and the settled community into which they are moving, and even between various elements within the refugee groups as they struggle to regain their land and reconstitute their communities (NCOORD 1996b: 4; Taylor 1998). New strategies for survival were necessary for those who returned, according to their situations. Those refugees who returned not to their home communities but to establish new communities, have received some humanitarian aid from NGO groups, including food supplies, medicines, and health services. This often created tension between the new community and their neighbors, or between the new community and the old one from which they had come, as both communities were poor and there was an inequity between them. In response some NGOs developed broader assistance plans, including both refugee and traditional communities in their cultural, educational, health, or development projects.

Those refugees who returned to their home communities were perceived as intruders and called "refugees" by those who had remained. Community members who stayed in Guatemala during the war years felt that the refugees were guerrilla supporters or at least had escaped civil patrol duty, leaving that onus on those who remained. In those communities resettled early in the return process, these divisions seem to be softening and the status of refugee is less often applied.

The Maya organizations promoting cultural revitalization, particularly the regional branches of the Academy of Maya

Languages, played an important role. They visited groups in both the refugee camps and the resettled communities and invited returnees as well as traditional community members to conferences and seminars concerning the local Maya language and the history of each region, reinforcing a common identity as Maya beyond the current divisions.

As of this writing early in 1998 most refugees still face the future with some hope, many memories of despair, and much anxiety about the next few years. Hope arises from the completion of the ten-year process of peace negotiations between the URNG and the Guatemalan government. Beginning in March 1990 with the signing of the Oslo Accord, which set a timetable for negotiations, work proceeded slowly as ten separate agreements were reached, all to be activated when the final Peace Accord was signed. In March 1994 a human rights accord was signed which went into effect immediately and allowed international verification by the United Nations. In June 1994 the Accord for the Resettlement of the Population Displaced by the Armed Conflict was signed. In March 1995, the Accord on the Indigenous Peoples' Identity and Rights was signed. This accord mandated constitutional reforms to make Guatemala a multicultural, plurilingual, and multiethnic state and promised official recognition of Guatemala's Maya languages and an end to official discrimination against the Maya, Garífuna, and Xinca people. In September 1996 the Accord on the Strengthening of Civilian Authority and the Role of the Army in a Democratic Society was signed. This restricted the army's role to defense of national sovereignty and protection of its borders. The civil patrols were to be disarmed and disbanded and the army's size and budget cut by one-third. Other accords covered constitutional and electoral reforms and the reincorporation of the URNG into legal life. On December 29, 1996, the Accord for a Firm and Lasting Peace was signed in Guatemala City, activating all the previously signed accords (CERIGUA 1997).

In these accords many of the important issues that underlay

the long and bitter conflict and drove the refugees over the border have been addressed, at least on paper. On the day the Accord for a Firm and Lasting Peace was signed, the parties also signed an agreement as to a timetable for implementing it, but it is too soon to say what the outcome will be and how it will affect the lives of Guatemala's majority Maya population. There is, however, hope that life will be changed for the better.

Mayas have faced much adversity throughout almost five hundred years of Western domination. They have met these extreme hardships with effective strategies of cultural survival, carried out by the many Maya ethnic groups that evolved from the macro-Maya underlying culture (the Maya Nation) since pre-Hispanic times. Each ethnic group has managed to save, transform, and continue different aspects of that ancient Mayan culture that gives all modern Maya people their common Maya identity. The Maya tradition as we know it today has undergone many dramatic changes and syncretic transformations. If the Mayas who confronted the Spanish invaders managed to rebuild and continue their cultural heritage in spite of the tremendous violence of the conquest, we, the modern Mayas, must take pride in our cultural traditions and make them an integral part of the building process of a Guatemalan national culture. Thus we Mayas insist that our culture must be taken as an important element in the remodeling of the Guatemalan nation, which, at present, is strongly oriented to the exaltation of imposed Western ideologies and traditions.

Some of this new thrust into national life can be seen in the Maya renaissance now under way in Guatemala. Spurred by the legitimation of our languages, publishing houses, radio stations, and periodicals have blossomed. Mayas who had lost the beauty of their mother tongue are relearning it. Maya cultural and ethnic organizations have proliferated, and importantly, there is talk of beginning work on a pan-Maya political party. But can everyone sit at this table? Will there be a growing divide between the Mayas who continue on the land as their ancestors have and those who become educated and move to the cities? Will there be a divide between those Mayas who return to Guatemala and those who find a new life in Mexico or Los Angeles or Florida or Vancouver? Will those who are now immigrants in other lands face greater pressures to assimilate to the dominant culture, or will they find ways to maintain their Mayanness?

In facing these issues, the immigrants are aided by two important factors. First, modern technology, in the form of tape and video recordings, frequent trips home, and the development of a Maya-language publishing house in Los Angeles (Yax Te' Press) will help to keep ties to the mother culture. And second, the experience of the "remembered community" that bound the refugees to their culture in exile will support and build a transnational Maya culture. Our ability to be Mayas is not limited to any one place or time. It is not forever rooted in the past. It can be our identity and our strength wherever we are. And that identity and strength can also guide Guatemala to a better future.

NOTES

Chapter One. The Anthropologist and the Other

1. Popb'al Ti' is the language of the Jakaltek people. Throughout this book Popb'al Ti' will be used to refer to the language and Jakaltek to the people or the region.

2. The content of this dream appears in an essay, "The Stones Will Speak Again: Dreams and Realities of an Ah Tzib' Maya," in Ortiz 1997.

3. *El Q'anil* was published in a limited edition in December 1982 by Signal Books. It is currently out of print, but a revised and expanded version is planned which will incorporate the Maya text.

4. Tracy Bachrach Ehlers criticized anthropology and anthropologists for their underrepresentation of Central American studies in major anthropological journals during the 1980s, when violence, ethnocide, and great suffering engulfed the region:

The reticence of anthropology as a discipline to legitimate policy-based research in Central America stems from a tendency that has characterized the field since its beginnings: studying communities as isolated, timeless cultures that are unaffected by regional, national and international events taking place outside their borders. This bias causes practitioners who wish to advance their careers to turn their backs on what may be considered controversial policy analysis and write instead about subjects endorsed by the discipline. (Ehlers 1990: 140–41)

5. These new archaeological interpretations reinforced the patterns of militarization taking place in Guatemala at that time, raising questions about causality in historical reconstructions. For a critique of the shifts in theories in Maya archaeology, see Wilks 1985.

6. The ties between the United States and the landed elite go back to the turn of the century. Ferris states that "in fact, the history of Guatemala in this century is the history of the United Fruit Company and close United States/Guatemala relations" (1987: 25).

7. I visited the Q'anjob'al Maya refugees in Immokalee, Florida, in summer 1991. For a study of the Florida Maya communities, see Burns 1993.

8. In the Kuchumatan highlands some ladinoized Maya communities were also affected by the violence, for example, Buena Vista in the municipio of Santa Ana Huista, Huehuetenango, where people had formerly spoken Popb'al Ti' but where the only language currently in use was Spanish.

9. These documents are located in the archives of the Catholic Diocese of San Cristóbal and at the national hospital at Comitán, Chiapas, Mexico. Officials of COMAR also keep records of their work among the refugees.

10. One collection of testimonies from these sources has been published in Montejo and Akab' 1992.

11. In addition to the CCPP and Mama Maquín, which promoted a left-of-center approach, a few other people more closely associated with the guerrilla movements made contact with the camps from time to time, soliciting funds and recruits. I have experienced the frustration of having my work and efforts to help the refugees countered because some politicized and leftist people who infiltrated the camps tried to stop me. During one of my visits I received an anonymous letter from such people threatening to ban me from the camps and to stop my research. They did not succeed. These people did not reinforce Maya identity or cultural revival and disapproved of any activities that did not promote their revolutionary cause. They continued to use the term "compañero" among themselves and with their few supporters.

12. For example, when a death occurred in the camp, the refugees' anxieties were intensified because of their yearning for their homeland and their fear of dying and being buried in a foreign land.

13. This videotaping project was made possible by the Onaway Fund through its director and trustee, John Morris, of London, England.

14. Ah Mayab' is known in English as the Association for Mayan Cultural Revival. It is a Popb'al Ti' term meaning "We, the Original People of the Maya Land."

15. This film project was supervised by Lavonne Poteet of Bucknell University and directed by Pamela Yates and Deborah Schaffer. As of this writing, the film has not been completed.

Chapter Two. Toward a Maya History of Guatemala

1. Nancy Farriss, in her classic work *Mayan Society under Colonial Rule* (1984), has discussed different forms of resistance Mayas developed for

their collective survival. She posits three types of population movements: flight, drift, and dispersal. "Flight" refers to the escape of Indians from colonial rule across the frontier into unpacified territory; "drift" refers to the migration to other communities within the area under more or less effective Spanish domination; and "dispersal" refers to the creation of satellite settlements by populations that have broken away from nucleated or congregated "parent" towns (1984: 200).

2. Rafael Carrera was thought to be at least part Indian and a poor man who visited rural communities buying and selling pigs. He identified himself with the people and placed indigenous leaders in high-ranking positions in his army in the Kuchumatan highlands. Both the historical record (Recinos 1954) and the oral tradition confirm these stories. John L. Stephens, while traveling through the Kuchumatan highlands, stated that "even on the borders of Central America, the name of Carrera was omnipotent" (1841: 238). Ralph Lee Woodward, Jr. (1993: 422 ff.), finds that Carrera's paternalistic approach to the Mayas was stronger in the earlier years of his presidency than in the latter ones. As coffee production expanded after midcentury, demands for Maya lands and labor increased again.

3. LaFarge reported for the Q'anjob'al of Santa Eulalia that "it is interesting that one finds the Indians, to this day, keenly aware of the fact that Carrera, dictator of Guatemala in the mid-nineteenth century, was an Indian, and this even in the Cuchumatanes section, which at the time was much isolated from the rest of the republic and had but little to do with the struggles by which he gained control of the country" (1947: 16).

4. Pushed to the limits of their tolerance, Mayas from the Kuchumatan region escaped this exploitation at various times by crossing the Mexican border and becoming permanent exiles. In 1928 Frans Blom found a group of Indians from Santa Eulalia living in Zapotal, Chiapas (LaFarge and Byers 1931: 175). The Chiapas settlement of Guadalupe Victoria (formerly San José Montenegro) was created by Jakaltek migrants who maintained their links to Jacaltenango. "Until recently, the Indians of San José came to Jacaltenango for the Year Bearer Ceremony, but now have their own church of Candelaria, the same patron as that of the parent town" (LaFarge and Byers 1931: 84). Juvenal Casaverde collected testimonies of Mayas who had abandoned their homelands in the Kuchumatan highlands:

An older informant in Guadalupe Victoria noted that her grandfather was an official of the alcaldes rezadores (prayer makers) of Jacaltenango during the late 1880s. At this time the departamento officials ordered the killing of a number of Jacaltecos, among them the informant's grandfather. She added that his body was cut into pieces and thrown over the cliff into the Río Azul. Older people of Jacaltenango also have memories of these killings. As a consequence, she says, many people from Jacaltenango decided to move out to Guadalupe Victoria to escape from the easy reach of the feared department authorities. (Casaverde 1976: 242)

5. The problem of nationalism and nation building in Guatemala is one of perennial debate. Although recognizing the injustices of the past, Miguel Angel Asturias described the nationalist and ethnic problem of the Indians in Guatemala in the "scientific" racist terminology of the early twentieth century:

How long will this disparity continue? The Indian represents a past civilization and the mestizo, or Ladino as we call him, a future civilization. The Indian who comprises the majority of our population lost his vigor during the long period of slavery to which he was subjected. He is not interested in anything, accustomed as he is to the first person who comes along taking away what he has, including his wife and children. He represents the mental, moral and material dearth of the country: he is humble, he is dirty, he dresses differently and he suffers without flinching. The Ladino, who comprises one-third of the population, lives a different historical moment. With spurts of ambition and romanticism, he aspires, desires and is, in the final analysis, the vital part of the Guatemalan nation. What a nation, where two-thirds of its population are dead to intelligent life! (1977: 65–66)

His work became the basis for an elitist ideology that persisted throughout most of the twentieth century.

6. Unlike the United States, where the vanished Indians can be portrayed romantically, as in the movies *Dances with Wolves* and *The Last of the Mohicans*, in Guatemala, where the Maya population is still the majority, a romantic view of the natives is only encouraged for commercial or promotional purposes. In common with most nations in the Western Hemisphere, the ongoing search for a Guatemalan national identity underwent a process that Anderson calls "indigenization": "But since by then the *real* aborigines of the Americas had been, if they were not exterminated, radically crushed and marginalized, and since the ascendency of creoles and mestizos was based on this historical obliteration, 'indigenization' almost everywhere was necessarily constructed in bad faith and as a kind of political theater" (1988: 404).

Maya identity is based on a specific sense of belonging to the land where they live and of tracing their links to the ancient Maya culture. There is a "Mayanness" that unites Guatemala's native people to their land and ancestors. Identity is therefore a process of history (Rojas Mix 1991). In contrast, the political identity of the mestizo/ladino group is ambiguous. They disdain the label "Indian," but they are not Europeans either; thus their identity is an imposed one. In this context the ladino elite, to legitimate their imagined community, appropriated Maya symbols (Tikal, the quetzal) of the past in order to be "Latin Americans."

7. The articulation of ethnicity, class structures, and state power (Worsley 1984) with the internationalization of the division of labor (Wolf 1982) is evident in Guatemala.

In many instances state elites have allied themselves with international corporations or agencies or foreign governments in order to maintain the domestic ethnic division of labor that guarantees perpetuation of the current state system. Just as states must be investigated in the context of the international system, so must ethnicity be investigated taking explicit account of the historical quality of international penetration. (Enloe 1986: 40)

This compromising of the local elite with foreign powers has increased the internal conflict and division of the country so that, in Eduardo Galeano's (1969) terms, Guatemala has become an "occupied country."

8. Or, as Larry Rohter reported in the *New York Times*, quoting an unnamed European diplomat, "'The exclusionary project of the Spanish-descended elite merged with the internal security concerns of the military,' leading to a situation in which 'each supported the other, and counterinsurgency merged with racism'" (1996: A5).

Chapter Three. The Advent of Violence in the Kuchumatan Highlands

1. This testimony and those that follow in this chapter are taken from my field notes or from transcriptions of tape recordings made during my research in the refugee camps. The speakers are not identified for reasons of their own personal safety.

2. This account has been previously published in Montejo and Akab' 1992.

3. One important note of discord in these northwestern Maya villages was introduced just before the violence began. It involved a religious movement called the Charismatics which provoked conflicts and created divisions among people and villages. Introduced to the region by a North American Catholic priest, it was a shock to the traditional Catholicism of the Maya people because its adherents claimed to see and talk constantly with Jesus, the Virgin, and the saints. Their major claims were that they had "gifts from God," such as speaking in tongues and curing. In their services people's religious fervor reached the point of convulsions and hysteria; their bodies trembled and some even undressed as they gave witness to their

faith. Villagers who rejected their brand of Catholicism were labeled pagans. Only a minority of people followed this movement, but it provoked a deeply disorienting conflict in those villages where it took root. In other areas the religious conflicts involved Evangelicals, Protestants, and traditional Catholics, groups with a longer history in the area whose friction was more familiar to the inhabitants (Stoll 1988).

4. For example, before the Spanish conquest in 1524, the dreams and prophecies of the Jaguar Priests were collected in the *Chilam Balam*, the Books of the Chilam. They foretold the hardships Mayas would suffer on the arrival of the Spanish:

> *Ay de vosotros, mis Hermanos Menores,*
> *que el 7 Ahau Katun*
> *tendréis exceso de dolor*
> *y exceso de miseria,*
> *por el tributo reunido*
> *con violencia,*
> *y antes que nada entregado con rapidez!*
> *Diferente tributo mañana*
> *y pasado mañana daréis;*
> *esto es lo que viene hijos mios . . .*

5. This was also the dream that I had during this time, just prior to the violence that engulfed our villages.

6. This young schoolteacher was my youngest brother, Pedro Antonio Montejo, who died at the hands of five soldiers on February 1, 1981. The following day he was to have begun his teaching assignment in a Q'anjob'al community.

7. The bombing of K'oya' occurred on a Sunday. I was talking with some friends in Jacaltenango when a helicopter passed over the town at a high altitude. A few minutes later, after the helicopter had disappeared behind the mountains, a warplane followed it, making a great deal of noise. Soon we could hear explosions behind the mountain. Later, when the K'oya' refugees began arriving dazed and bleeding in Jacaltenango, we knew that it had been the army's target.

8. This account was told to me by "Juan," one of the survivors in the refugee camp in Mexico where he had fled for fear of being recognized by his captors. The testimony is taken from my interview with him.

9. I was in La Laguna at this time, gathering up the corn that had just been harvested from some land I had there. Although I taught school in another village, my father and I hired workers to look after my field there

and harvest my corn. The corn from this harvest had to be abandoned when the entire community left the village and sought refuge in Mexico.

10. This testimony comes from a fifty-year-old woman who survived the massacre and made her way to La Laguna the next day seeking help.

11. A person wanting to construct a house informs his neighbors and "hires" the expert builders by offering them a ball of dough for pozol made of ground corn and chocolate. If the dough is accepted, they have accepted the job. On an agreed day all the people asked assemble at the building site and work until the task is finished.

12. This event was witnessed by a young woman who was fifteen years old at the time it took place. She had remained behind in the village to care for her sick father. When the army approached her house, her father escaped, but the young woman was captured by the soldiers. Young and pretty, she was taken by the army officers to "enjoy" her, as they told her. Six days later they released her in the town of Santa Ana Huista. She related the stories of Gilbertino, the five men and their donkeys, and Tumax and Pilín to me in a refugee camp in Chiapas.

13. Other accounts of the massacre at Finca San Francisco can be found in Stoll 1988; Falla 1983; and Montejo and Akab' 1992.

Chapter Four. Military Control of the Highlands

1. These programs were, in large measure, funded by international agencies, including the UN World Food Program, and administered by regional military officers and thus cost the Guatemalan government relatively little (Black 1983: 24).

2. In addition to the testimonies presented here, I personally witnessed the formation of the civil patrol by the army in the Kuchumatan highlands in 1982. Some of this material originally appeared in Montejo and Akab' 1992.

3. This and the succeeding stories are taken from my field notes of interviews with refugees in the camps in Mexico.

4. After a decade (1982–92) this road had not been completed. A present tripartite, community-municipality-government effort to finish the road has been initiated, but the majority of the work is being done by the communities.

5. Manz reported that the civil patrols were never heavily armed: "In Huehuetenango, patrollers were sometimes armed only with sticks in the shape of rifles" (1988a: 242).

6. This testimony was originally recorded in Popb'al Ti'. Akuxh Lenam has lived in exile with his family since July 1982.

7. I have experienced the Guatemalan army as just such a "killing machine," as the kaibiles chant in their training (see Montejo 1987).

8. The Civil Patrol Code of Conduct is as follows:

1. *I will defend my family, home and community against any subversive attack or natural catastrophe.*

2. *I will never allow subversion to penetrate my community.*

3. *I will support the Guatemalan army in all its actions.*

4. *I will deny support to subversion and whoever acts against the peace and security of the honorable nation.*

5. *I will capture any suspicious-looking person who enters or pillages my community and I will inform the nearest Military Commander.*

6. *I will inform the Military Commander, Military Commissioner or the head of the Civil Patrol about any subversive hiding place, encampment or movements.*

7. *I will never abandon my civil defense companions when they are in difficult situations, whether it is antisubversive combat or any other kind.*

8. *I will not abuse the authority I have as a member of the Civil Defense.*

9. *I will not misuse the arms and munitions given to me for use in the Civil Patrol.*

10. *I will respect community customs and traditions as well as the Civil and Military authorities.*

11. *I will protect and not harm the crops where I walk.*

12. *I will always fight to maintain peace, tranquility and the well-being of my community.*

13. *While on my watch I will be responsible for the lives of my companions in the community; I will carry out my duties thoroughly and safely and be an example to the person who relieves me.*

14. *I will support all the plans that encourage community development and progress.* (Americas Watch 1986: 99–100)

Chapter Six. The Journey to Mexico

1. The most widely discussed case among the refugees was that of three girls (14, 13, and 12 years of age) who were taken by a Mexican woman all the way to the city of Puebla and forced to "work" in a house of

prostitution run by this woman. Two other girls found themselves in the same situation in Tijuana.

2. COMAR was actually formed in July 1980 to provide assistance, within the framework of Mexican law, to the Salvadoran refugees, then a growing group in Mexico City (GHRSP 1992: 3).

3. Elected political officials in Mexico serve a single six-year term in office. For many, public service is seen as an opportunity to increase wealth and, after six years, to move on to another position to do the same. In Mexico's bloated bureaucracies, functionaries and department heads are constantly shifted around to make room for newer political or familial favorites. This rapid turnover was true of COMAR in Chiapas during this time.

4. Of all the states of Mexico Chiapas experienced the fewest land reforms of the Mexican revolution. In some parts of Chiapas there are large coffee fincas, similar to the haciendas that the land reforms of the 1930s restricted elsewhere in Mexico. In other areas cattle ranchers have taken over large tracts of cleared land from the Lacandón Selva and established huge estates. All this has limited the land available for the growing Mexican Maya populations, and they too have been pushing into the Lacandón rain forest in search of land to grow corn and beans. The arrival of the Guatemalan refugees exacerbated an already tense situation in Chiapas over land. This larger struggle erupted into public view on January 1, 1994, when the Zapatista National Liberation Army made its presence known to the world (EPICA 1994).

5. This account was related to me by Kaxh Pasil (a pseudonym). As a Jakaltek schoolteacher who fled into exile, he personally experienced the refugee ordeal in all its cruelty. I recorded this description in visits to the refugee settlements in 1982 and 1983. Part of Kaxh Pasil's testimony has been previously published in Spanish (Montejo and Akab' 1992).

6. Field notes, 1988. The testimony of Kaxh Pasil concerning this problem with Mexican immigration authorities has been confirmed by other testimonies, particularly those compiled by the Grupo de Apoyo a Refugiados Guatemaltecos in 1983.

7. These groups added to the large number of unrecognized or undocumented refugees in Mexico. In 1988 Mexican authorities and nongovernmental organizations working with refugees estimated that there were one-hundred fifty thousand Guatemalan refugees dispersed throughout Mexico (Salvadó 1988).

8. One specific case came to my attention while I was doing research in the refugee camp of Guadalupe Victoria, close to the border. The

unfortunate man was named Lalo, and he, like others, has been forgotten. Most of those Mexicans who were mistakenly abducted were poor campesinos who did not have family, economic means, or power to pursue the cases or to prosecute the offenders.

9. Most Mayas entered the United States illegally and then had a very difficult time receiving political asylum during the 1980s. U.S. immigration officials, more used to people fleeing communist countries, were not willing to listen to stories of village massacres that were not backed up by threats to individual persons, provable with written documents. In this reluctance to grant asylum, they were encouraged by the Republican tenants of the White House who persisted in seeing the Guatemalan government and army as engaged in a mighty war against communism.

Chapter Eight. Strategies of Cultural Survival

1. Most of the data in this chapter were gathered in the Guadalupe Victoria, Villa Cocalito, and Las Maravillas camps and have been confirmed by my primary Maya collaborator, Kaxh Pasil, and by previous ethnographic reports on the refugee situation (see Earle 1988; Falla 1992; Freyermuth Enciso and Hernandez Castillo 1992; Manz 1988a).

2. The ethnographic literature includes Cox de Collins 1980; Davis 1968; LaFarge 1947; LaFarge and Byers 1931; Lovell 1985b; Oakes 1951; and Watanabe 1992.

3. This resistance is another expression of the ongoing revival of all Maya cultures within Guatemala, within the Mexican Maya communities, and within the transnational Maya groups, which gained impetus from the Quincentennial, the anniversary of our five hundred years of indigenous resistance and survival.

4. Tz'ibinh means "the spotted ones," and refers to the camouflage uniforms worn by soldiers in regular units of the Guatemalan army. Xoltelaj means "the ones from the forest or mountains," and refers to the places where the guerrillas had their operational bases. Neither of these terms was secret. They became known and integrated into the regular vocabulary of these groups.

5. For another aspect of the Florida situation, I recommend *Mayan Voices: American Lives*, a film by Olivia Carrescia (First Run/Icarus Films, New York).

6. See, for example, the film *When the Mountains Tremble*, directed by Pamela Yates and Thomas Siegal (Skylight Pictures, New York).

7. As an example, the former archbishop of Guatemala, Mario Casariegos, took no notice of the massacres directed by his friends, the generals, against the Maya population. He even criticized priests for abandoning their parishes because of threats to their lives (Fried et al. 1983: 222).

8. This ethnocidal strategy of model villages, a modern term for the older strategy of reducciones applied by the Spanish conquistadors and missionaries to control Maya populations, has been criticized by those concerned with human rights. Forcing people to live in those concentration camps, as refugees and political observers have called the model villages, is seen as the continuation of the violence of conquest and the reinforcement of the colonial domination and exploitation of the indigenous population (see Krueger and Enge 1985: vii).

9. In 1991 the refugee women united to form an organization named Mama Maquín in honor of a elderly woman who was killed by the army while defending her land in the Qeqchi' Maya region during the Panzós massacre in May 1978. The Mama Maquín organization, working in local groups in each of the camps, has stressed the role of women as equal partners with men in household activities and of education for women so that they can be more competent political actors in their camps and more effective maintainers and transmitters of Maya culture and values. The organization was strongly supported by feminist and international solidarity groups, particularly from Spain, the United States, and Canada. They participated in the negotiations for the collective return. Their central offices were in Comitán, and they maintained contact with women in the camps through regular meetings with camp delegates.

10. The lands of the Q'anjob'al and the Mam of Todos Santos have become badly eroded from the overuse of the agricultural technique of making their hoed furrows run downhill.

11. For example, during the patronal festival of the neighboring community of San Marcos in 1950, a Q'anjob'al man got drunk and bragged about his adventures, claiming to be a "man" because he managed to reach Los Angeles, California. He shouted while he was dancing, "Qué viva los Ankeles Kalipornia, ¡Chingado!" This story was told to me by my father. Since then the Q'anjob'al people have realized that the United States was not the other end of the world and that people could go there and come back alive.

12. This strategy might be seen to be the result of the market forces operating in the region. But it also reflects some deliberate supraeconomic choices. In 1980 the Jakalteks began to produce large quantities of potatoes, so much that the Mam of Todos Santos could not sell a pound of their

potatoes during a Sunday market. They were practically forced to give them away and had to return home without buying the corn they needed. The Jakalteks decided not to cultivate potatoes anymore, in part because they too could not sell their corn, but also because of their awareness that they were taking away the means of survival of their neighbors.

13. Life in the camp of Rancho Tejas where several ethnic groups were present could have been a model for Maya social unity and the global construction of Maya culture, but unfortunately the camp was dismantled by immigration authorities in late 1982.

14. In the slack season (May to October), the Mam women produced their weaving. Mam weaving is highly prized because of its intricate Maya designs, especially seen on the woman's traditional huipil, which may take several months to complete.

15. Among the most visible Maya cultural organizations promoting Maya culture in exile are the International Maya League based in Costa Rica, the IXIM cultural group in Los Angeles, and Corn Maya in Florida. These groups have promoted Maya culture by continuing to celebrate important festivals and using the marimba as a resource.

Chapter Nine. Ethnic Relations and Cultural Revival in the Refugee Camps

1. There are also non-Maya indigenous people, the Xinca and the Garifuna (Caribbean blacks), along the Atlantic coast.

2. The best example of this is seen in the materials prepared by INGUAT, the tourist information bureau of the Guatemalan government. Maya maidens smile out from tourist posters and brochures, beckoning tourist dollars that never reach Maya pockets. This is not limited to the Guatemalan government, as one can see from the *National Geographic*'s promotion of "La Ruta Maya" (1989) and the hundreds of non-Guatemalan tour groups that use Maya images to promote their tours.

3. This was especially the case of Operación Ixil (Ixil Campaign), a massive military operation conducted against the Ixil Maya who were suspected of being strong supporters of the EGP guerrilla group (Cifuentes 1982).

4. From an interview videotaped at the refugee camp of Villa Cocalito in 1992.

5. I conducted short-term fieldwork among the Q'anjob'al and Jakaltek refugees and migrants in Immokalee and Indiantown, Florida, during the summer of 1990. These problems in social relations were also confirmed by

Geronimo Camposeco, a paralegal aide working with Maya farmworkers and migrants there.

6. Guatemalitas means "little Guatemalans"; *chakuates* is a compound Q'anjob'al word meaning "friend." Both are used in Florida in a patronizing way.

7. Ah Mayab' is a term from Jakaltek and Q'anjob'al that encompasses the cultural concepts of identity, origin, and persistence. With this name we can include all the linguistic groups that make up the great pan-Mayan culture.

8. The debates originating from the Quincentenary commemoration and the Nobel Peace Prize awarded to Rigoberta Menchú, a K'iche' Maya woman, have also helped to create this ethnic consciousness of belonging to a greater Maya culture among all Mayas, in Guatemala, in the refugee camps, and among the migrants to more distant places.

Chapter Eleven. Returning Home

1. Between 1984 and 1987 the flow of individuals seeking voluntary repatriation was quite light. By UNHCR's count there were 794 (area of departure unspecified) in 1984, 205 (65 from Chiapas) in 1985, and 343 (132 from Chiapas) in 1986. In 1987, 874 people sought voluntary repatriation. Their camp locations are not specified, but Huehuetenango was given as the destination for 80 percent of them. In 1988, 1,830 people sought voluntary repatriation, almost all from the Campeche/Quintana Roo camps and headed back to the Ixcán cooperatives. No figures are available for 1989. In 1990 the political instability generated by the presidential election campaign virtually stopped repatriation in that year (Nolin Hanlon 1995: 200).

2. The Director of the Instituto Nacional de Transformación Agraria (INTA), Gustavo Adolfo Búcaro González, was quoted as saying,

During the years of violence entire communities abandoned their lands. There is a clause [in the Guatemalan constitution] that states that if lands are abandoned the state will take those lands. That's what happened. Two or three years went by and the refugees would not appear. So the land was given to new people. For the time being there have not been problems because the refugees have not returned, and those that have returned have been put in "development poles." (Manz 1988a: 143)

BIBLIOGRAPHY

Adams, Richard N.
  1990   "Ethnic Images and Strategies in 1944." In *Guatemalan Indians and the State, 1540–1988*, edited by Carol Smith. Austin: University of Texas Press.

Alvarado, Pedro de
  1969   *Documents and Narratives Concerning the Discovery and Conquest of Latin America.* New York: Kraus Reprint Co. Originally published by Cortes Society, New York. No. 3.

Aguilera Peralta, Gabriel
  1988   "The Hidden War: Guatemala's Counterinsurgency Campaign." In *Crisis in Central America: Regional Dynamics and U.S. Policy in the 1980s*, edited by Nora Hamilton, Jeffrey A. Friedsen, Linda Fuller, and Manuel Pastor. Boulder, Colo: A PACCA Book, Westview Press.

Ah Mayab'
  1992   Newsletter, no. 2 (October-November).

Americas Watch
  1986   *Civil Patrols in Guatemala.* New York: Americas Watch.

Amnesty International
  1987   *Guatemala: The Human Rights Record.* London: Amnesty International.

Anderson, Benedict
  1988   Afterword. In *Ethnicities and Nations: Processes of Interethnic Relations in Latin America, Southeast Asia, and the Pacific*, edited by Remo Guidieri, Francesco Pellizzi, and Stanley J. Tambiah, 402–6. Austin: A Rothko Chapel Book, distributed by University of Texas Press.

1990   *Imagined Communities: Reflections on the Origin and Spread of Nationalism.* London: Verso.

Anderson, Ken, and Jean-Marie Simon
  1987   "Permanent Counterinsurgency in Guatemala." *Telos*, no. 73 (Fall 1987): 9–46.

Anderson, Marilyn, and Jonathan Garlock
  1988   *Granddaughters of Corn: Portraits of Guatemalan Women.* Willimantic, Conn: Curbstone Press.

Arias, Arturo
  1990   "Changing Indian Identity: Guatemala's Violent Transition to Modernity." In *Guatemalan Indians and the State: 1540 to 1988*, edited by Carol A. Smith, 230–57. Austin: University of Texas Press.

Asad, Talal
  1988   *Anthropology and the Colonial Encounter.* Atlantic Highlands, N.J.: Humanities Press.

Asturias, Miguel Angel
  1977   *Guatemalan Sociology: The Social Problem of the Indian.* Tempe: Arizona State University, Center for Latin American Studies.

Barry, Tom
  1989   *Guatemala: A Country Guide.* Albuquerque, New Mex.: Inter-Hemisphere Education Resouce Center.

Barry, Tom, and Deb Preusch
  1986   *The Central America Fact Book.* New York: Grove Weidenfeld.

Bazzy, Derril
  1986   "Guatemalan Refugee Children: Conditions in Chiapas." *Cultural Survival Quarterly* 10(4): 45–47.

Black, George
  1983   "All Change, No Change." *NACLA Report on the Americas*, 17, no. 2 (March–April 1983): 11–24.

Boothby, Neil
  1986   "Uprooted Mayan Children." *Cultural Survival Quarterly* 10(4): 48–50.

Bossen, Laurel Herbenar
  1984   *The Redivision of Labor: Women and Economic Choice in Four Guatemalan Communities.* Albany: State University of New York Press.

Bricker, Victoria
1981   *The Indian Christ, The Indian King: The Historical Substrate of Maya Myth and Ritual.* Austin: University of Texas Press.

Brinton, Daniel G.
1969   *The Maya Chronicles.* Library of Aboriginal American Literature, no. 1. New York: AMS Press.

Britnall, Douglas E.
1979   *Revolt Against the Dead: The Modernization of a Mayan Community in the Highlands of Guatemala.* New York: Gordon and Breach.

1983   "The Guatemalan Indian Civil Rights Movement." *Cultural Survival Quarterly* 7, no. 1 (Spring 1983): 14–16.

Bunzel, Ruth
1972   *Chichicastenango: A Guatemalan Indian Village.* Seattle: University of Washington Press.

Burgos-Debray, Elisabeth, ed.
1984   *I, Rigoberta Menchú: An Indian Woman in Guatemala.* London: Verso.

Burns, Allan F.
1993   *Maya in Exile: Guatemalans in Florida.* Philadelphia: Temple University Press.

Cambranes, Julio C. (also Castellanos Cambranes)
1997   "Hacia le recuperación de nuestra historia: Sobre la invasión española de Noj Petén, Guatemala en 1697". *Mesoamérica,* no. 33 (June 1997): 217–40. Antigua, Guatemala: CIRMA; South Woodstock, Vt: Plumsock Mesoamerican Studies.

Campbell, Lyle, and Terrence Kaufman
1985   "Mayan Linguistics: Where Are We Now?" In *Annual Review of Anthropology* 14: 187–98, edited by Bernard J. Siegal. Palo Alto, Calif.: Annual Review.

Camposeco, Jerónimo, and David Griffith
1990   "Anchors of Identity: Migration and Transnationalism among Guatemalans, Jamaicans and Puerto Ricans in Florida." Paper presented at the 89th Annual Meeting of the American Anthropological Association, New Orleans.

Carlsen, Robert
1997   *The War for the Heart and Soul of a Highland Maya Town.* Austin: University of Texas Press.

Carmack, Robert M.

1981   *The Quiché Mayas of Utatlán: The Evolution of a Highland Guatemala Kingdom.* Norman: University of Oklahoma Press.

1995   *Rebels of Highland Guatemala: The Quiché-Mayas of Momostenango.* Norman: University of Oklahoma Press.

Carmack, Robert M., ed.

1988   *Harvest of Violence: The Maya Indians and the Guatemalan Crises.* Norman: University of Oklahoma Press.

Carmack, Robert, Janine Gasco, and Gary H. Gossens, eds.

1996   *The Legacy of Mesoamerica: History and Culture of a Native American Civilization.* Englewood Cliffs, N.J.: Prentice-Hall.

Carta Pastoral Colectiva del Episcopado Guatemalteco

1988   *El clamor por la tierra.* Guatemala City: Nueva Guatemala de la Asunción.

Casaverde, Juvenal

1976   *Jacaltec Social and Political Structure.* Ann Arbor, Mich.: University Microfilms International.

Castellanos Cambranes, Julio (also Cambranes)

1988   *Sobre los empresarios agrarios y el estado en Guatemala.* Cuaderno no. 1. Guatemala City: Centro de Estudios Rurales Centroamericanos (CERCA).

CCPP (Comisiones Permanentes)

1986   *Crossroads.* Occasional newsletter. Chiapas, Mexico.

CERIGUA

1996   "CERIGUA Weekly Briefs," no. 33, August 12, 1996.

1997   "CERIGUA Weekly Briefs," no. 1, January 2, 1997. Special Edition for the Peace.

Cifuentes H., Juan Fernando (Capitán de Navió DEM G-5)

1982   "Apreciación de asuntos civiles (G-5) para el area Ixil." *Revista Militar,* September-December. Guatemala City: Centro de Estudios Militares (CEM).

Cojtí Cuxil, Demétrio

1991   *Configuración del pensamiento político del pueblo Maya.* Asociación de Escritores Mayances de Guatemala. Quetzaltenango, Guatemala City: Impreso en Talleres de "El Estudiante."

1988–89 *Nuevo Día.* Boletín de las Comisiones Permanentes de Representantes Refugiados Guatemaltecos en México, nos. 1–5.

COMAR (Comisión Mexicana de Ayuda a Refugiados)
1985   *Refugiados guatemaltecos.* Mexico City: COMAR.

Comité Cristiano de Solidaridad de la Diócesis de San Cristóbal
1983   *Refugiados guatemaltecos en la Diócesis de San Cristóbal de las Casas.* Chiapas, México: Reporte preparado por el Comité Cristiano de la Diócesis de San Cristóbal de las Casas.

Cox de Collins, Anne
1980   "Colonial Jacaltenango, Guatemala: The Formation of a Corporate Community." Ph.D. dissertation, Tulane University.

Davis, Shelton H.
1968   *Santa Eulalia: Tierra de nuestros antepasados y esperanza para nuestros hijos.* Guatemala City: Instituto Indigenista Nacional.

1988a   "Introduction: Sowing the Seeds of Violence." In *Harvest of Violence: The Guatemalan Indians and the Guatemalan Crisis,* edited by Robert M. Carmack, 3–36. Norman: University of Oklahoma Press.

1988b   "Agrarian Structure and Ethnic Resistance: The Indian in Guatemalan and Salvadoran National Politics." In *Ethnicities and Nations,* edited by Remo Guidieri, Francesco Pellizzi, and Stanley J. Tambiah, 78–106. Austin: A Rothko Chapel Book, distributed by University of Texas Press.

Davis, Shelton H., and Julie Hodson
1982   *Witness to Political Violence in Guatemala.* Oxfam America, Impact Audit no. 2. Boston: Oxfam America.

Davis, Wade
1983   "Observations from Guatemala." *Cultural Survival Quarterly* 7(2): 55–57.

Diócesis de San Cristóbal
1986   "La Vida de los Campamentos." *Caminante* (newsletter).

Earle, Duncan
1988   "Mayas Aiding Mayas: Guatemalan Refugees in Chiapas, Mexico." In *Harvest of Violence: The Maya Indians and the Guatemalan Crisis,* edited by Robert M. Carmack, 256–73. Norman: University of Oklahoma Press.

Edwards, David B.
1988   "Marginality and Migration: Cultural Dimensions of the Afghan Refugee Problem." *International Migration Review* 20(2): 313–26.

Ehlers, Tracy Bachrach
  1990   "Central America in the 1980s: Political Crisis and the Social
          Responsibility of Anthropologists." *Latin America Research
          Review* 25(3): 141–53.

England, Nora
  1992   *Autonomía de los idiomas Mayas: Historia e identidad
          Rukutamil, Ramaq'il, Rutzijob'al Ri Mayab' Amaq'*. Guatemala
          City: Editorial Cholsamaj.

England, Nora, and Stephen Elliot (eds.)
  1990   *Lecturas sobre la lingüística Maya*. Antigua, Guatemala:
          Centro de Investigaciones Regionales de Mesoamérica
          (CIRMA).

Enloe, H. Cynthia
  1978   "Ethnicity, Bureaucracy and State-building in Africa and Latin
          America." *Ethnic and Racial Studies*, 1(3): 336–51.

EPICA (Ecumenical Program on Central America and the Caribbean)
  1993   *Out of the Shadows: The Communities of Populations in
          Resistance*. Washington, D.C.: EPICA.

  1994   *Chiapas: The Rebellion of the Excluded*. Washington, D.C.:
          EPICA.

Falla, Ricardo, S.J.
  1983   "The Massacre at the Rural Estate of San Francisco, July,
          1982." *Cultural Survival Quarterly* 7(1): 43–44.

  1992   *Masacres de la Selva: Ixcán, Guatemala (1975–1982)*.
          Colección 500 Años, vol. 1. Guatemala City: Editorial
          Universitaria, Universidad de San Carlos de Guatemala.

Farriss, Nancy M.
  1984   *Maya Society under Colonial Rule: The Collective Enterprise of
          Survival*. Princeton: Princeton University Press.

Ferris, Elizabeth G.
  1987   *The Central American Refugees*. New York: Praeger.

  1989   "The Churches, Refugees, and Politics." In *Refugees and
          International Relations*, edited by Gil Loescher and Laila
          Monahan, 159–77. Oxford: Oxford University Press.

Frank, Luisa, and Philip Wheaton
  1984   *Indian Guatemala: Path to Liberation*. Washington, D.C.:
          EPICA Task Force.

Freyermuth Enciso, Graciela, and Rosalva Aida Hernández Castillo
  1992   *Una decada de refugio en México: Los refugiados guatemaltecos*

y los derechos humanos. México, D.F.: Centro de
Investigaciones y Estudios Superiores en Antropología Social,
Ediciones de la Casa Chata.

Fried, Jonathan L., Marvin E. Gettleman, Deborah T. Levenson, and
Nancy Peckenham, eds.

1983   *Guatemala in Rebellion: Unfinished History.* New York:
Grove Press.

Galeano, Eduardo

1969   *Guatemala: Occupied Country.* New York: Monthly Review Press.

GARG (Grupo de Apoyo a Refugiados Guatemaltecos)

1983   *La contrainsurgencia y los refugiados guatemaltecos.* México,
D. F.: Federación Editorial Mexicana.

GHRSP (Guatemala Health Rights Support Project)

1992   *Unfinished Stories: Guatemalan Refugees in Mexico.* Issue
Brief, Summer 1992. Washington, D.C.: Guatemala Health
Rights Support Project.

Giddens, Anthony

1995   "Epilogue: Note on the Future of Anthropology." In *The
Future of Anthropology: Its Relevance to the Contemporary
World,* edited by Akbar Ahmed and Chris Shroe, 272–77.
London: Athlone Press.

Gleijeses, Piero

1991   *Shattered Hope: The Guatemalan Revolution and the United
States, 1944–1954.* Princeton: Princeton University Press.

González, Jorge R.

1992   "De Panzós a el aguacate, sobre la ruta del Quinto
Centenario." In *Una década de refugio en México: Los
refugiados guatemaltecos y los derechos humanos,* 119–33.
México, D.F.: Centro de Investigaciones y Estudios Superiores
en Antropología Social, Ediciones de la Casa Chata.

Gossen, Gary H.

1974   *Chamulas in the World of the Sun: Time and Space in a Maya
Oral Tradition.* Prospect Heights, Ill: Waveland Press.

Guatemala Human Rights Commission/USA

1986   *Guatemalan Children Today.* September. Washington, D.C.:
GHRC/USA.

Guatemalan Church in Exile

1987   *Guatemala: Refugiados y repatriación.* Año 7, num. 2.
Managua, Nicaragua.

Gupta, Akhil, and James Ferguson
  1992   "Beyond 'Culture': Space, Identity, and Politics of Difference."
           Cultural Anthropology 7 (1): 6–23.

Hagan, Jacqueline M.
  1987   "The Politics of Numbers: Central American Migration During
           a Period of Crisis, 1978–1985." M.A. thesis, University of
           Texas, Austin.

Haines, David W., editor
  1989   *Refugees as Immigrants: Cambodians, Laotians and Vietnamese
           in America.* Totowa, N.J.: Rowman and Littlefield.

Handy, Jim
  1984   *Gift of the Devil: A History of Guatemala.* Boston: South End
           Press.

  1994   *Revolution in the Countryside: Rural Conflict and Agrarian
           Reform in Guatemala, 1944–1954.* Chapel Hill: University of
           North Carolina Press.

Hastrup, Kirsten
  1992   "Writing Ethnography: State of the Art." In *Anthropology and
           Autobiography,* edited by Judith Oakley and Helen Callaway,
           116–33. ASA Monograph 29. London: Routledge.

Hawkins, John
  1984   *Inverse Images: The Meaning of Culture, Ethnicity and Family
           in Postcolonial Guatemala.* Albuquerque: University of New
           Mexico Press.

Henderson, John M.
  1981   *The World of the Ancient Maya.* Ithaca: Cornell University Press.

Hendrickson, Carol
  1985   "Guatemala: Everybody's Indian When the Occasion's Right."
           Cultural Survival Quarterly 9(2): 22–23.

Hernández Castillo, Rosalva Aída
  1992   "Los refugiados guatemaltecos y la dinámica frontera en
           Chiapas." In *Una década de refugio en México: Los refugiados
           guatemaltecos y los derechos humanos,* 93–105. México, D.F.:
           Centro de Investigaciones y Estudios Superiores en
           Antropología Social, Ediciones de la Casa Chata.

Hinshaw, Robert
  1975   *Panajachel: A Guatemalan Town in Thirty-Year Perspective.*
           Pittsburgh: University of Pittsburgh Press.

JRS/USA (Jesuit Refugee Service/USA)
1996   *The Mustard Seed,* no. 41 (Spring 1996).

Justice and Peace Committee on Guatemala
1986   *Human Rights in Guatemala.* November. Guatemala City:
        Report prepared and published with the support of the World
        Council of Churches.

Krueger, Christine
1986   "Re-education and Relocation in Guatemala." *Cultural
        Survival Quarterly* 10(4): 43–44.

Krueger, Christine, and Kjell Enge
1985   *Security and Development Conditions in the Guatemalan
        Highlands.* Washington, D.C.: Washington Office on Latin
        America.

LaFarge, Oliver
1947   *Santa Eulalia: A Religion of a Cuchumatan Indian Town.*
        Chicago: University of Chicago Press.

LaFarge, Oliver, and Douglas Byers
1931   *The Year Bearer's People.* Tulane University Middle American
        Research Series, Publication no. 3. New Orleans: Tulane
        University.

1940   "Maya Ethnology: The Sequence of Cultures." In *The Maya
        and Their Neighbors,* edited by Clarence L. Hay, 281–91.
        New York: Appleton-Century.

Landa, Diego de
1983   *Relación de las cosas de Yucatán.* Mexico: Ediciones Dante.

1978   *Yucatan Before and After Conquest.* Translated by William
        Gates. New York: Dover.

Las Casas, Bartolomé de
[1552]1974   *In Defense of the Indians: The Defense of the Most
        Reverend Lord, Don Fray Bartolomé de Las Casas, of the Order
        of Preachers, Late Bishop of Chiapa, Against the Percesutors
        and Slanderers of the Peoples of the New World Discovered
        Across the Sea.* Translated by Stafford Poole. Chicago:
        Northern Illinois University Press.

Laughlin, Robert M.
1988   *The People of the Bat: Mayan Tales and Dreams from
        Zinacantán.* Washington, D.C.: Smithsonian Institution Press.

Loescher, Gil, and Laila Monahan
    1989   *Refugees and International Relations*. Oxford: Oxford
            University Press.

Lovell, W. George
    1985a   "From Conquest to Counterinsurgency." *Cultural Survival
            Quarterly* 9(2): 46–49.

    1985b   *Conquest and Survival in Colonial Guatemala: A Historical
            Geography of the Cuchumatanes Highlands, 1500–1821*.
            Kingston, Canada: McGill-Queen's University Press.

Lovell, W. George, and Christopher Lutz
    1994   "Conquest and Population: Maya Demography in Historical
            Perspective." *Latin American Research Review* 29(2): 133–40.

McClintock, Michael
    1985   *The American Connection*. Vol. 2: *State Terror and Popular
            Resistance in Guatemala*. London: Zed Books.

McCreery, David J.
    1994   *Rural Guatemala, 1760–1940*. Stanford: Stanford University
            Press.

Malkki, Liisa
    1992   "National Geographic: The Rooting of Peoples and the
            Territorialization of National Identity among Scholars and
            Refugees." *Cultural Anthropology* 7(1): 24–44.

Manz, Beatriz
    1988a   *Refugees of a Hidden War: The Aftermath of Counter-
            insurgency in Guatemala*. Albany: State University of New
            York Press.

    1988b   *Repatriation and Reintegration: An Arduous Process in
            Guatemala*. Washington, D.C.: Hemispheric Migration
            Project, Center for Immigration Policy and Refugee
            Assistance, Georgetown University.

    1988c   "The Transformation of La Esperanza, an Ixcán Village." In
            *Harvest of Violence: The Mayan Indians and the Guatemalan
            Crisis*, edited by Robert M. Carmack, 70–89. Norman:
            University of Oklahoma Press.

Martínez Peláez, Severo
    1971   *La patria del criollo: Ensayo de interpretación de la realidad
            colonial guatemalteca*. Guatemala City: Editorial Universitaria.

Montejo, Victor D.

1984   *El Q'anil: The Man of Lightning.* Carrboro, N.C.: Signal
         Books.

1987   *Testimony: The Death of a Guatemalan Village.* Willimantic,
         Conn.: Curbstone Press.

1995   *Sculpted Stones/Piedras Labradas.* Willimantic, Conn.:
         Curbstone Press.

1997   "The Stones Will Speak Again: Dreams and Realities of an
         Ah Tz'ib' Maya (Writer) in the Maya Land." In *Speaking for
         the Generations,* edited by Simon Ortiz, 196–216. Tucson:
         University of Arizona Press.

Montejo, Victor, and Q'anil Akab'

1992   *Brevísima relación testimonial de la contínua destrucción del
         Mayab' (Guatemala).* Providence, R.I.: Guatemala Scholars
         Network.

Moors, Marilyn M.

1988   "Indian Labor and the Guatemalan Crisis: Evidence from
         History and Anthropology." In *Central America: Historical
         Perspectives on the Contemporary Crises,* edited by R. L.
         Woodward, Jr., 67–84. New York: Greenwood Press.

Motzafi-Haller, Pnina

1997   "Writing Birthright: On Native Anthropologists and the
         Politics of Representation." In *Auto/Ethnography: Rewriting
         the Self and the Social,* edited by Debora E. Reed-Danahay,
         195–222. Oxford: Berg Press.

National Geographic

1989   "La Ruta Maya." Vol. 176, no. 4 (October): 424–79.
         Washington, D.C.: National Geographic Society.

NCOORD (National Coordinating Office on Refugees and Displaced of
         Guatemala)

1996a   *NCOORD Newsletter* 4, no. 2 (March).

1996b   *NCOORD Newsletter* 4, no. 3 (July).

1996c   *NCOORD Newsletter* 4, no. 4 (September).

Nolin Hanlon, Catherine

1995   "Flight, Exile and Return: Place and Identity among
         Guatemalan Mayan Refugees." M.A. thesis, Queen's
         University, Kingston, Ontario, Canada.

Oakes, Maud
  1951   *The Two Crosses of Todos Santos: Survival of Mayan Religious Rituals.* New York: Pantheon Books.

Obispos de la Región Pastoral Pacífico-Sur
  1984   *Sobre la situación de los refugiados.* Documento no. 2, Mayo 23, 1984.

Ortiz, Simon, ed.
  1997   *Speaking for the Generations.* Tucson: University of Arizona Press.

Otzoy, Irma
  1992   "Identidad y trajes mayas." *Mesoamérica* 12(23): 95–112. Antigua, Guatemala: Centro de Investigaciones Regionales de Mesoamérica; South Woodstock, Vt: Plumsock Mesoamerican Studies.

Paul, Benjamin D., and Demarest, William J.
  1988   "The Operation of a Death Squad in San Pedro La Laguna." In *Harvest of Violence: The Maya Indians and the Guatemalan Crisis,* edited by Robert M. Carmack, 119–54. Norman: University of Oklahoma Press.

Pellizzi, Francesco
  1988   "To Seek Refuge: Nation and Ethnicity in Exile." In *Ethnicities and Nations: Processes of Interethnic Relations in Latin America, Southeast Asia, and the Pacific,* edited by Remo Guideri, Francesco Pellizzi, and Stanley J. Tambiah, 154–71. Austin: A Rothko Chapel Book, distributed by University of Texas Press.

Perera, Victor
  1983   "Guatemalan Indian Refugees: Pawns in the Political Game." *Nation,* November 12, 1983.

  1993   *Unfinished Conquest: The Guatemalan Tragedy.* Berkeley: University of California Press.

Recinos, Adrián
  1954   *Monografía de Huehuetenango.* 2a edn. Guatemala City: Ministerio de Educación Pública.

Recinos, Adrián, and Delia Goetz, trans.
  1953   *The Annals of the Cakchiquels.* Norman: University of Oklahoma Press.

Reed, Nelson
  1964   *The Caste War of Yucatán.* Stanford: Stanford University Press.

Reed-Danahay, Deborah E., ed.
1997   Auto/Ethnography: Rewriting the Self and the Social. Oxford: Berg Press.

Robert F. Kennedy Memorial Center for Human Rights
1993   Persecution by Proxy: The Civil Patrols in Guatemala. New York: Robert F. Kennedy Memorial Center for Human Rights.

Rodríguez Guaján, Demétrio, comp.
1989   Cultura Maya y políticas de desarrollo. Guatemala City: Departamento de Investigaciones COCADI, Editorial Cholsamaj.

Rohter, Larry
1996   "Maya Renaissance in Guatemala Turns Political." New York Times, August 12, 1996.

Rojas Mix, Miguel
1991   "Reinventing Identity." NACLA: Report on the Americas: Inventing America 1492–1992 24(5): 29–33.

Ruíz García, Samuel
1992   "Los refugiados y los derechos humanos." In Una década de refugio en México: Los refugiados guatemaltecos y los derechos humanos. México: Centro de Investigaciones y Estudios Superiores en Antropología Social, Ediciones de la Casa Chata.

Said, Edward
1979   Orientalism. New York: Vintage Books.

Salvadó, Luis Raúl
1988   The Other Refugees: A Study of Nonrecognized Guatemalan Refugees in Chiapas, Mexico. Washington, D.C.: Hemispheric Migration Project, Center for Immigration Policy and Refugee Assistance, Georgetown University.

Sam Colop, Luis E.
1991   Jub'aqtun omay kuchum k'alesmal/Cinco siglos de encubrimiento -A Propósito. Seminario Permanente de Estudios Mayas, SPEM. Cuaderno no. 1. Guatemala City: Editorial Cholsamaj.

Sanford, Victoria
1994   "Reproducing the Culture of Terror: The Forced Recruitment of Maya Youth into the Guatemalan Military." Paper presented at the Congress of the Latin American Studies Association, March 10, 1994.

Santoli, Al
    1988   "Their Dreams Are for the Children." *Parade Magazine,*
            October 23, 1988, 16–17.

Schlesinger, Stephen, and Stephen Kinzer
    1982   *Bitter Fruit: The Untold Story of the American Coup in
            Guatemala.* Garden City, N.Y.: Anchor Books.

Scott, James C.
    1985   *Weapons of the Weak: Everyday Forms of Peasant Resistance.*
            New Haven: Yale University Press.

Secretaría de Ayuda a Refugiados Guatemaltecos
    1991   *1992: El retorno de un pueblo?* Boletín no. 27. Dic. México.

Shahrani, Nazif M.
    1994   "Honored Guest and Marginal Man: Long-Term Field Research
            and Predicaments of a Native Anthropologist." In *Others
            Knowing Others: Perspectives on Ethnographic Careers,* edited
            by Don D. Fowler and Donald L. Hardesty, 15–67.
            Smithsonian Series in Ethnographic Inquiry. Washington,
            D.C.: Smithsonian Institution Press.

Sherman, William L.
    1979   *Forced Native Labor in Sixteenth-Century Central America.*
            Lincoln: University of Nebraska Press.

Skinner-Klee, Jorge
    1954   *Legislación indigenista de Guatemala.* México, D.F.: Ediciones
            especiales del Instituto Indigenista Interamericano.

Smith, Carol A., ed.
    1990   *Guatemalan Indians and the State: 1540 to 1988.* Austin:
            University of Texas Press.

Smith, Waldemar
    1977   *The Fiesta System and Economic Change.* New York: Columbia
            University Press.

Stephens, John L.
    1841   *Incidents of Travel in Central America, Chiapas and Yucatán.*
            Vol 1. New York: Harper Brothers.

Stoll, David
    1988   "Evangelicals, Guerrillas, and the Army: The Ixil Triangle." In
            *Harvest of Violence: The Maya Indians and the Guatemalan
            Crisis,* edited by Robert M. Carmack, 90–116. Norman:
            University of Oklahoma Press.

Taylor, Clark
1998   *The Return of Guatemala's Refugees: Reweaving the Torn.*
        Philadelphia: Temple University Press.

Tumin, Melvin
1952   *Caste in a Peasant Society: A Case Study in the Dynamics of
        Caste.* Princeton: Princeton University Press.

Tyler, Stephen A.
1992   "On Being Out of Words." In *Rereading Cultural Anthropology,*
        edited by George Marcus, 1–7. Durham, N.C.: Duke
        University Press.

UNHCR (United Nations High Commission for Refugees)
1984a   *Refugees Magazine,* no. 4 (April).

1984b   *Refugees Magazine,* no. 46 (June).

1986   *Refugees Magazine,* no. 34 (October).

U.S. Committee for Refugees
1993   *El Retorno: Guatemalans' Risky Repatriation Begins.*
        Washington, D.C.: American Council for Nationalities Service.

Van Praag, Nicholas
1986   "The Relocation Experience: Refugees in Campeche and
        Quintana Roo." *Refugees Magazine,* no. 34 (October): 19–31.
        New York: UNHCR.

Wagley, Charles
1949   *The Social and Religious Life of a Guatemalan Village.* Memoir
        no. 71. *American Anthropologist* 51, no. 4. Washington, D.C.:
        American Anthropological Association.

Wallace, Anthony F. C.
1956   "Revitalization Movements." *American Anthropologist* 58: 264–81.

Warren, Kay B.
1978   *The Symbolism of Subordination: Indian Identity in a
        Guatemalan Town.* Austin: University of Texas Press.

1993   "Interpreting *La Violencia* in Guatemala: Shapes of Kaqchikel
        Resistance and Silence." In *The Violence Within: Cultural and
        Political Opposition in Divided Nations,* edited by Kay B.
        Warren, 25–46. Boulder, Colo.: Westview Press.

1997   "Narrating Cultural Resurgence: Genre and Self-Representation
        for Pan-Maya Writers." In *Auto/Ethnography: Rewriting the Self
        and the Social,* edited by Deborah E. Reed-Danahay, 21–45.
        Oxford: Berg Press.

274 • BIBLIOGRAPHY

Watanabe, John M.

1990   "Enduring Yet Ineffable Community in the Western Periphery
        of Guatemala." In *Guatemalan Indians and the State, 1540 to
        1988*, edited by Carol A. Smith, 183–204. Austin: University
        of Texas Press.

1992   *Maya Saints and Souls in a Changing World*. Austin: University
        of Texas Press.

Wiesel, Elie

1990   *Dimensions of the Holocaust: Lecture at Northwestern
        University*. Evanston, Ill.: Northwestern University Press.

Wilk, Richard R.

1985   "The Ancient Maya and the Political Present." *Journal of
        Anthropological Research* 41, no. 3 (Fall) 307–26.

Wilson, Richard

1991   "Machine Guns and Mountain Spirits." *Critique of
        Anthropology* 11(1): 33–61.

WOLA (Washington Office on Latin America)

1989   *Uncertain Return: Refugees and Reconciliation in Guatemala*.
        Washington, D.C.: WOLA.

Wolf, Eric

1957   "Closed Corporate Communities in Mesoamerica and Central
        Java." *Southwestern Journal of Anthropology* 13: 1–18.

1982   *Europe and the People without History*. Berkeley: University of
        California Press.

Woodward, Ralph Lee, Jr.

1993   *Rafael Carrera and the Emergence of the Republic of
        Guatemala*. Athens: University of Georgia Press.

Worsley, Peter

1984   *The Three Worlds: Culture and World Development*. Berkeley:
        University of California Press.

Zimmerman, Marc

1995a   *Literature and Resistance in Guatemala: Textual Modes and
        Cultural Politics from El Señor Presidente to Rigoberta
        Menchú*. Vol. 1: *Theory, History, Fiction and Poetry*. Athens:
        Ohio University Center for International Studies.

1995b   *Literature and Resistance in Guatemala: Textual Modes and Cultural Politics from El Señor Presidente to Rigoberta Menchú.* Vol. 2: *Testimonio and Cultural Politics in the Years of Cerezo and Serrano Elías.* Athens: Ohio University Center for International Studies.

INDEX

DATE DUE